A SOCIAL HISTORY OF THE CINEMA IN WALES, 1918–1951

PULPITS, COAL PITS AND FLEAPITS

PETER MISKELL

UNIVERSITY OF WALES PRESS
CARDIFF
2006

Published by the University of Wales Press

University of Wales Press
10 Columbus Walk
Brigantine Place
Cardiff
CF10 4UP

www.wales.ac.uk/press

ISBN-10 0-7083-1878-9
ISBN-13 978-0-7083-1878-2

British Library Cataloguing-in-Publication Data.
A catalogue record for this book is available from the British Library.

The publishers wish to acknowledge the financial support of the Higher Education
Funding Council for Wales and of the Arts Council of Wales in the publication of
this book.

Printed in Great Britain by Antony Rowe Ltd, Wiltshire

To Bethan, Rhys and Sean

CONTENTS

ACKNOWLEDGEMENTS

This book began life as a Ph.D. thesis at the University of Wales, Aberystwyth, which was funded by the Arts and Humanities Research Board. In the course of researching and writing the thesis I received support, advice and encouragement from many quarters. Above all, credit must go to my supervisor, Dr Sian Nicholas, who was patient and supportive throughout. Her careful guidance and constructive criticism was invaluable. I must also mention Professor Aled Jones, whose advice and enthusiasm gave me the confidence to embark on this project in the first place, and also Peter Stead who was willing to share with me some of his vast knowledge of this subject area. The encouragement and support I received from the teaching and secretarial staff at the Department of History and Welsh History at Aberystwyth was also important – and appreciated.

The transition from thesis to book has taken longer than I would have liked, but along the way I have received valuable input from a number of people. Feedback and encouragement from Jeffrey Richards, who acted as external examiner for the Ph.D., was particularly appreciated, as were the suggestions of an anonymous referee who read through an earlier draft of the book. Constructive advice has also been received from those who have listened to me present at workshops and conferences, or who have commented on previous research papers. I would particularly like to thank Paul O'Leary and Neil Evans, the editors of *Llafur*, and also Lina Galvez-Munoz and Mattius Kipping, the organizers of the 'Business of Addiction' conference at Reading University. They have helped me to re-assess my work from differing perspectives. Support and encouragement has also been forthcoming from my (current and former) colleagues at the Centre for International Business History at Reading, who have helped to create the research-friendly environment in which I am fortunate enough to work.

Research for this book was carried out at a number of institutions. My endeavours have been greatly facilitated by help from the staff at the Public Record Office, the National Library of Wales, the Glamorgan Record Office, the Museum of Welsh Life, Swansea City Archives, Denbighshire Record Office, Gwynedd Archives, Ceredigion Museum, the British Film Institute and the archives of the Wisconsin Historical Society.

Finally, I must acknowledge the emotional and material assistance I have received from those closest to me. My family, and especially my parents, have been generous in their support. I must thank Ian, for putting me up on my early research trips to London, and most importantly Bethan, Rhys and Sean for just being there. To all those I have lived and studied alongside in the last few years who have taken an interest in my studies and who have contributed their own ideas and suggestions, many thanks.

ABBREVIATIONS

ABC	Associated British Cinemas
BBFC	British Board of Film Censors
BFI	British Film Institute
CEA	Cinematograph Exhibitors Association
ETU	Electrical Trades Union
GRO	Glamorgan Record Office
MU	Musicians' Union
MWL	Museum of Welsh Life
NACO	National Association of Cinematograph Operators
NAT(K)E	National Association of Theatrical (and Kine) Employees
NLW	National Library of Wales
PEP	Political and Economic Planning
PFI	Progressive Film Institute
TNA	The National Archives
TUC	Trades Union Congress
UAA	United Artists Archive

INTRODUCTION

This book provides a history of film-going in Wales, not a history of Welsh film. The history of Wales's contribution to the cinematic medium has already been rigorously and comprehensively compiled.[1] The present volume explores the contribution made by the cinema to Welsh society in the period of its greatest appeal. It examines cinema's role as a social and economic institution in Wales, the nature of the entertainment it provided, and the responses it generated from the guardians of older cultural traditions within Wales. In certain respects, the typical film-going experience was no different for Welsh audiences than for those in many other parts of Britain, but the primary concern of the book is how cinema functioned as a local, rather than a national, institution.

Global entertainments: local institutions

The development of the film industry in the early decades of the twentieth century has been described as a process by which public entertainment became industrialized.[2] For the first time, visual entertainments, recorded on celluloid, could be mass-produced and shipped around the world to be transmitted simultaneously to audiences in their millions. The economics of the film industry were such that virtually the whole cost of production went into creating the original celluloid reels. Once a film had been made, the extra cost to the film-maker of producing a further fifty or hundred copies was almost negligible. Yet the returns available to a producer were increased enormously if a film could be shown simultaneously in fifty or a hundred cinemas rather than just one. The logic of the industry encouraged producers to seek as wide as possible a distribution for their films. This meant that almost as soon as film-makers began producing feature films, these products were exported to international markets. If the cinematograph enabled public entertainments to become industrialized, it also paved the way for entertainment to become truly global.

The internationalization of the film industry predates the First World War, and in this early period European films were more widely distributed than American ones. The collapse of European film industries during the war, however, enabled US firms to develop, unchallenged, at a critical period of rapid growth in the industry. By the 1920s a small number of large firms had emerged in the US that controlled the production and distribution of between 60 and 75 per cent of all films shown around the world. From the mid-1920s the governments of many European countries sought to protect their domestic film industries by restricting imports of American made films. Such policies were often successful and enabled national film industries to develop in Europe to serve their home markets. No country, however, was able to develop an industry capable of competing with American firms on an international level. Between the 1920s and the 1950s the internationalization of the film industry was driven forward by American firms. In this period, if not in earlier ones, the process of globalization seemed almost indistinguishable from that of 'Americanization'.

The question this book addresses is how audiences in local communities, far removed from the centres of film production, received, and responded to, this new form of mass-produced entertainment. After all, had there not been a demand on the part of audiences for this industrialized entertainment, it is hard to see how the industry could have evolved on a global scale. From the perspective of film producers, the strategy of global expansion made clear economic sense; but what was the appeal for consumers of foreign-made films over existing forms of entertainment?

Film historians have only recently begun seriously to address this question by exploring the social composition of audiences and the cultural experience of film consumption.[3] Our understanding of cinema audiences, however, remains underdeveloped compared to the extensive research conducted into processes of film production.[4] This has led one leading film historian to call on colleagues to 'explore the archival records of distribution and exhibition, and produce more accounts of the specific contexts of picture-going to amplify our understanding of the diversity of both Hollywood's audiences and of the programmes they viewed'.[5] This book answers such a call. It draws on the archival records of film exhibitors in Wales, and one of the major US film distributors, along with the personal recollections of film-goers themselves, to provide an account of cinema audiences in a specific regional context. In doing so it portrays a film industry that was as much a local institution as an agent of 'Americanization'. This is not to deny that some degree of Americanization took place: the movies provided millions of film-goers with their first, and perhaps only, experience of American characters, lifestyles and fashions. Yet if films appealed to audiences in part because they seemed so different, glamorous, exotic, so *foreign*; individual cinemas were often popular for precisely the opposite reasons: because they were so conveniently accessible, familiar, *local*.

This book examines the provision, and reception, of global entertainments in local communities in Wales. How was cinema entertainment consumed? What was the basis of its popular appeal? How easily did this new form of public entertainment sit alongside older cultural traditions?

Pulpits, coal pits and fleapits

The terms 'pulpit' and 'coal pit' are used in the title of this book to symbolize two quite different, but nonetheless connected aspects of modern Welsh society. The society represented by the pulpit was that of chapel-going, Nonconformist, Liberal Wales. It was a society in which Welsh was the most commonly spoken language, and whose leaders in the late nineteenth and early twentieth century were proud of their distinctly *Welsh* identity. Men such as David Lloyd George and Tom Ellis were convinced that politically Wales belonged in, and was an important part of, the British Empire. The cultural distinctiveness of Wales, however, was something that they felt needed to be properly recognized and more confidently expressed. The single most lasting political accomplishment of Liberal Wales was Disestablishment of the Church; another of its legislative achievements was the 1881 Welsh Sunday Closing Act ('the first distinctively Welsh act of parliament'[6]). As well as providing Wales with a much more significant voice in Westminster, the 'Welshness' of Liberal Wales was also expressed in the national institutions which it established: the National Library of Wales, the National Museum and the University of Wales being the most prominent. The heartland of this Liberal Wales was not the large towns of the south or north east, but the more rural areas of mid- and north-west Wales. These were the areas where the sermons preached from pulpits were most influential, where sabbath observance was most strict, and where Welsh was most commonly spoken as a first language.

If the 'pulpit' represents an essentially Liberal-voting, non-industrial, Welsh-speaking Wales led by a self-confident and politically influential middle class, the 'coal pit' symbolized a Wales centred on an industrial economy, largely (though not exclusively) English speaking, and peopled by a large working class who overwhelmingly supported the Labour Party. Important similarities did exist between these two societies: Nonconformist religion was a common element in both, as was the value attached to respectability in appearance and personal advancement through self-education. The 'national' educational and cultural institutions established by Liberal Wales may not have attracted many south Walian miners or steel workers, but well-stocked libraries were one of the key features of the many south Wales miners' institutes built in the early twentieth century. For all the similarities between the societies of the pulpit and the coal pit, however, a key difference was that of nationality. Many of the political efforts of Liberal Wales were aimed at strengthening or creating national institutions that gave expression to a distinct Welsh culture and identity. The politics of Labour Wales, on the other hand, was firmly associated with British socialism in which the identity of class outweighed that of nation. There were certainly those within the Labour Party in Wales who maintained a strong sense of national identity, but nationality was not a defining characteristic of the labour movement as it had been of Liberal Wales.[7] Aneurin Bevan, for instance, was just as fervent in his opposition to the idea of Home Rule as Lloyd George had been in support.

The societies of Liberal and Labour Wales (of the pulpit and the coal pit) co-existed and shared many similarities. Politically, a dramatic shift took place in the 1920s as the dominance of the Liberal Party in Wales was replaced by that of Labour (at least in the most industrial areas). Culturally, however, continuity was as important as change.[8] As Gwyn A. Williams memorably put it: 'the new Labour people were still children, even if bastard children, of imperial Wales.'[9] The leaders of both these societies had reasons to be sceptical of the cultural and educational value of the cinema. The secular, commercial and mostly American entertainment it provided did as little to promote class consciousness and political activism as it did to celebrate Welsh culture, language and identity. Yet the immense popularity of film-going in Wales suggests that the cutural values commonly associated with Liberal or Labour Wales were far from universal. Passions for politics, learning, music and rugby football were real enough, but they were not all-pervasive. For the hundreds of thousands of men and women across Wales who went to the cinema on at least a weekly basis, entertainment took priority over education; the pictures meant as much as party politics; movie stars provided more inspiring role models than Methodist ministers. Cinemas were as much a focal point of Welsh communities as chapels or miners' institutes in the period covered here: the 'fleapit', in other words, was as much a symbol of twentieth-century Welsh society as the pulpit or coal pit. The type of society it symbolized was perhaps that which Alfred Zimmern, writing in 1921, identified as 'American Wales'.[10]

American Wales?

In coining the term 'American Wales' Zimmern did not dwell on what this actually meant. The phrase was little more than a throwaway line in a lecture given to the Cambrian Society at Oxford University. Yet his description of industrial south Wales is one that has been taken up and explored in more detail by subsequent historians who have seen fit to draw parallels between the emergence of industrial society in Wales in the nineteenth century and the forging of modern America.[11] What concerns us here is not the degree of similarity (or otherwise) between the two countries, but the extent to which the popular culture generated by, and for, US society also appealed directly to Welsh audiences. Does the popularity of the cinema, and of Hollywood films in particular, provide tangible evidence that the Welsh working class were as willing to embrace the popular entertainment of the new world as they were to rely on local or national traditions? If film-going can be taken as an indicator of 'American Wales', this was not something confined to the industrialized south of the country. 'Fleapits', as local institutions providing mostly American entertainment, were popular throughout the country by the 1920s. If the society of the fleapit can be equated with American Wales, this needs to be understood not as a geographically specific region within Wales, but as a type of culture or mentality that was distinct from, but also interacted with those of the pulpit and coal pit.

One account of the process by which new forms of entertainment emerged to rival the more traditional pursuits associated with pulpit or coal pit has been provided by Walter Haydn Davies. Davies attributed the initial demand for modern, professional entertainments to immigrant communities in the south Wales valleys, but his description of the appeal of such amusements can perhaps be applied more generally:

> Pulpit 'hwyl' and Pantycelyn's 'Feed me till I want no more' ecstasy made no appeal to them, and local fairs, travelling shows, cock fights, prize fighters, and even the excellence of the Rhymney and Taff Vale brews were not enough. They had tasted the nectar of the newer, professional forms of entertainment on playing field and music hall outside the valley's confines and needed this pleasure more and more as economic stresses multiplied as they strove to earn their daily bread . . . Indoor entertainment became wide and varied so as to suit all tastes, and the music hall ditty became as popular as the hymn.[12]

As economic stresses intensified during the inter-war period, the cinema stood out as the most affordable, accessible and popular form of public indoor entertainment. As Davies remembers it: 'no entertainment enlivened the minds of the masses more than the film whether it was shown in Palace, Electric Theatre, hut or marquee.'[13]

These reminiscences are corroborated by other autobiographical accounts of those who grew up in Wales in the first half of the twentieth century. For the young Emlyn Williams, living in Connah's Quay in the 1920s, life revolved around twice-weekly visits to 'the Hip'. 'As the weeks passed, the Pictures dominated my life: the week rose to Wednesday, sank, rose to Saturday, sank for Sunday and rose again.' For Williams, as for many of his generation, 'the Pictures' held a magical allure quite lacking in other forms of entertainment – including the variety turns that appeared on stage between films. 'I was left cold by the comics in front of a painted Chester street with the local references.' Occasional dance troupes offered a more appealing distraction 'but such rarities could not oust the Silver Screen. It occupied the foreground of my life, vibrant and near, while fuzzy in the background was the Quay'.[14]

Such accounts bear testament to the intensity of the appeal the silver screen held for audiences, but also point to the diversity of cinema-going experiences they enjoyed. In larger towns, particularly, film-goers were able to choose from a range of cinemas: each with its own local reputation. Recalling his childhood years in Newport, for example, Leslie Thomas contrasted a visit to the 'Gem' (on his return from which he was searched for fleas by horrified parents) with the more respectable alternatives of the Odeon or the Maindee Super Cinema.[15] In smaller communities there was often only a single cinema, but even these halls could offer a variety of film-going experiences for different audiences. The anarchy of the children's Saturday morning matinee, for example, was not repeated in the evenings when a more civilized environment was strictly enforced by torch-wielding usherettes. Even during the evenings, however, audiences within the same hall were carefully segregated. The most obvious distinction was between the balcony and the stalls. Indeed, if one was to gauge a person's social status through acts of consumption, rather than their role in the process of produc-tion, their choice of seat at the cinema was probably as accurate an indicator as any. For those wishing to set themselves above and apart from 'the masses', the balcony was the only place to sit, and as acts of conspicuous con-sumption go, this was more affordable than most. Even below the balcony, seats were graded into several price brackets, each attracting a slightly dif-ferent audience.

Cinema entertainment was regarded by some commentators in the 1930s as a symbol of American culture: providing as it did a type of luxury that, by being mass-produced, was cheap and accessible for all. The degree of social segregation within cinemas, however, casts doubt on the notion that these were essentially modern democratic institutions providing exactly the same entertainment for all types of consumers. For writers such as Priestley and Orwell concerns about the pace of modernization, or Americanization, were confined mostly to southern England,[16] yet film-going in Britain was actually most popular in the north of England, Scotland and Wales. Audiences in these regions had clearly developed a taste for American films, but were they 'Americanized'?

Cinema entertainment was largely American entertainment. It was embraced enthusiastically by Welsh audiences, but in their own way and on their owns terms. As we shall see, most of the Rialtos, Plazas, Tivolis and Gems were owned and controlled by local businessmen, or in the case of many valleys cinemas, by miners' institutes. These halls were prominent architectural features of their communities. As well as being relatively large, they were also essentially public spaces and people often felt a sense of own-ership of their local cinema as they did of their local pub.

The purpose of this book is not to demonstrate how cinema changed, or Americanized, Welsh society, but to explore how film-going added to and enriched the existing popular culture. Throughout our period, it must be stressed, cinema remained just one of a range of activities and attractions that kept people amused and entertained during decades of real economic and social stress. Rugby football, of course, was already something of a national obsession by the beginning of the twentieth century, its status being further reinforced with the national side's famous victory over the touring New

Zealand All Blacks in 1905. The period covered by this book was far from being a golden age of Welsh rugby, but leading players remained local heroes in their own communities. Growing up in Llanelli in the 1920s Frederick (later Lord) Elwyn-Jones recalled a local vicar expressing concern 'that the people of his parish were getting too obsessed with rugby. His verger told him: "Don't worry about it. Just mention Albert Jenkins once or twice in your sermon and you'll be all right".'[17] Similar anecdotes have passed down into the folklore of towns and villages across south Wales.

Rugby was not the only provider of local heroes. Boxing was another sport that held a powerful grip on men's imagination, never more so than when a local champion challenged for a world title. The Welsh boxers who achieved the status of world champion in the early twentieth century were Percy Jones, Jimmy Wilde and Freddie Welsh. The latter, according to Gareth Williams, 'embodied that American Wales that was at the same time intensely local and enterprisingly Atlantic in its outlook'.[18] Something similar might be said of Wilde, who invested his hard-earned prize money in a cinema in the south Wales valleys.[19] Welsh boxers achieved less international success in the 1930s and 1940s than in previous decades, but the strength of their following at home was undiminished.

Rugby football and boxing were sports that seemed to hold a particularly strong appeal in Wales, to the extent that rugby has actually become a defining feature of national identity. Yet these were by no means the only sports that people chose to watch or participate in. Walter Haydn Davies's account of social and cultural life in the south Wales valleys in this period gives greater prominence to association football than to rugby, and there is little doubt that soccer was a strong rival to rugby in terms of popularity – if not in its capacity to serve as a vehicle for national self expression. Similarly cricket, although not a sport commonly associated with Welshness, was as popular there as in most other parts of Britain.

Aside from sporting attractions, the cultural activity most often associated with the Welsh in our period was music, or more precisely choral singing. The leading choirs were as much an embodiment of local communities as were rugby or soccer teams, and the rivalry between them could be just as intense. Victory in regional or national competitions were occasions for public celebrations, with conductors elevated to the status of local heroes. The appeal of choral singing was arguably broader than that of rugby or boxing in that it straddled more comfortably the societies of pulpit and coal pit, while capturing the interest of women as well as men. Its popular appeal, however, had probably peaked before our period begins. Gareth Williams concludes his account of the *Valleys of Song* in 1914, and autobiographical accounts of life in Wales in the inter-war period do not provide much sense of choral traditions dominating the cultural life of local communities.

This is not to suggest, of course, that musical or other cultural pursuits were in danger of dying out altogether. Data on consumer expenditure from the 1930s indicate that the average Welsh household in this period spent more per week on music lessons than households in almost every other region of Britain, despite having the lowest overall level of income.[20] The boyhood experience of Harry Libby (a future mayor of Swansea) was no doubt common to many others: 'An aunt gave the Libby family a piano and offered to pay for lessons . . . After three months we gave it up, I was a dismal failure, and my sister decided she would follow my example.'[21] Those with more dedication, or talent, were not short of opportunities to play and to perform. Silver or brass bands were almost as common a feature of Welsh communities as male voice choirs. Bands were sometimes associated with collieries, but were not confined to mining areas. Mumbles, for example, boasted two bands of its own. As well as providing their own musical entertainment, local communities in many parts of Wales maintained a strong tradition of amateur dramatics. Few Welsh towns were large enough to support a permanent theatre, and theatrical entertainments had traditionally been regarded with suspicion by Nonconformist religious leaders. By the inter-war period, however, popular demand for stage plays was catered for by a plethora of local drama and theatrical societies, as well as occasional visits by professional touring companies.[22]

Sporting, musical, and theatrical entertainments were an important feature of social life in Wales in our period which, along with the public house, offered an alternative means of spending leisure time than visiting the cinema. During holiday periods, the range of rival attractions increased. Summer excursions to the seaside were eagerly awaited and provided those from the most industrialized areas, in particular, with some treasured memories. For a young Robert Morgan growing up in Penrhiwceiber a visit to Barry Island 'was the greatest day out of all, a day of wonders, sand to dig holes in, ice-cream to eat, fizzy pop to drink, rock to suck, and a vast sea to play in'. For his parents the attraction was more the opportunity to 'look at the beautiful sea, doze and breathe the fresh air devoid of coal dust'.[23] A day at the seaside would often be concluded with a visit to a fair, but fairground attractions were not restricted to seaside resorts only. Travelling fairs were hugely popular attractions in the inter-war period which for one week in the year would provide the main source of entertainment for a community. Looking back on his Cardiff upbringing Roy Denning described the annual visit of the fair as 'a crowd pulling event of much excitement and merry making'.[24] Against this even cinemas found it hard to compete. The recently appointed manager of one hall in Porth wrote confidently to his employer in 1920 that the 'advantage of a cinema in the Rhondda [is that] it is the only form of amusement the people have'.[25] The arrival of the annual fair soon disabused him of this notion: 'I did not believe that this could possibly interfere with trade until I paid a personal visit. I really think the whole population of Porth remain there from afternoon till 11 pm.'[26]

By the 1920s cinema was the dominant form of publicly consumed indoor entertainment in Wales. Music hall and variety performances had either disappeared or been incorporated into cinema programmes as films, and their stars, provided a more appealing and glamorous attraction. Other forms of public entertainment, however, remained as popular and as important as ever. Cinemas therefore, competed with, and complimented, the wide range of other entertainments available to the public. This book examines how it did so by addressing three sets of questions. The first section considers the social context in which cinema entertainment was brought to Welsh consumers: who were these consumers; what type of cinemas did they go to; and how were these institutions managed? The second section explores the appeal of cinema-going: why did people choose the cinema over other forms of entertainment; what type of entertainment did they receive when they got there? The third, and final, section considers how cinema, as a cultural form and a social institution, was received and regulated. How did the societies of the pulpit and coal pit respond to the mass appeal of moving pictures? What do these responses tell us about changes in Welsh society in the mid-twentieth century?

I

Social-Economic Context of Film-Going in Wales

The film industry has traditionally been divided into three distinct areas: production, distribution and exhibition. Film production is the creative process of film-making itself, involving writers, actors, directors, technicians and a host of other staff working mainly in film studios. Distribution is the process by which completed films are marketed and sold to the network of cinemas stretching across a country, or indeed the world. The exhibition side of the business is that responsible for providing filmed entertainment to the public. In the period with which this book is concerned there was a high degree of international business activity in the production and distribution sides of the film industry. American companies, in particular, proved highly effective in producing films that appealed to international audiences, though the popularity of US films in non-English speaking markets was diminished after the coming of the 'talkies' at the end of the 1920s. By this time leading US film companies had set up distribution subsidiaries in national markets around the world, to ensure that their films were widely available. The exhibition side of the industry, however, remained largely under the control of national companies, not international ones. US film companies operated a handful of cinemas in key international markets, but the vast majority of cinemas around the world were not foreign owned.

In Britain in this period, while all but a handful of cinemas were British owned, the majority of films they screened were American, leading one commentator to observe that 'to be an Englishman in the film industry is to know what it's like to be colonised'.[1] In fact, the proportion of British films screened in UK cinemas did increase significantly – from 5 per cent in the mid-1920s to around 25 per cent for most of the 1930s and 40s – largely as a result of protective legislation introduced by the British government in 1927. British films proved no match for American competition, however, outside the protected British market.

In Wales, in the period covered here, there were no significant film production or distribution companies to speak of, nor were there any major Welsh cinema chains. The leading British cinema circuits did operate a limited number of venues in Wales in this period but most film exhibition in Wales was controlled by small, locally owned firms operating between one and ten halls in a geographically confined area.

In most historical accounts of the British film industry the small independent exhibitor is seen as a peripheral figure. This is quite understandable in any account based around the products themselves: the films. The key to success for any individual picture was usually to be found in a combination of production values, distribution arrangements and, crucially, a booking with a major cinema chain. British film historians have shown how the growth of large domestic production, distribution and exhibition companies in the 1930s (on the back of the Cinematograph Films Act of 1927) helped to restore the economic (if not necessarily the cultural) fortunes of the UK industry.

This book is not a history of the film production, however, but a history of film-going. Its main point of focus is not the films themselves, but the consumers who gathered in their thousands to see them. Since Wales did not have a functioning commercial film industry, there can be no attempt here to analyse the success or failure of Welsh films. The emphasis instead will be on who went to the cinema, why they went, and the implications of this for our understanding of Welsh culture and society. In such a study the small independent film exhibitor is not a marginal figure. He (and they were mostly men) represented, and controlled, the point of contact between the consumers and the products. In Wales, the small exhibitors may not have been able to determine which films were successful, but they played a key role in shaping the experiences of a generation of habitual cinema-goers.

Histories of Wales centred on the societies of the coal pit or the pulpit have seldom conceived of the Welsh people as consumers. Communities whose economic stability was shaken by the collapse of their major industries, and whose cultural traditions, based around strict religious observance and an instinctive scepticism of secular commercialism, appear quite at odds with the notion of a consumer society. A combination of inter-war depression, wartime shortages and post-war rationing meant that in the period covered here, Wales was certainly never an affluent consumer society. People may not have been able to define an individual identity for themselves on the basis of consumer spending decisions, yet they were surely consumers nonetheless. For all the political solidarity of the mining communities, or the sermonizing in the chapels, audiences across Wales flocked to the picture houses to experience, albeit fleetingly, another (more glamorous) lifestyle, just as their children and grandchildren demanded designer 'brands' later in the century.

The first section of the book will analyse consumer spending on film-going in Wales, and compare patterns of cinema attendance with other parts of Britain. How often did people go to the cinema, and how much did they spend? From here the analysis moves beyond the consumers themselves, to the industry that emerged to supply and sustain their patterns of consumption. What did the film (exhibition) industry look like, and what effect did it have on the economy and society of Wales?

1

CONSUMERS

In most accounts of economic development in Wales in the first half of the twentieth century, the process of production (or lack of it) has taken priority over the role of consumption. This is understandable, since the economic health of just a few industries, most notably coal, iron and steel, had an enormous impact on levels of employment and overall living standards for a large part of the Welsh population. A great deal has been written about the decline of the coal industry, in particular, in the inter-war decades, and the problems of unemployment this caused – most notably in the eastern part of the south Wales coalfield.[1] Historians have also examined industrial relations in these industries, which were as politically charged in Wales as in any other part of Britain.[2] Much attention has been devoted to the creation of a strong working-class identity on the part of Welsh labour,[3] but rather less is known about the Welsh in their economic role as consumers.

How does one begin to construct a consumer's eye view of economic and social history in Wales? Discussions of consumption can lead in many different directions, and terms such as 'consumerism' or 'consumer society' mean different things to different people.[4] One recent study of the subject has argued that 'the central problem of the polymorphic meaning of the terms consumer and consumption can be overcome by categorizing goods according to three distinct types: those associated with luxury, with necessity and with affluence'.[5] Each of these three fields of consumption has led to the creation of specific forms of consumer politics.[6] In many discussions of the rise of modern consumer societies, however, emphasis tends to be placed on patterns of consumption related to affluence – be it among middle-income groups in the eighteenth century, or working-class communities in the late nineteenth or twentieth centuries.[7] In his attempt to pin down what social historians really meant when they used the term 'consumer society', John Benson managed to identify three discernible trends: 'they are societies, it emerges, in which choice and credit are readily available, in which social value is defined in terms of purchasing power and material possessions, and in which there is a desire, above all, for that which is new, modern, exciting and fashionable.'[8]

Between 1918 and 1951 Wales was not an affluent consumer society. Far from it. Much of the period covered here was one of crisis and decline for the industries of coal, iron and steel that dominated the economy of south Wales in particular. The 1920s witnessed rising levels of unemployment in many parts of Wales, and the onset of the depression in the early 1930s was more acutely felt in Wales than in almost any other part of Britain. This was not a society of which it could be said that 'choice and credit were readily available'. Nor was it one where social status was necessarily bestowed by purchasing power or material possessions. The desire, however, to embrace modernity and to keep up with the latest trends and fashions was evident in even the most economically deprived communities. As Thorstein Veblen observed in his *Theory of the Leisure Class* in 1899: 'No class of society, not even the most abjectly poor, forgoes all conspicuous consumption. The last items of this category are not given up except under stress of the very direst necessity.'[9]

The Welsh may not have been affluent, but this is not to say they were not consumers. With economic prosperity restricted to only a small proportion of the population of Wales, many consumer products and entertainments remained beyond the means of the average Welsh household. Yet, the people of Wales were still able to keep in touch with a world of 'conspicuous consumption' through newspaper and magazine articles and advertising, popular literature and, of course, the cinema. A visit to the local picture house was the closest many people would get to experiencing the consumption of products associated with luxury or even affluence. It allowed audiences to suspend disbelief and, for a few hours at least, forget about mundane 'necessities'. Hollywood, in Hortense Powdermaker's famous phrase, was a 'dream factory',[10] and with cinema tickets costing as little as a few pence, the dreams and desires it offered were affordable for almost everyone.

This chapter will examine how much the average Welsh household spent on cinema-going, and compare levels and patterns of cinema attendance in Wales with the rest of Britain. First, however, cinema consumption will be placed in the context of overall household spending in both Wales and Britain. Even those on the lowest incomes had to make choices about the allocation of weekly expenditures. How did they choose to spend their (limited) disposable income: and what were they getting for their money?

Consumers and consumer expenditure in Wales

Reliable statistics providing a detailed breakdown of consumer expenditure in Wales do not exist for the whole of the period covered here.[11] However, two surveys conducted by the Ministry of Labour in 1937/8[12] and 1953/4,[13] do allow a comparison to be made between consumption patterns in the middle, and at the end, of our period. The two dates are significant because they measure consumer expenditure under very different economic conditions. For much of the inter-war period Wales was among the most economically depressed areas of the United Kingdom, a fact reflected in the absolute levels of expenditure reported in 1937/8 – which were lower in Wales than any other part of Britain. By the early 1950s, in contrast, the Welsh economy had been transformed: unemployment was down to two per cent, average incomes in Wales were in line with the national average, as was household expenditure.[14] The data examined here do not provide a complete picture of consumer spending in Wales (or Britain), and the two surveys are not directly comparable. The 1937/8 survey looked at working-class households only, whereas the 1953/4 enquiry was broader in scope. Some attempt has been made to correct this difference, at least at the UK level, by providing figures for the working-class households covered by the 1953/4 survey though it was not possible to identify and isolate such households within Wales.

Another difficulty in comparing the two surveys is that in each case the results were presented quite differently. Spending was broken down into ten separate categories in 1953/4, but only five in 1937/8. To overcome this problem both sets of survey data were examined at the level of the most detailed units of analysis, and nine broadly comparable categories were drawn up. Not all of the categories correspond exactly, but they match each other closely enough to allow general trends to be identified. The results of these two surveys do not provide an exact picture of how household spending patterns changed in Wales between the 1930s and the 1950s, but they do provide the most reliable indication possible about consumption trends in this period.

Table 1
Average weekly household expenditure in
Wales and the UK (in d at 1953 prices)

	Wales		UK		W-C Households in UK	
	1937/8	1953/4	1937/8	1953/4	1937/8	1953/4
Housing	263	272	314	336	314	263
Food	962	977	989	958	989	1017
Clothing	231	395	235	339	235	317
Fuel and light	172	140	186	148	186	142
Household goods and services	141	385	160	391	160	361
Tax, insurance and welfare	202	335	226	374	226	339
Travel	44	172	66	201	66	182
Recreation	176	509	216	489	216	539
Other	55	77	75	85	75	77
Total	2246	3262	2467	3321	2467	3235

Source: Ministry of Labour, 'Weekly expenditure of working-class households in the UK in 1937/8'; Ministry of Labour, *Report of an Enquiry into Household Expenditure in 1953–54.*

What, then, do the results of these two surveys tell us? The first and most basic finding is that, after allowing for inflation, total weekly expenditure increased significantly over the period (see table 1). Among working-class households in the UK, average weekly spending was 31 per cent higher in 1953/4 than it had been in 1937/8. In Wales, average household expenditure reported in the 1953/4 survey was 45 per cent higher than in that of 1937/8. Whereas average household spending in Wales had been 9 per cent below the UK average in 1937/8, it was within 2 per cent by the 1950s.

Given the overall growth in household expenditure, it is not surprising to find real terms increases in spending in every category, in both Wales and the UK as a whole. Some categories, however, grew much faster than others. If we look at the proportion of total expenditure allocated to each of the categories in the two surveys some clear trends emerge (see table 2). We see a noticeable decline in the proportion of expenditure allocated to housing costs and also to fuel and lighting. There is a much more dramatic decline in the proportion of the household budget spent on food. On the other hand we see an increasing proportion of household spending going on travel, and household goods and services. More importantly, for the purpose of this book, we see something close to a doubling in the relative importance of recreational spending. By the early 1950s 'recreation' accounted for a larger proportion of household expenditure than any other category except food. All of these trends are clearly identifiable in both Wales and the UK as a whole, and all are equally apparent when we look at working-class households only. In fact, the increasing prominence of recreational spending is even more pronounced when only working- class households are considered.

Table 2
Breakdown of weekly household expenditure in Wales and the UK (%)

	Wales		UK		W-C Households in UK	
	1937/8	1953/4	1937/8	1953/4	1937/8	1953/4
Housing	11.7	8.4	12.7	10.1	12.7	8.1
Food	42.8	29.9	40.1	28.8	40.1	31.4
Clothing	10.3	12.1	9.5	10.2	9.5	9.8
Fuel and light	7.7	4.3	7.6	4.5	7.6	4.4
Household goods and services	6.3	11.8	6.5	11.8	6.5	11.1
Tax, insurance and welfare	9.0	10.3	9.1	11.3	9.1	10.5
Travel	2.0	5.3	2.7	6.1	2.7	5.6
Recreation	7.8	15.6	8.7	14.7	8.7	16.7
Other	2.5	2.4	3.1	2.6	3.1	2.4
Total	100.1	100.1	100	100.1	100	100

Source: Ministry of Labour, 'Weekly expenditure of working-class households in the UK in 1937/8'; Ministry of Labour, *Report of an Enquiry into Household Expenditure in 1953–54.*

The following section will examine expenditure on recreation in more detail, with a particular focus on the relative importance of the cinema.

Consumer expenditure on cinema and other forms of recreation

The evidence from the Ministry of Labour surveys suggests that in the 1930s the average Welsh household could not afford to allocate as much expenditure to recreation as the typical British household. By the 1950s this had changed, and the proportion of household budgets devoted to recreational pursuits was higher in Wales than the UK as a whole. Recreation appeared to be the fastest growing area of household expenditure between the 1930s and the 1950s, and in Wales the rate of growth was faster than in the rest of Britain.

While spending on leisure and recreation was growing rapidly, however, the increased spending on cinema-going was much less pronounced. Among working-class households in the UK, recreational spending rose by 150 per

Table 3
Average weekly expenditure on recreation in Wales
and the UK (in d at 1953 prices)

	Wales		UK		W-C Households in UK	
	1937/8	1953/4	1937/8	1953/4	1937/8	1953/4
Tobacco	68	197	74	191	74	222
Alcoholic drink	12	94	22	98	22	108
Radio, TV and musical instruments	–	52	–	33	–	35
Books, newspapers and periodicals	30	43	35	46	35	45
Cinema	24	31	26	29	26	35
Theatre and sport	9	23	14	26	14	25
Licences (TV, radio etc.)	15	10	14	8	14	8
Library and other entertainment	–	8	–	7	–	6
Holiday	7	22*	19	25	19	20*
Betting	–	29	–	27	–	35
Total	165	509	204	489	204	539

* Holiday expenditure was included in a category with trade union subscriptions and church collections in 1953/4, which was disaggregated at a UK level. These figures have been estimated by assuming that the proportion of expenditure on holidays, relative to other items in the category, was the same across the UK.

Source: Ministry of Labour, 'Weekly expenditure of working-class households in the UK in 1937/8'; Ministry of Labour, Report of an Enquiry into Household Expenditure in 1953–54.

Table 4
Breakdown of expenditure on recreation in Wales and the UK (%)

	Wales		UK		W-C Households in UK	
	1937/8	1953/4	1937/8	1953/4	1937/8	1953/4
Tobacco	41.3	38.7	36.2	39.1	36.2	41.2
Alcoholic drink	7.2	18.5	10.9	20.1	10.9	20.1
Radio, TV and musical instruments	–	10.3	–	6.7	–	6.5
Books, newspapers and periodicals	18.2	8.5	17.0	9.3	17.0	8.3
Cinema	14.4	6.0	12.7	5.8	12.7	6.6
Theatre and sport	5.7	4.5	7.0	5.3	7.0	4.5
Licences (TV, radio, etc.)	8.8	2.0	7.0	1.6	7.0	1.4
Library and other entertainment	–	1.5	–	1.5	–	1.1
Holiday	4.4	4.4	9.1	5.2	9.1	3.8
Betting	–	5.7	–	5.5	–	6.5
Total	100	100.1	99.9	100.1	99.9	100

Source: Ministry of Labour, 'Weekly expenditure of working-class households in the UK in 1937/8'; Ministry of Labour, *Report of an Enquiry into Household Expenditure in 1953–54.*

cent in real terms between the late 1930s and the early 1950s, the corresponding figure for cinema spending was only 37 per cent. The breakdown of expenditure on recreational pursuits is provided in tables 3 and 4.

As these tables suggest, not all of the items classified here as recreational expenditure were measured in both of the surveys. While data exists from 1953/4 for spending on television and radios, betting, and also a category called 'library and other entertainments', no comparable figures are available from 1937/8. The total figure for recreational spending in 1953/4 is thus based on more comprehensive data than that available for 1937/8. While this clearly makes a difference to the figures, it does not distort the overall picture. Even if we deduct spending on these three categories from the 1953/4 figures, we still find that among working-class households in the UK spending on recreation increased by 127 per cent in real terms between the late 1930s and the early 1950s. The vast majority of this increase in recreational spending, both in Wales and the UK as a whole, was accounted for by a quite dramatic leap in expenditure on tobacco and alcoholic drinks.

Spending on cinema-going, like that on books, newspapers and periodicals (a category that would have included film related magazines), though rising faster than the rate of inflation, did not increase at anything like the same rate as spending on drink or tobacco. This, in addition to the emergence of new recreational categories in the 1953/4 survey, meant that the proportion of recreational spending allocated to film-going was much lower in the later survey.

In the late 1930s, although Welsh households could not afford to spend as much on recreation as those in other parts of the UK, the proportion of this expenditure devoted to cinema-going (14.4 per cent) was well above the national average. By the early 1950s the typical Welsh household was spending more on recreation than the average British one, but the proportion of this (much higher) level of expenditure going on the cinema had fallen to just 6 per cent, which was in line with the national average. In Wales, spending on film-going as a proportion of all expenditure fell from 1.1 per cent in 1937/8 to 0.9 per cent by 1953/4.

Cinema-going, then, was not an especially important economic activity in terms of the amount of money people spent on it. However, this strictly economic measurement of the cinema's importance does not reflect the significance of its social and cultural role. Judged purely in terms of consumer spending, cinema-going became relatively less important between the late 1930s and the early 1950s. Yet this is not to say that the relative importance of cinema as a form of recreation also declined for consumers in Wales (or the rest of Britain) during this period. Indeed, the popularity of film-going was at its peak at precisely this time. If we are to understand how important cinema-going was for consumers, it is necessary not just to examine how much they spent but how frequently they went.

The level of cinema attendance in Wales and Britain

Reliable statistics for cinema attendance in Britain only exist for the period from 1934 onwards. For the period between the First World War and the early 1930s we must rely on estimates drawn mainly from the trade press. These suggest a dramatic surge in cinema admissions during the First World War followed by a levelling off in attendance levels during the inter-war period, and then a second upswing in cinema-going in the 1940s. One study of film-going in Britain has suggested that the average weekly number of cinema visits *per household* declined substantially between 1919 and 1929, before rising once again in the 1940s.[15] The overall attendance figures, however, suggest a level of cinema-going in the inter-war period that was only slightly below the First World War peak, but very substantially below the level achieved in the 1940s and early 1950s (see table 5).[16]

The proportion of household expenditure allocated to film-going may have dropped between the late 1930s and the early 1950s, but this clearly did not mean that it had become less popular, or less important a part of peoples' lives. Levels of cinema attendance were, in fact, 45 per cent higher in 1952 than they had been in 1934. Indeed, in the early 1950s the British were, by some margin, the world's most avid film-goers.[17]

How much of this increase in cinema attendance in the 1940s can be attributed to ticket prices becoming cheaper? Between the 1930s and the 1950s the
average price of a cinema ticket did increase more slowly than the rate of
inflation, and much more slowly than the increase in household income.[18]
The increase in cinema admissions, however, cannot be attributed solely to
falling prices. Tickets were cheaper in real terms in 1952 than they had been
in the mid-1930s, but during the period of the Second World War itself, when
attendance levels soared, the real-terms cost of a cinema ticket also increased.
This was due, almost entirely, to an extraordinary hike in the level of entertainment duty charged on cinema admissions. The average rate of tax
increased from little more than 13 per cent in the late 1930s to just under 36
per cent by the mid-1940s. As the rate of entertainment tax levelled off at
around 35 per cent from the mid-1940s prices stabilized, and fell in real

Table 5
Cinema admissions and average ticket prices in Britain, 1914–1952

Year	Weekly cinema admissions (millions)	Av. ticket price in d (nominal)	Av. ticket price in d (1953 prices)	Av. rate of entertainment tax (%)
1914	7.0	n/a	n/a	0
1917	20.6	4	8.5	n/a
1925	20.0	n/a	n/a	n/a
1929	18.0	n/a	n/a	n/a
1934	17.4	10.3	27.3	16.5
1935	17.4	10.2	26.7	15.0
1936	17.6	10.1	25.6	13.5
1937	18.2	10.1	24.4	13.5
1938	19.0	10.1	24.1	13.3
1939	19.0	10.1	22.3	13.4
1940	19.8	10.6	20.2	14.9
1941	25.2	11.9	20.7	19.7
1942	28.7	14.0	24.3	26.6
1943	29.6	16.1	28.1	33.5
1944	30.3	17.0	29.3	35.5
1945	30.5	17.3	28.4	35.7
1946	31.4	17.4	25.0	35.8
1947	28.1	17.3	23.2	35.8
1948	29.1	17.2	21.5	35.7
1949	27.5	17.3	20.9	35.3
1950	26.8	18.1	21.5	35.0
1951	26.3	19.0	20.5	35.4
1952	25.2	20.1	20.7	34.7

Source: Hiley, ' "Let's go to the pictures" '; Browning and Sorrell, 'Cinemas and cinema-going in
Great Britain'.

terms.[19] The average price of a cinema ticket, when adjusted for inflation, was 25 per cent lower in 1951 than it had been in 1934, despite the rise in tax.

Unfortunately, neither the price of cinema admission, nor the level of cinema attendance, is broken down by region in the 1930s or 40s. The surviving records of one cinema exhibitor, however, reveal exactly how much the audience of one picture house in the south Wales valleys paid for their cinema tickets in the 1920s and the 1940s.[20] For the years 1924–8 and 1944–6 the cash books of Porth's Central Cinema recorded not just the gross and net receipts, but also the weekly admissions figures broken down by price of ticket (see table 6). The data reveals that patrons of this cinema (typical of many across the south Wales valleys) were even more likely to sit in seats costing 7d or less than the average British audience.

The increasing proportion of Porth's film-goers paying over 1s for their tickets by the 1940s (and the declining proportion paying 7d or less) can be accounted for at least in part by inflationary pressures – particularly during the Second World War. Between the mid-1920s and the mid-1930s, however, Britain underwent a period of deflation which means that, if anything, an even greater proportion of this cinema's audience would have occupied cheap seats in 1934 than had been the case in the 1920s.

The effect of inflation on the price of cinema tickets, and the comparison between ticket prices in the south Wales valleys and the rest of Britain, can be seen more clearly when the average cost of cinema admission is calculated, as in table 7.

The falling (real terms) price paid for cinema tickets in Porth in the mid-1920s is partly attributable to a decline in the level of entertainment duty, and partly to the economic hardship caused by the miners strike of 1926. In the second half of 1926 attendance levels at this cinema fell significantly, and almost two-thirds of the audience occupied seats costing less that 7d. Ticket prices were higher in the 1940s than they had been in the 1920s, but not by very much. The years 1944–45 saw ticket prices across the country reach a peak as the rate of entertainment tax more than doubled from its pre-war level (see table 5). In Porth, however, patrons of the Central paid approximately 30 per cent less for cinema tickets than the average British film-goer

Table 6
Attendance at Porth's Central Cinema by price of ticket (nominal prices)

Price	1924–1928* %	1944–1946* %	British average in 1934 (%)
7d and under	53.9	33.4	42.7
8d – 1s	38.5	44.2	37.3
Over 1s	7.6	22.3	20.0

* These figures based on sample weeks from each quarter of the years in question.

Source: Central Cinema Cash Books, GRO D/D A/B 41/2–7.

Table 7
Average price paid for admission to Porth's Central Cinema

Year	Average ticket price (d)	Average at 1953 prices (d)	British average at 1953 prices (d)
1924	7.6	16.2	n/a
1925	7.1	15.1	n/a
1926	6.3	13.7	n/a
1927	6.6	14.7	n/a
1928	6.5	14.6	n/a
1944	11.9	20.5	29.3
1945	12.4	20.3	28.4
1946	12.3	17.7	25.0

Source: Central Cinema Cash Books, GRO D/D A/B 41/2–7.

in the mid-1940s, and the average price of a ticket in 1946 was barely any higher in real terms than it had been in 1924, despite the higher rate of tax.

The Central in Porth may not, of course, be representative of cinemas in Wales more generally. Figures from the early 1950s, however, clearly illustrate that the areas where average ticket prices were lowest were the ones where admissions were highest. In Wales, levels of attendance matched the British average exactly. Here, attendances were lower than in northern England or Scotland, but higher than in the midlands or the south of England. Conversely, prices of admission were on average higher in Wales than northern regions or Scotland, but lower than in the midlands or the south (see table 8).

The nature of the film-going experience meant that people could pay very different amounts of money to watch the same film. Some cinemas charged more for admission than others, and as we have seen, even within the same hall ticket prices varied widely according to where one chose to sit. The average price paid for cinema tickets in any given area, therefore, was determined not just by the admission prices charged by cinemas, but by the consumption patterns of audiences themselves.[21] In Wales, for example, average ticket prices were lower than in south-west England, but this does not necessarily mean that the typical cinema in Wales charged a lower rate of admission than its equivalent in the south-west. The differential may be due to more film-goers in Wales choosing to visit cheaper types of cinema or sit in cheaper seats. The final part of this chapter looks at the composition of cinema audiences, and compares patterns of film-going in Wales with other parts of Britain.

Table 8
Cinema admissions and average prices by region, 1950–1951

Region	Admissions per person (April 1950–March 1951)	Average Admission Price in d (January–March 1951)
Northern regions	37	15.4
East and West Ridings	34	16.1
North west	35	16.2
Scotland	36	15.9
North midlands	25	18.2
Midlands	26	18.6
Eastern regions	17	21.3
London and south east	26	22.8
South	20	22.5
South west	19	21.8
Wales	28	17.7
Great Britain	28	18.5

Source: Browning and Sorrell, 'Cinemas and cinema-going in Great Britain'.

Patterns of cinema attendance in Wales and Britain

A 1952 report into the film industry in Britain explained that

> For cinema-going purposes the population of Great Britain can be divided into three groups: those who are regular cinema-goers, that is to say those who go once a week or more often, occasional cinema-goers who go less than once a week; and those who 'never go to the pictures'.[22]

Rising levels of cinema attendance in the 1940s were probably not the result of any increase in the number of film-goers as such, but of the proportion of these who went to the cinema on a regular basis.[23] Even in 1946, the peak year for cinema admissions in Britain, film-going was far from a universal activity. In that year a survey of 'the cinema and the public' found that 27 per cent of the sample population never went to the cinema at all, and a further 22 per cent visited the cinema less than once a month. High attendance levels were attributable in large part to those who went to the pictures once a week or more, who constituted approximately one third of those questioned.[24] A similar picture emerged from a survey conducted in 1943.[25] The results of the two surveys are compared in table 9.

The 1943 survey was conducted in the summer months (a relatively quiet period for cinemas) and the 1946 one in October of that year. This seasonal difference is reflected in the higher proportion of people in 1943 claiming not to go the cinema at that time of year. Seasonal variation appears to have had

Table 9

Frequency of cinema attendance in Britain

'How often do you go to the cinema at this time of year?'	1943 %	1946 %
More than twice a week	4	3
Twice a week	8	10
Once a week	20	19
Once a fortnight	6	9
Once a month	6	10
Less than once a month	26	22
Don't go now	9	3
Never go	21	24
Sample size	5639	3137

Source: Moss and Box, 'The cinema audience'; Box, 'The Cinema and the Public'.

much less influence on the most committed film-goers, however, with 32 per cent of respondents in both surveys claiming to be regular film-goers. The higher overall attendance figures for 1946 may be the result of a slightly higher proportion of this 'regular' group actually going to the pictures twice a week or more.

The extraordinary levels of cinema attendance in mid-twentieth-century Britain are explained not by the breadth of the cinema's appeal, but by its intensity. Perhaps only half the population went to the cinema on anything like a regular basis, even in the 1940s, but for many of those people film-going had become a deeply ingrained habit. On the basis of the figures in table 9 we can estimate that at least half of the typical cinema audience in the 1940s would have consisted of people who went to the pictures at least twice a week. The importance of these most committed film-goers to the industry as a whole was crucial: 'if this small group cut its visits from twice a week to once a week' one report warned, 'total cinema attendances would drop by 25 per cent.'[26]

When cinema-going patterns are broken down on a regional basis, we see a correlation between the proportion of regular film-goers and overall levels of attendance. Northern England and Scotland tend to have a higher proportion of regular cinema-goers than the national average, while most southern regions have a lower one. The north/south divide is perhaps less important in this respect, however, than the urban/rural one, with regions such as London and the Midlands having more regular film-goers than Scotland or the north east. Wales had a lower proportion of regular film-goers than either the northern regions or the main urban conurbations, though it had more than most other regions in the southern half of Britain (see table 10).[27] Unfortunately, these figures do not tell us what proportion of regular film-goers in each region went to the pictures twice a week or more.

Table 10
Frequency of cinema attendance in Britain by Region, 1943

	Once a week or more (%)	Less than once a week (%)	Not at all (%)	No information (%)
Scotland	33	35	30	2
North	44	30	26	–
North west	38	41	20	–
North east	29	39	31	1
North midlands	23	41	36	–
Midlands	37	38	25	–
East Anglia	19	44	37	1
South	23	40	37	–
South west	21	32	46	–
South east	26	40	34	–
London	38	39	22	1
Wales	26	36	38	–
Britain	32	38	30	–

Source: Moss and Box, 'The cinema audience'.

The mass appeal of the cinema in the period from the 1920s to the 1950s cannot be attributed just to the attraction of individual films: the practice of film-going itself had become habitual for a significant minority of the population. This is not to say, of course, that the films themselves were unimportant or that audiences failed to exercise any critical judgement over the entertainment before them.[28] Film-goers clearly preferred some pictures to others, most had the favourite 'stars', and audiences were certainly not slow to express their disapproval when a film was not up to the expected standard.[29] How, then, do we reconcile the notion that film-goers were discerning customers with the statistical evidence which tells us that at least half of all film-goers were people who went to the pictures at least once a week, every week?

One recent study of cinema audiences in Britain in the 1950s identified three distinct groups: indiscriminate, regular and occasional cinema-goers. The 'indiscriminate' group, which declined significantly in number and importance in the 1950s, were those who attended the cinema irrespective of the film being shown. 'Regular' film-goers were more discerning in their choice of film but, nonetheless, for this group 'a visit to the cinema was part of their weekly routine'. 'Occasional' film-goers, on the other hand, only visited the cinema if there was a particular film they wanted to see.[30] The 1946 survey of cinema-going allows us to identify what proportion of film-goers fell into each of these categories (see table 11).

Table 11 does not include those people who went to the cinema less than once a month, but it does indicate the film-going habits of the vast majority

Table 11
Cinema-going habits, 1946

Habit	% of film-goers
Generally go to the same cinema regularly, whatever the film	23
Go to a cinema regularly, choosing from those available the one with the best film	48
Generally go to the same cinema, but only if they think they will like the film	10
Only go to the cinema when there is a film they particularly want to see	19
Sample (those who go once a month or more)	1206

Source: Box, 'The cinema and the public'.

of cinema audiences. Less than 30 per cent of film-goers only went to the cinema when there was a film showing that they thought they would like. For the remainder, the decision whether or not to go to the cinema was not determined by the film being shown, but more by force of habit. The majority of these habitual film-goers did exercise choice over the films they saw by visiting the cinema with the most appealing film. The choice of film for these people, however, was a secondary one which came after the decision to go to the cinema itself. Finally there was a significant group of film-goers, almost a quarter, who apparently exercised no discretion at all over the films they saw, visiting the same cinema on a regular basis irrespective of the film being shown.

The reliability of the demand for weekly screen entertainment, consumed as a matter of routine by audiences who were happy to keep coming back for more, enabled a multitude of local village or suburban halls to survive even though they could not compete with big town-centre cinemas in terms of new releases. As such, much film-going in our period was concentrated in local halls which were often a focal point for their communities.[31] A visit to a small local hall provided a very different type of film-going experience to that on offer at the largest showpiece cinemas.[32] As attendance levels declined in the 1950s and 1960s most of these smaller local halls closed and the habit of going to the local cinema was lost.[33] From the 1920s to the early 1950s, however, the cinema succeeded in becoming an established part of many peoples' weekly routine, and was by far the most popular form of publicly consumed entertainment. In Wales, more than in any other part of Britain, the film-going culture that developed in this period was based around small, local cinemas. It is to these sites of consumption that our attention now turns.

2

CINEMAS

The statistical measurement of consumer expenditure, cinema admissions and patterns of attendance provides a sound empirical base for assessing the popularity of film-going. If we are to understand *why* film-going was popular, however, or assess its importance as a social or cultural institution, a much clearer picture of the actual process of film consumption is required. This chapter begins to provide such a picture by examining the environment in which films were screened.

Nicholas Hiley has argued that between the First World War and the 1940s, two distinct patterns of cinema consumption can be identified.[1] The first of these was mainly associated with the silent period, when film was still in its infancy and only beginning to be established as a 'respectable' form of entertainment. During this period audiences were almost exclusively working-class, tickets were extremely cheap, and films were shown in small auditoria that often were not purpose-built as cinemas at all – such as old skating rinks.[2] Programmes consisted of a range of short films, perhaps a weekly serial, and one longer 'feature' film. The cinemas themselves were public spaces that working-class audiences were able to dominate and control. In this early pattern of film-going the site of consumption, and the social environment in which films were viewed, played at least as important a part of the cinema experience as the pictures themselves.[3]

Such a pattern of film consumption began to change, according to Hiley, in the 1930s. This decade witnessed the construction of new cinema buildings across many parts of Britain that were specifically designed to attract a new, and decidedly more up-market, class of film-goer. Audiences in these new, and usually much larger, auditoria were segmented into cheaper and more expensive seats, and the behaviour of audiences was closely monitored by cinema staff.[4] Programmes of entertainment tended to be longer, with fewer short films and two main features. During the 1930s

> the traditions of silent film presentation – dominated by working-class attendance, small local auditoria, and many elements of live performance – gave way to a new style of sound film presentation – in larger and more imposing auditoria, before a socially mixed audience whose sense of communal identity was much reduced. In the large sound cinemas, a docile audience was expected to attend, rather than to participate, and the routines were imposed by management.[5]

The 1930s, according to the seminal work on film-going in the period, was 'the age of the dream palace'.[6]

Such a transformation in film exhibition may have taken place in many parts of Britain, but it was much less evident in Wales. Hiley does recognize that in some parts of the country older patterns of consumption persisted, and several commentators have pointed to differences between film audiences in the north and south of Britain.[7] In Wales, older patterns of film-going did not just persist, they remained the norm. In no part of Britain were there fewer 'dream palaces' constructed in the 1930s. Small local cinemas, or fleapits, remained as much a part of film-going culture in Wales in the 1940s as they had been twenty years earlier. Film-going, as we have seen, was as popular in Wales as the rest of Britain, but here rising levels of attendance in the 1930s and 40s cannot be attributed to the emergence of a new pattern of film exhibition based around large modern cinemas.

This chapter will examine the nature of cinema provision in Wales. What types of cinema did most people attend? Did this change to any great extent between the 1920s and the early 1950s, and were there significant regional variations within Wales? Before dealing with these questions, and to put them in context, a survey of the main trends in cinema design in Britain will be provided.

Cinema architecture in Britain up to the 1930s

The period between the cinematograph's invention and the end of the First World War witnessed two discernible routes of development as far as the provision of cinema entertainment was concerned. The first of these involved films being shown as part of a general programme of entertainment in variety theatres or music halls. There has been some dispute over just how popular the early films were with variety or vaudeville audiences,[8] but they did well enough to survive, and in many cases they became an integral part of the programme. One Edinburgh showman recalled using them to maintain continuity throughout the show:

> A whistle was blown and a large linen graph sheet was pulled across the proscenium and pegged down, while a five or six minute Felix the Cat or a single reel Chaplin short was screened. Meanwhile the stage was being prepared behind for acts – a conjuror, monocyclist or equilibrist. The screen pulled off – on with the act – and at its conclusion another whistle . . .[9]

Before long films were the main attraction at variety theatres, and these halls began to devote themselves entirely to the screening of films as early as 1908.[10] Many of the buildings used as cinemas in Wales in our period were in fact old theatres or music halls.

A second line of development in cinema architecture begins with the medium's fairground origins. In the earliest days of the cinematograph people lined up outside a showman's booth to catch a glimpse of the 'miracle' of living pictures. As the cinema's enormous popularity became apparent, the showmen sought to cash in by screening their films in larger (though no more salubrious) 'penny gaffs'.[11] It was not until at least a decade after the cinema's arrival that its popularity was recognized by the trade as much more than a passing fad, and showmen began to plan for the longer term. Rather than packing the public into 'penny gaffs', they began to invest in purpose-built cinemas that claimed to offer comfort and refinement, as well as a full programme of films.

Purpose-built cinemas appeared at about the same time as variety theatres started to devote themselves entirely to the screening of films. Those halls which were designed specifically as cinemas, however, were seldom noted for their architectural quality or distinctiveness.[12] According to Dennis Sharp, 'The Grosvenor, All Saints, built in 1912, is a perfect surviving example of the pre-war picture house, with cream and green faience tiled elevations on two streets, a small copper dome over the corner entrance and an interior that is more like an Edwardian music hall than a cinema.'[13] These early cinemas lacked a discernible identity but, thanks partly to the Cinematograph Act of 1909, they were an improvement on what had gone before. The act's provisions dealt with safety regulations, particularly in the event of fire, but as Rachael Low has pointed out: 'More and more effort was spent in impressing the audience with comfort and elegance, and proving the pictures worthy of better-class audiences.' This was even reflected in the names of the cinemas with Gem, Palace, Pictorium, Jewel and Imperial being popular choices. Although as Low suggests: 'Such inept efforts to be dignified may have made a more favourable impression on the working-class public than on the classes for whom they were intended.'[14] The quality, and safety, of cinema buildings had clearly come a long way by 1914, yet developments seem to have been restricted by continuing doubts as to how long the popularity of moving pictures would last. One commentator in 1913 was adamant that '[t]he limitations of this form of entertainment, already eked out in the larger palaces with music-hall varieties, will soon appear, and the interest even of the threepenny public be exhausted.' It was not until after the First World War that such doubts finally evaporated, and 'the long rectangular hall with a minimum of pre-auditorium space was replaced by the larger cinema that seated audiences in thousands instead of hundreds and which copied American ideas on size, planning and decoration.'[15]

Architectural and cinema historians have linked trends in cinema design in the inter-war decades to the medium's growing social respectability.[16] The connection between cinema architecture and the esteem in which the film industry was held was fully recognized at the time.[17] By the 1920s cinema was established as an important medium of popular entertainment with a long-term future. Showmen no longer needed to cram as many people as possible into fairground booths or 'penny gaffs' in order to maximize their profits while the popularity of the medium lasted. As the cinema's appeal came to be regarded as permanent, exhibitors were more concerned with attracting both a better class of patron, and crucially, a *regular* audience. A greater emphasis came to be placed on providing audiences with what they wanted: warmth, comfort and refinement.[18]

These developments were most pronounced in the USA, where the sheer scale and grandeur of many cinemas was quite startling. The Fox cinema in San Francisco, for instance, cost $5,000,000 to build and seated 5,000. Even bigger, and more costly, was New York's Roxy with a capacity of 6,000. Nothing on this scale was ever constructed in the UK,[19] although the basic concepts that underpinned the work of leading American architects such as Thomas Lamb and C. Howard Crane were incorporated into British cinema design in the 1920s. New buildings became ever larger, and much more attention was given to making the interiors not just comfortable, but sumptuous. Exteriors also became more flamboyant, with facades in the Egyptian, Chinese or Assyrian styles particularly popular. In the USA John Eberson was taking some of the trends already evident in 1920s cinema design a stage further. More than simply being grand and spacious, his 'atmospheric' halls encouraged the audience to believe that they were actually in some distant exotic setting. The concept was clearly outlined by Eberson himself in 1927:

> We visualise and dream a magnificent amphitheatre under a glorious moonlit sky in an Italian garden, in a Persian Court, in a Spanish patio, or in a mystic Egyptian temple-yard, all canopied by a soft moonlit sky . . . The very nature of the pastel colouring executed in hundreds of desired shades and colours, lends itself so well to the imagination of the average person, and as we linger and look about, our fancy is free to conjure endless tales of romance.[20]

Eberson's influence was limited to interior design, and externally many of the buildings still resembled theatres. The influence of the theatre was, in fact, clearly evident in most 1920s cinema architecture. This may owe something to American influence where the terms 'cinema' and 'theatre' were indeed synonymous. Perhaps more importantly, some of the leading British cinema architects of the 1920s, such as Frank T. Verity, had started their careers by designing theatres, which must surely have provided the obvious starting point when it came to planning a cinema.

The 'atmospherics' adapted features of theatre design specifically for the movies. David Atwell makes the point that theatres were an obvious choice of building to convert to cinema use 'with their ready made "fantasy" atmospherics and sense of occasion'. He implies that for most people a visit to the cinema was a special event, an opportunity to escape from reality to a new, imagined world, and that cinemas should help to foster the audience's imagination. Indeed, he goes on to argue that it was the 'public clamour for even bigger and better picture palaces that resulted in many of the larger and more elaborate theatres being turned over to permanent cinema use in order to realise their most profitable potential'.[21] The public demand for more ornate and elaborate cinemas has also been connected to the nature of the entertainment provided therein. Ross McKibbin observes that

> the so-called 'atmosphere' cinemas, [were] appropriate for the decade's 'atmospheric' films: vamps, sheiks, Latin lovers, romantic adventurers in far-away places. The 'super-cinemas' of the 1930s, in their turn, reflected the greater matter-of-factness of 1930s movies: as the vamps and Latin lovers departed the cinema, so did the architectural ebullience.[22]

Whether 1930s films were really any more 'matter-of-fact' than those of the preceding decade is open to debate. However, the similarity between the criticism levelled at 1920s cinema architecture by highbrow British critics and that directed at the films themselves is striking.[23] The following comes from a 1931 survey of cinema and theatre architecture by P. Morton Shand:

> Came the 'atmospherics' as Mr. H. G. Wells would say. The phrase is well suited to the nature of this nauseating stick-jaw candy, so fulsomely flavoured with the syrupy romanticism of popular novels and the 'see Naples and die' herd nostalgia which speeds Cook's conducted tours on their weary ways . . .[24]

This condemnation reflects more than simply dissatisfaction with the state of existing cinema design. It shows that there was a growing intellectual interest in, and therefore criticism of, the cinema generally. When Shand referred to H. G. Wells, he did so knowing that the writer was also a leading figure in the London-based Film Society. Through bodies such as the Film Society and journals such as *Close-Up* and *Cinema Quarterly*, the cinema came to be viewed in certain intellectual quarters not just as the amusement of the masses, but as the century's newest art form. Shand was certainly no enemy of the cinema itself, claiming that it was only 'the soured and aged [who] declare that the spread of the cinema-going habit is responsible for the decay of home life.' He felt that shortcomings of cinema design were caused largely by the fact that the buildings were not being designed by qualified architects: 'In more cases than not the wrong men are being entrusted with the job of building and decorating our cinemas.'[25] Greater intellectual and professional involvement in cinema design, then, was felt to be essential if the latest architectural principles were to be applied to the homes of the newest art form.

By the 1930s this was beginning to happen, with cinema buildings being treated seriously in periodicals such as *Architectural Design and Construction* and the *Architects Journal*. The growing professional and intellectual interest being taken in cinema design, rather than the changing nature of the films themselves, lay behind the extension of (matter-of-fact) modernist principles to the design of cinema buildings in the 1930s. Shand set out his vision of a new style of cinema architecture thus:

> The cinema ought to be one of those types of building most characteristic of our age, if only because our age is identified both with the invention of the cinematograph and the phenomenal expansion of the film industry. Unfortunately, however, in England its design still wearily rings out the changes of already obsolescent theatre models. With the possible exception of Non-conformist chapels, no class of edifice represents quite such a degraded general level of design. But what was true of yesterday need not be true of tomorrow.[26]

To Shand, the theatre provided an entirely inappropriate model on which to base cinema architecture because the experience of watching a play was very different from that of going to the cinema. 'There is something formal and ceremonial about going to the theatre. It is an occasion, an event. It implies more careful attire, if not evening dress. We do not say casually "Let's go to the theatre?" as we say "Let's go to the pictures?" ' According to this view, a visit to the cinema was not a special event that needed to be invested with a sense of occasion. Rather, the cinema was 'primarily a sort of public lounge'[27] which needed no elaborate decoration. The notion of the cinema as 'public lounge' neatly captures the spirit of film consumption that Nicholas Hiley associates with the First World War and the decade following it. The very informality of film-going, however, was employed as an argument in favour of the construction of more 'modern' cinemas in the 1930s.

The modern 'super-cinema' became a common feature of town centres and suburbs in many parts of Britain in the 1930s. The 'atmospherics', which were confined almost exclusively to London, had a limited impact on British cinema design with only a handful of examples ever built. Out, also, went the facades in Egyptian or Oriental styles that had been a feature of 1920s cinema design. Exteriors, while often imposing, now tended to be far less ornate, which enabled the purpose of the buildings to be more clearly advertised. The name of the cinema, and the titles of the films being shown were usually prominent, and the walls of the cinemas could be plastered with posters advertising forthcoming attractions.

The cinemas of the 1930s were, perhaps, best typified by the Odeons of Oscar Deutsch. The company had a policy of building new cinemas rather than simply taking over the running of existing premises, and these soon developed a distinctive house style. The buildings were moderate in size by the standards of the 1930s (usually seating around 1,400–1,800) and they were more noted for their practicality and simplicity than any architectural over-elaboration.[28] As David Atwell put it:

> They were above all a complete break away from the traditional school inspired in America by Thomas Lamb and in Britain by Frank Verity, and from

the atmospherics which grew out of John Eberson. The Modern Movement theatres and cinemas of Scandinavia and Europe, but more especially Germany, were the source of influence.[29]

All this had been the intention of Mr Deutsch himself who expressed his thinking in the architectural press:

> With regard to design, it was always my ambition to have buildings which were individual and striking, but which were always objects of architectural beauty . . . We endeavour to make our buildings express the fact that they are specially erected as the homes of the latest, most progressive entertainment in the world today, and I think the entertainment with the greatest future.[30]

Acclaim for these, and other, cinemas was by no means universal in the 1930s. Robert Cromie, a respected cinema designer of the period, appeared to be concerned that cinema architecture was more reflective of European ideas than of British traditions. He felt that there was 'no reason why cinemas should not present, in mien and form, something of the comfortable elegance and repose of our best domestic work. It is strange that an industry which includes so many people of artistic perception has not seen to this'.[31] J. R. Leathart, another professional architect, was even more critical in 1935:

> Some few years ago an observant but irresponsible traveller returned from the Continent with the tale of a new simplicity in cinema design which he fatuously labelled 'modern' and which has since provided some of our cinema architects with yet another opportunity of second-hand self expression.

Leathart did, at least, concede that there were a few buildings which 'bear the impress of an intelligent interpretation of elegant simplicity'.[32] Dennis Sharp, however, in his 1969 history of cinema architecture in Britain, agreed with John Betjeman's assessment, in the same year, that 'the truly modern kinema has yet to be built in England'.[33]

Other commentators have taken a different view. Audrey Field, for instance, points out that while many British cinemas tended to be rather conservative in nature, which 'was a source of dissatisfaction to many sophisticated people', film-goers themselves had few complaints. 'If, as was soon all too sadly clear, we could not make a world fit for heroes to live in, a substitute Valhalla for an occasional festive afternoon or evening out was better than nothing, especially if, besides seeing a picture, you could dance and feast in the same marble halls.'[34]

David Atwell concurs, pointing out that audiences 'were hardly likely to be impressed or moved if the influence of Le Corbusier were to find its way into the cinema auditorium'.[35] To the extent that cinemas were in touch with popular taste, then, they clearly were reflective of their times – throughout their development, not just in the 1930s. What distinguished the buildings of this decade was that for the first time they developed a distinctive style of their own. An article in a supplement to Kine Weekly in 1934 summed up the development succinctly:

> Today the kinema architect does not attempt to outdo all the other buildings in the street merely by excess of architectural detail. He is content to make his facade effective by means of distinction. That is to say, he allows it frankly to express his own particular line of business, and rather than cause the kinema to masquerade as something else, he may often emphasise or exaggerate those characteristics which a kinema possesses and other buildings do not.[36]

Developments in British cinema architecture in the 1920s and 30s reflected a number of social, economic and cultural trends. The size, and the number of buildings erected was clearly determined by the popularity of cinema-going itself. Yet as attendance levels reached their peak in the 1940s cinema building ground to a halt, as economic resources were directed to the war effort and demands of post-war recovery. Cinema design was also influenced by technical innovations: before the widespread introduction of reinforced concrete in the 1920s, for example, it simply was not possible for architects to design a two-tier auditorium seating 3,000 spectators, each with an uninhibited view of the screen. Parliamentary legislation was another area which had a bearing on cinema design: the safety regulations in the 1909 Cinematograph Act introduced considerable alterations to early cinema buildings. Changes in cinema design were hardly imposed upon a reluctant trade, however. Showmen, and later cinema companies, were eager to build halls that would both house and appeal to as broad a range of the cinema-going public as possible. Yet it was not only commercial interests that could influence cinema design, but also contemporary intellectual opinion. In the early years of its development the cinema had been unable to attract the interest of academics or professional architects. By the 1930s this was no longer the case and the influence of another social group had to be taken into account. The challenge by then was to design buildings that were both architecturally interesting, and popular with the general public.

Cinema buildings in Wales

In Wales, social and economic conditions contrasted strikingly with those in many other parts of Britain and developments in inter-war cinema architecture had a very limited impact. In his study of British cinema design, David Atwell does draw attention to a couple of Swansea's pre-1914 buildings as being architecturally interesting,[37] but no study of cinema building in the UK has acknowledged any important innovations coming from Wales in the inter-war period. This is explained, in part at least, by the reluctance of the major cinema companies to invest in Wales in this period.[38] Moreover, the conditions which deterred the likes of Gaumont and Associated British Cinemas (ABC) from building new halls in Wales (economic instability and population decline) would also have influenced local speculators. The provision of cinema buildings in Wales by the end of the 1930s, therefore, was quite different to that in the more prosperous areas of Britain.

The contrast between Wales and other parts of Britain in terms of cinema provision emerges clearly from statistical surveys of the cinema industry.[39] Table 12 compares the proportion of large and small cinemas in Wales with other regions in Britain.

Not only did Wales have a much higher proportion of small cinemas (and of seats in small cinemas) than any other part of the country in 1934, patterns of cinema building only served to increase the discrepancy. Table 13 shows that relatively few cinemas were being built in Wales in the 1930s.[40] It also illustrates that whereas most new cinemas built in Britain at this time were larger than 1,000 seats, in Wales the great majority were smaller halls.

In Britain as a whole, the construction of large new 'super-cinemas' in the 1930s, allied with the closure of some older, smaller halls, meant that by the early 1950s the average cinema was larger than it had been in 1934 (see table

Table 12

The breakdown of cinema provision in Britain by region, 1934 (%)

Region	Under 1000 seats		1000–2000 seats		Over 2000 seats	
	Cinemas	Seats	Cinemas	Seats	Cinemas	Seats
London	55	31	32	41	13	28
South and Midlands	77	58	21	37	2	5
Northern England	70	54	27	39	3	8
Scotland	64	45	32	44	4	10
Wales	86	73	13	24	1	4
Britain	72	53	25	38	4	10

Source: Rowson, 'A statistical survey of the cinema industry in Great Britain in 1934'.

Table 13

New cinemas built between 1932 and 1934

	Wales		Britain	
	No.	%	No.	%
Under 1000 seats	8	80	131	43
1000–2000 seats	2	20	124	41
Over 2000 seats	–	–	33	11
Unknown	–	–	14	5
Total	10	100	302	100

Source: Rowson, 'A statistical survey of the cinema industry in Great Britain in 1934'.

14). This trend was particularly pronounced in the southern half of England and the Midlands, but it was not evident elsewhere in the country. In Scotland, cinemas remained almost the same size on average in 1950 as they had in the early 1930s. In the north of England and in Wales average cinema size actually fell quite significantly over the same period. For many of those parts of Britain where the cinema-going habit was most deeply ingrained, the 'age of the dream palace' turns out to have been one in which cinemas actually got smaller. In Wales this is even more remarkable because the average size of cinemas there was already well below the national average in the early 1930s.

This is not to say that modern 'super-cinemas' were not built at all in Wales in this period. However, visits to halls such as the Plaza in Swansea (the largest cinema to be built in Wales in the 1930s) were rare for the majority of Welsh cinema-goers.

Cinema building in Britain in the inter-war years clearly reflected economic conditions, with the greatest concentration of 'super-cinemas' in the more prosperous regions of southern England and the Midlands. Yet this does not explain why cinemas were so much smaller in Wales than in the north or Scotland.[41] Part of the reason for this was geographical. Cinemas, understandably, tended to be much smaller in rural areas than in urban ones, and in 1934 at least, north Wales was the region with the smallest cinemas of all.[42] A much smaller proportion of the Welsh population lived in towns of over 100,000 inhabitants than was the case in Scotland, the north-west, the Midlands or the south-east.[43] This relative lack of large towns and cities, perhaps more than any other single factor, explains the limited number of large cinemas in Wales. Even in an industrialized and heavily populated area such as the south Wales coalfield, many people still lived in small and relatively isolated communities. As one prominent historian of modern Wales has explained, south Wales Valleys communities were 'as separated by language, routes of development and geography as they were united by occupation, popular culture and shared experience'.[44]

If the small size of cinemas in Wales was largely the result of geography, the age of these buildings was determined more by the economy. The extent of the inter-war depression in Wales was such that even the most expansive and ambitious cinema circuits were seldom prepared to erect new cinemas there. Equally important, perhaps, is the *contrast* between the remarkable economic growth in Wales in the decades leading up to the First World War (a period when many small cinemas were being built, and other buildings were converted to cinema use), and the ensuing collapse. As Philip Jenkins puts it: 'From 1870 to 1914, the Welsh economy had grown at a dizzying rate; from the 1920s, the image is almost of a film suddenly thrown into reverse, as the country entered a period less of slump than of deindustrialisation.'[45] Peter Stead has claimed that in the early years of the twentieth century, 'as far as the commercial exhibition of films was concerned, Cardiff and

Table 14
Average cinema size, 1934–1951

	1934			1950[46]		
	Cinemas (no.)	Seats (000)	Average size	Cinemas (no.)	Seats (000)	Average size
London, Southern England and Midlands	1925	1697	882	2045	1960	958
Northern England	1537	1421	925	1597	1413	885
Scotland	522	511	979	603	591	980
Wales	321	243	757	352	256	727
Britain	4305	3872	899	4597	4221	918

Source: Rowson, 'A statistical survey of the cinema industry in Great Britain in 1934'; Browning and Sorrell, 'Cinemas and cinema-going in Great Britain'.

Swansea were as advanced as any other towns outside the major centres of London, Paris and New York'.[47] Part of the reason, it seems, why relatively few cinemas were being built between the wars was that the generous provision of halls from the pre-1918 era was sufficient to satisfy the demand of a declining population.

The contrast between rapid growth and startling decline, however, does not apply to the whole of Wales. The towns along the south Wales coastal strip, the south Wales Valleys, and the communities of mid- and north Wales were areas with quite a different provision of cinemas, and the remainder of this chapter will examine the nature and extent of these differences. For the purpose of clarity the different types of cinema hall that existed across Wales have been divided into three categories.

First, there were the minority of newly built cinemas. These looked very much like others in the rest of the UK, often with striking facades and interiors which claimed to provide 'the last word in luxury'. They ranged in size from little more than 500 seats right up to 3,000. The building of new 'super-cinemas' in Britain may have been an attempt to lure a new, more affluent and 'respectable' audience to the cinema. Attracting a middle-class audience, however, was probably not central to guaranteeing commercial success for Welsh cinema managers (even though the most expensive seats could cost up to four times that of the cheapest). More important was that the features designed to appeal to the middle class were extremely popular with people from lower social groups.[48] This explains why Swansea was able to support a modern 3,000 seat 'super-cinema' like the Plaza.

A second strand of inter-war cinema development took the form of improvements to existing facilities rather than the building of new ones. A number of large theatres and music-halls were converted into cinemas, and many of those older buildings already used as cinemas at the beginning of our period underwent substantial renovations in the 1930s. In terms of their interior decoration, these cinemas often resembled the newly-constructed dream palaces. Their exteriors, however, reflected no signs of modernist influence and looked much as they had done when first built – in many cases before the cinematograph's invention.

Finally there were the smaller cinemas built between *c.*1910 and 1915. While a number of these were forced to close as a result of competition from larger and more modern rivals in the 1920s and 30s many, perhaps the majority, survived at least until the Second World War with virtually no alterations. Such venues, which charged less for admission than larger and more modern alternatives, appealed particularly to the lowest paid, the young and unemployed. They also benefited from the regular patronage of 'locals' who would have been unwilling to spend extra time and money travelling to more distant picture shows – at least on a regular basis.

These different types of cinema embody variations not only in social and economic conditions, but also in the attitudes and requirements of different groups of cinema-goers. For many people visits to the pictures were frequent and habitual: the cinema, in effect, performed a social function which was later to be provided by television. For such purposes the local 'fleapit', which was both cheap and informal, was ideally suited. For middle-class audiences, however, and for those who wanted their visits to the cinema to be separate from a weekly routine (courting couples, perhaps, or children enjoying a birthday treat) the larger, more glamorous halls were more suitable.[49] Yet these halls could only exist where social and economic circumstances permitted. In the south Wales Valleys, where the contrast between pre-1914 prosperity and inter-war depression was most dramatic, the old 'fleapit' halls continued to make-up the bulk of cinema provision. In many parts of mid- and north Wales, where permanent cinema provision had been very limited before the First World War, more modern cinemas were constructed – but on nothing like the grand scale seen in the major towns and cities of Britain. In the larger towns of south Wales, however, the biggest and most impressive cinemas tended to be the converted theatres and music halls, not the modern 'super-cinemas'. The precise nature of the cinema buildings available to Welsh audiences, therefore, is best examined by dealing separately with different parts of Wales.

The south Wales coastal strip

A useful gauge of the kinds of building being used as cinemas in the larger south Wales towns in this period can be provided by examining the situation in Cardiff. The city was an extremely important port in the early part of the twentieth century, from where much of the produce of the south Wales coalfield was shipped across the globe.[50] As coal production soared, so more work was created in the city. At the turn of the century there had even been suggestions that its economy would eventually outstrip that of London.[51] The rate of its population growth was certainly impressive. Between 1891 and 1901 the population increased from 128,915 to 164,333, by 1921 it was well over 200,000.[52]

As might be expected, the city was well catered for in terms of cinemas, with eighteen at the end of the First World War. This number changed remarkably little during the inter-war period. It did rise to twenty-one during the 1920s but had dropped to twenty by the end of the 1930s.[53] Cardiff's virtually unchanging number of cinemas in the inter-war years was apparently out of line with the pattern in Britain as a whole which, according to the *Kinematograph Year Book* in 1921, needed another 2,000 cinemas to satisfy public demand. Birmingham, for example, had fifty-seven cinemas during the First World War, and its population was far greater than three times that of Cardiff's. However, these figures increased to seventy-four in 1928, 100 in 1935 and 109 in 1939.[54] Cardiff's totals of three newly built cinemas in the 1920s and three in the 1930s seem almost negligible in comparison.[55] To some extent this reflects the rapidity of cinema's growth in Cardiff up to 1918. Of the eighteen picture houses operating in this year eleven had been purpose-built as cinemas. Furthermore, a number of the buildings which had been converted to cinema use by 1918 were fairly large, prestigious halls. The Empire, Grand, Andrew's Hall, Park Hall and Philharmonic, which had been built in the late nineteenth century as theatres, were all being used, in part at least, for film exhibition. This, again, bears testament to the popularity of the cinema in Cardiff by the beginning of our period, but it also meant that as well as having a lot of cinemas, the city was well provided for in terms of seating capacity. A number of these older buildings had 2,000 seats or more and all had over 1,000, therefore they were certainly much larger than the purpose-built cinemas in the city at this time.

This is not to say, however, that the nature of Cardiff's cinemas remained unchanged throughout the inter-war period. Admittedly, only six new cinemas opened in these decades, which combined with a handful of closures meant that the total number of venues remained fairly constant. Further, many of the buildings used as cinemas in the 1920s and 30s were based on Edwardian, or even Victorian designs. Yet while cinema buildings themselves tended not to be new, they were frequently subject to renovation. Of the twenty cinemas open in Cardiff at the end of 1939 nine had received some kind of renovation since 1918. This usually involved the building having to close for several weeks as the interior was redecorated, and occasionally some alterations were made to the facade. When we add to this number the cinemas newly constructed since 1920, we find that three-quarters of Cardiff's cinemas in 1939 had either been built or renovated in the inter-war period. When measured in terms of available seating, 86 per cent of Cardiff's cinema capacity had been either built or renovated in the inter-war era.[56]

Two points emerge from all of this. First, that Cardiff's cinemas did change considerably during the 1920s and 30s, such that the experience of visiting many of them in 1939 was quite different to what it would have been twenty years previously. This comment in the *South Wales Echo* in 1935 was typical of the way in which cinema openings, or reopenings, were reported in the local press:

> When the Olympia Cinema, Queen Street, Cardiff, re-opens tomorrow after-noon, after being closed since May for complete rebuilding, patrons of the hall with the most interesting history in Cardiff will not recognise the palace of entertainment which will be revealed to them . . . The Olympia of old was an admirable hall, but the proprietors, S. Andrews and Sons Ltd., felt that it was not all that the modern cinema-goer demanded. He had learned to expect comfort with the showing of the super-film, and the company felt that if the Olympia was to maintain its proper place in the scheme of entertainment in the city it had to be the most luxurious and best equipped cinema that money could provide. Orders were given immediately for drawing up of plans, and the task fell to Mr. Howard Williams ARIBA, of Pembroke Terrace, Cardiff, who planned a theatre which incorporated the finest features of British and American practice.[57]

Second, the majority of new developments took the form of alterations to existing buildings, rather than to the construction of completely new ones. Even the Odeon circuit, which had a policy of erecting new buildings, rather than renovating old ones, made an exception in Cardiff's case. The building, on the site of the former New Imperial on Queen Street, had an extremely narrow front and looked nothing like the majority of other cinemas from this famous chain.[58] It seems then, that for all the growth in cinema's popularity and the corresponding expansion in Cardiff's picture houses, the city's archi-tecture was far from transformed in the inter-war years. Many of the city-centre halls were able to keep up with the latest trends in *interior* design, but they continued to look much as they always had done from the outside.

For the most part the alterations made to Cardiff's cinemas in the 1920s and 30s were incorporated into the city's existing facilities. Continuity with the past and preservation of local traditions was a more important feature of Cardiff's inter-war cinema development than the influence of continental, modern styles of architecture. The press report on the reopening of the Olympia, significantly, drew attention to the building's place in the city's 'history'; it stressed that the architect was a local man; and his influences were not German or Scandinavian, but from Britain and America. While the journalist claimed that patrons would not recognize the new auditorium, given the improvements in decoration, comfort and facilities, the name, structure and location of the building remained unchanged. Here, then, we see developments in British and American practice indeed being 'incorporated' into the existing facilities – facilities which happened to pre-date the age of cinema itself. The press report greeting the re-opening of the Park Hall makes the point even more clearly:

> One of Cardiff's first cinema theatres, the Park Hall, has always had a character and atmosphere all its own. There was that elusive quality about it that gave a homely warmth sometimes missing from the more imposing 'Picture Palaces'. Those who attended the re-opening last night were probably relieved, as I was, to find that not even the housebreakers, the builders and the decorators, or the glitter of modernity, has robbed it of its old character.[59]

It seems clear that modernity was demanded *inside* the halls in terms of space, comfort, and practicalities like sightlines, sound quality and ventilation systems – even in the old Park Hall. Indeed, it is a common feature of local press reports of cinema openings across Wales that such practical facilities are described in immense detail. But it is equally clear that audiences also cherished the familiarity, 'homely warmth' and 'old character' of their favourite cinemas. Of all Cardiff's main city-centre cinemas, interestingly, only the Capitol was built in the inter-war period, opening in 1921.

All new cinemas built in Cardiff after this were in the suburbs; it was here rather than in the city centre that modern cinema architecture established itself. Avoiding any similarities with theatre design, these buildings had fairly plain, yet striking, exteriors which could loudly advertise both the name of the cinema and the films being screened. The most notable examples were the Monico in Rhiwbina, the County in Rumney, the Regent in Ely, the Plaza in Gabalfa and the Tivoli in Llandaff. It was in these areas, outside the city centre, where the cinema made its greatest architectural impact – in so far as a recognized new style of design, conceived of elsewhere, was introduced into the local townscape.[60] These newly constructed suburban halls, however, were not exactly worthy of description as dream palaces. For one thing they were much smaller than the city-centre halls. Their average capacity was a moderate 1,140 seats, and the smallest of them – Llandaff's Tivoli – held only 600. The fact that these halls were built in outlying residential areas, rather than the city centre, suggests that they were designed to meet a demand, not for prestigious showpiece cinemas, but for more modest, local buildings whose chief attractions would be cheapness and convenience.

The admission prices charged by the different kinds of cinema is discussed in chapter 4, but it is important to note that in this respect modern, suburban cinemas were, in fact, closer to those of the local fleapit than to the larger, city-centre halls. The difference in price between the suburban and city-centre halls may not have been spectacular, but it was certainly significant for those on the lowest incomes and youngsters, who formed the bulk of the regular, cinema-going audience.[61] Indeed, the saving probably amounted to more than just a few pennies since the bus fare would have added further to the cost of a visit to a city-centre cinema for many people. The opening of the Regent in Ely, it was claimed by the local press, would 'enable the population of about 15,000 to "go to the pictures" at the price they formerly paid to travel to the city by bus or tram'.[62]

It was not just the cost of visiting the modern, suburban cinemas which set them apart from the larger city-centre halls. The nature of the entertainment they provided was also slightly different. The likes of the Capitol and the Park Hall were first-run cinemas – that is to say they were the first in the area to screen new releases. The suburban cinemas were second- or third-run halls, unable to screen the major releases until weeks, or even months, after main city-centre venues. Furthermore, a number of the largest and most prestigious halls, such as the Capitol, supplemented their programmes of films in this period with live variety entertainment on stage. The modern halls, in keeping with their size and their admission prices, offered a more modest programme of entertainment.[63]

Cardiff's modern suburban cinemas, were in no way in competition with the larger (and older) city-centre halls. Rather, they offered substantial improvements for the existing, once or twice-weekly cinema-going public. The new halls were certainly eager to distance themselves from the 'fleapits'. Advertisements in the local press stressed that their interior design offered the 'last word in luxury', and it was also pointed out that car parking space was available – a clear indication that more affluent patrons would be welcomed. Yet it was an essentially local, working-class public for which these halls catered. It is significant that whereas the large city-centre halls provided those able to pay the most with superior balcony seats, in the suburban cinemas more effort was made to provide comfortable and spacious conditions *throughout* the hall.

> Care has been taken to make the seating arrangements as comfortable as possible, with ample leg room and it is a fact that no matter where one sits, cheap or dearer sections of the hall, the seats are equally comfortable. The sound system installed is absolutely the latest and best, and conveys the dialogue to any part of the hall with equal clarity and range.[64]

As well as appealing to an essentially local, working-class public, these cinemas were also built by a local firm – the Splott Cinema Company. This was a company that had pursued a policy of building new cinemas rather than buying existing ones ever since running into difficulties over its acquisition of the Canton cinema in 1925.[65] Their activities brought about an improvement in the cinema facilities available to many people. They simply did not have the resources, however, to construct cinemas to rival city-centre venues such as the Capitol or the Park Hall, much less the 'dream palaces' constructed by Gaumont and ABC.

Just as significant as the *type* of building constructed by the Splott Cinema Company, arguably, was their location. None of the cinemas built by this company in the inter-war years were in areas that already had a picture house.[66] The social function performed by these modern suburban halls actually had much in common with the third type of cinema considered here: the ageing 'fleapits'. The intention of the Splott Cinema Company was clearly to meet a demand for more local cinemas, not to compete directly with existing ones. What this meant was that quite a number of Cardiff's small, pre-war cinemas such as the Central, Coliseum, Globe and Coronet faced little new competition in the period covered here. These halls offered little by way of glamour or even comfort, but they were an established and a popular feature of the local community. Their familiarity, convenience and cheapness appealed to a working-class public for whom visits to the cinema were habitual, rather than a special event. For the whole of the period covered by this book the older 'fleapit' cinemas formed an important part of Cardiff's cinema provision.

The situation in Wales's second largest town, Swansea, was broadly similar. The relative diversity of Swansea's economic base meant that the town's economy was less badly hit by the depression than many other parts of Wales. Unemployment in the town did reach 24.1 per cent in 1931, but this was well below the figures seen in some of the worst black spots. Neither Cardiff nor Swansea suffered from the kind of population exodus which afflicted the valleys in the inter-war years and their relative economic security was reflected in the state of their cinemas.

As with Cardiff, Swansea had plenty of cinemas by the end of the First World War. There seem to have been around seventeen separate venues, of which approximately half were purpose-built as cinemas.[67] Also like Cardiff, the absolute number of cinemas altered very little in the inter-war years – rising to nineteen by 1939. Again, however, there were significant developments in this period. Six new cinemas were built and a number of others were altered significantly. The tendency toward using existing theatres for film exhibition was also evident in Swansea where both the Albert Hall and Grand were converted into cinemas. In Swansea, however, such halls were not necessarily the most prestigious town-centre venues. The town's premier cinema was undoubtedly the Plaza, built in 1931, while a theatre like the Theatre Royal, rather than simply having a 'face-lift' in the 1930s, was totally demolished and rebuilt – opening in 1932 as the Rialto.

With regard to the town-centre cinemas, at least, it seems that new buildings and styles of architecture were developed to a much greater extent than in Cardiff, although some older traditions did remain. Moreover, no clear distinction existed between town-centre and suburban developments: throughout we find a blend of old and new buildings. Pre-war cinemas such as the Castle (1911) and Carlton (1913), as well converted theatres like the Albert Hall and Grand were able to compete with the recently built Plaza and Rialto cinemas in the town centre. Further out, the Maxime in Sketty and Tower in Townhill were products of the late 1930s, the Tivoli and Regent were built in Mumbles in the mid-to-late 1920s, while residents of the Uplands and Morriston had local cinemas since before 1914.

Where new cinemas were built they tended to follow trends evident elsewhere in the UK. It was claimed in the local press, for instance, that '[t]hose who were present at the opening of the [Maxime] cinema on Saturday must have been impressed with the modern developments in cinema practice which are embodied in the building'. Increasingly imposing and distinctive exteriors were developed, providing an identity quite separate from traditional theatres. In the Maxime's case 'an imposing facade' was 'carried out in coloured glass, illuminated with neon lighting'.[68] The interiors became ever more decorative and comfortable; each new building claiming to offer 'the last word in luxury'. They were also bigger than their pre-war counterparts with an average of 1,634 seats as compared with 773 in those earlier purpose-built cinemas.[69] Converted theatres also tended to be fairly large, usually between 1,000 and 2,000 seats. Much the biggest of Swansea's cinemas, however, was the Plaza: with over 3,000 seats this was, in fact, the largest picture house in Wales. The Plaza was built by a local firm and, though impressive in many respects, was not a typical example of 1930s British cinema design. Serious consideration was clearly given to the interior design in terms of lighting, seating arrangements, acoustics and decoration. One press report claimed that 'internally one can almost describe it as artistically perfect'. Both interior and external decorations, however, were said to have been 'in the Renaissance style with Celtic motifs'. This is clearly some way from an austere, modernist design, and it is interesting that a Welsh flavour should have been added. Yet the sheer scale, as well as look, of the building made a considerable impression on the local townscape. As it was claimed in the press: 'From the exterior the cinema presents an imposing appearance, facing on what is destined to become the town's main thoroughfare.'[70]

As well as attempting to combine modern architectural principles with a Welsh theme, the Plaza was also a good example of a theatre which made its appeal as all-inclusive as possible. This was reflected in the pricing policy, which was similar to that seen in Cardiff's modern cinemas. In most of Swansea's cinemas admission charges ranged between 6d and 1s 6d by the late 1930s. Visiting the cinema was thus within the range of all sections of society, although the more affluent could spend an extra shilling and sit in the balcony. In the Plaza and the Albert Hall the price range was slightly wider, going up to 2s; these halls were the ones which probably appealed most to the middle-class audiences. It was not even necessary to be a film fan to be able to enjoy the facilities on offer here. Both contained large cafés, and the Plaza advertised itself in the *South Wales Evening Post* as 'Swansea's popular rendezvous' rather than just a place of entertainment.

At the other end of the market, the Scala, Uplands and Landore cinemas, which fell into the third ('fleapit') category, charged prices of between 4d and 1s 4d. The difference is not great, but it does seem that these halls were catering largely for those with the least to spend on entertainment. These so-called 'bug houses' were almost inevitably survivors from pre-war days. They were not necessarily the oldest buildings used for showing films. They were, however, early examples of purpose-built cinemas erected to meet a working-class demand for moving pictures, the longevity of which could not be predicted. In south Wales a considerable proportion of these were able to survive, with minimum alterations, into and beyond the inter-war period, competing alongside the modern 'super-cinemas' and offering an alternative experience for film-goers.

Much of what has been seen in Cardiff and Swansea, applies equally to other towns along the south Wales coastal strip. Newport's tally of cinemas rose from eight in 1918 to ten in 1940. Of these ten, just two were built in the inter-war period, and two had been converted to cinema use during these years, leaving six survivors from before 1918. The four new cinemas had an average capacity of 1,271 seats and were able to provide the latest standards of comfort, convenience and decoration. Of the older halls only two, the Gem and the Plaza, conformed to the 'fleapit' stereotype, with much smaller capacities and cheaper prices. The other existing cinemas adapted very well to modern developments. The Olympia was taken over by ABC, and the Coliseum by Gaumont British, both undergoing improvements in the 1920s. The other two pre-war halls were not purpose-built cinemas but large buildings converted from other uses, and thus more adaptable for the demands of inter-war audiences. Newport's cinemas were thus able to keep abreast of the latest developments without radically altering the architecture of the town.[71]

A similar picture emerges in Port Talbot where the small pre-war cinemas such as the Electric Palace and Picturedrome were able to coexist in the inter-war years alongside new constructions such as the 1,500-seat Majestic, and the Regent, as well as converted theatres like the Grand and New Empire. The same was true of Llanelli where the large newly built cinemas, namely the Odeon (1,450 seats) and the Regal (1,778), were joined by the Hippodrome, a converted theatre of 1,000 seats. Alongside these halls, however, were the likes of the Llanelli Cinema and the Palace, both survivors from the pre-war era.[72]

These south Wales towns were hardly in a position to support the kind of explosion in cinema building witnessed elsewhere in Britain. The difficult economic circumstances no doubt deterred the major cinema companies from investing here, and the fact that many of these towns were already well served in terms of cinema provision by 1918 meant that there were limited opportunities for local firms to exploit. By the end of the inter-war period, however, we can see that there were three types of cinema in the larger south Wales towns, (the newly built halls, the converted theatres and the ageing fleapits), which each had a significant role to play.

The south Wales Valleys

In the Valleys, too, there was evidence of all of the above types of cinema, although here the overwhelming majority fell into the third category. Indeed, it was the Valleys, far more than the coastal belt, which was responsible for the preponderance of small cinemas in south Wales. The boom-bust economic cycle in the first half of the century, which helps explain the limited amount of new cinema building in Wales, was nowhere more acutely felt than in the south Wales coalfield. In the century leading up to the First World War this area had developed from a quiet, largely rural backwater, to one of the most important industrial regions in Britain. Between 1901 and 1921 the population of Glamorgan had increased by 46 per cent; the population of Rhondda by 69 per cent. By 1923 there were 252,617 miners working in the south Wales coalfield and the area was producing over a million tonnes of coal a week.[73] The economic collapse of the following decades, however, was every bit as spectacular as this meteoric growth. With unemployment levels reaching 50 or 60 per cent in many areas there seemed little alternative, especially for young people, but to migrate to more prosperous new industrial communities.[74] Young women fled into domestic service in London, the Home Counties and the Midlands, while schoolboys embarked upon what Gwyn A. Williams described as the 'examination obstacle race'.[75] By 1951 the population of Rhondda was back below its 1901 level; the population of Merthyr fell from 80,116 in 1921 to 61,142 in 1951; in Aberdare the figures were 55,007 and 40,932. Given that the younger generation were the most regular cinema-goers, and that those who remained in these areas generally had less to spend on entertainment, it must have seemed inevitable that cinema, like much else, would be a victim of the depression – and in a sense it was.

The explosion in cinema building in inter-war Britain simply did not happen in the south Wales Valleys. It is perhaps ironic, though hardly surprising, that this most vibrant and radical working-class culture, once described as 'the most active and thriving community in Great Britain or the world',[76] failed to witness any significant improvement in its provision of cinemas – homes to the most popular medium of public entertainment. On the other hand, the cinema industry existing in this area was able to cope with the economic conditions remarkably well; far better, in fact, than most other businesses, or forms of popular culture.[77] One of the most striking features of the valleys cinemas was not just that they tended to be old and relatively small, but that so many actually survived throughout the 1920s and 30s. The writer Jack Jones, visiting one valleys town in 1938, was astounded that '[t]oday, in this most distressed borough in Britain, there are half a dozen cinemas, with a seating capacity of six thousand, with a mid-week change of programme. The largest does three shows daily.'[78] Evidence from trade directories of the period tells us this must have been an exaggeration. However, they also show that at a time when the population and economy of most valleys' communities was being crippled, the cinemas were able to survive.

For the inhabitants of most valleys' communities picture-going did not involve a visit to modern 'super-cinemas', but to the local fleapit, or perhaps a workman's institute. Where cinema building did take place in this region between the wars it tended to be in larger towns such as Merthyr and Aberdare. Here, the general pattern was similar to that seen in Cardiff and Swansea, though on a much reduced scale. Merthyr, for example had four cinemas at the end of the First World War, and the same number twenty years later. Of the four cinemas open in 1939, two were survivors from the pre-1914 era: the Palace (897 seats) and the Temperance Hall (600). The remaining two were the Castle Super Cinema (1,600 seats), built in 1929, and the Theatre Royal (1,217), converted to cinema use in the early 1920s. The two that had closed were the Penydaren Cinema and the Electric Theatre. Despite its declining population, then, Merthyr's cinema provision actually increased in terms of seating capacity between the wars. As with other south Wales towns there was a mix of new and old cinema buildings, and in the design of the Castle cinema itself there was a combination of American and local influences. The interior seems to have been designed along the lines of an 'atmospheric' – with the setting of medieval Wales rather than of a Mediterranean resort: 'The walls are beautifully decorated by mural paintings of singular beauty and charm. Large landscape panels, designed by Mr. J. Jones, a local artist . . . show stately castles in medieval settings, and across the ceiling is colour-washed a brilliant sky, illuminated from two light-ray domes.'[79] In terms of comfort and decoration, then, the most up-to-date practices in cinema design were adopted here. Yet the cinema was very much a local institution. The Castle was originally locally owned and run (by Merthyr Cinemas Ltd), and its local identity was confirmed by its name – it stood on the site of the old Castle hotel on Castle street.

In Aberdare a broadly similar picture emerges with the Rex, the only cinema to be built between the wars, although this did not open until 1939.[80] Many valleys towns witnessed no such developments in the 1920s and 30s. In places such as Mountain Ash and Tredegar no new cinemas were built in this period at all. Similarly, the numerous small mining communities scattered across the Valleys saw very little change in their cinema provision in the inter-war years. Not only were very few new cinemas ever built, there was seldom any attempt to refurbish or redecorate existing ones. In terms of interior design, therefore, as well as external appearance, valleys cinemas had undergone little change in this period. Much of this, of course, was due to social and economic conditions caused by the depression. For the major cinema circuits, it would surely have been a far greater risk to invest in the south Wales Valleys than most other parts of the country. Authors of social surveys dealing with life in distressed areas were attracted to towns like

Brynmawr;[81] Oscar Deutsch was not. This is understandable. While the 'super-cinemas' were felt to be offering the entertainment of the future, it was far from clear for how long such communities would continue to exist. Where new cinemas were built, such as the Castle at Merthyr, the investors were usually a local firm. The depression, however, had meant that there was less money in the local economy to be invested. When the mayor opened the Castle cinema he said that he 'looked upon the venture as a magnificent gesture of faith in Merthyr's future. To build so fine and so costly a hall today needed great courage.'[82] Such courage, not to mention resources, must have been a scarce commodity at this time. Nevertheless, a great many existing cinemas were able to survive, and new ones tended to do quite well. Merthyr's Castle cinema was even taken over by ABC in November 1932.

The geography of the south Wales Valleys, as much as the area's depressed economy, can be held responsible for the lack of inter-war cinema construction. The vast majority of valleys cinemas were located in small communities with a population of between four to eight thousand. These communities also tended to have a strong local identity, largely because they were so isolated from one another. The cinemas built in these communities were local institutions: they did not (and could not) serve a wider regional audience. Even if the inhabitants of some of the smaller communities had wanted to visit cinemas in larger towns like Maesteg or Merthyr, they would have faced transport difficulties. Geographical, as well economic limitations made the south Wales coalfield a risky area in which to build large, modern cinemas.

This, however, only served to strengthen the local identity of the picture halls which did exist in the area. The cinema had become firmly incorporated into the culture and traditions of the south Wales coalfield. This was reflected in the buildings themselves, which were frequently housed in miners' institutes and run by the local workmen, not large circuits based in London.[83] It was the valleys, more than the coastal strip, that was responsible for high proportion of small cinemas found in south Wales in the 1930s. While there were some similarities between the two parts of the region, the differences in cinema provision must be accounted for in terms of geographical and cultural forces, as well as economic ones.

Mid and north Wales

As with the south, it would be misleading to generalize too freely about cinema building in north Wales. According to Rowson's study in 1934, north Wales had an even greater proportion of small cinemas than the south. This is not to say, however, that cinema development here followed a similar pattern to that set in the valleys. Social and economic conditions, for one thing, were rather different. In much of rural Wales the population was declining between the wars, but this was nothing new. Population had been steadily falling since around 1850 in these areas, providing much of the labour in newly-industrialized regions. There was not such a stark contrast between economic hardships here in the inter-war period and the prosperity of previous decades, as had been the case in the industrialized south. In north Wales towns the depression was certainly felt, (the proportion out of work in the Wrexham area, for instance, almost reached 40 per cent in 1931), but the high rates of unemployment were not as widespread as in the south. The county of Flintshire actually witnessed considerable industrial development in these years, its population increasing by about 10,000 between 1921 and 1938.[84] Further, the social structure of the towns tended to be quite different. While Wrexham had a certain amount in common with Cardiff and Swansea, in terms of the proportion of the population in unskilled or semi-skilled occupations, the resorts of Colwyn Bay and Llandudno contained not only more people in work, but a far higher proportion in professional positions. The towns of the north were home to some of the most impressive 'super cinemas' constructed in inter-war Wales. The differences between towns in the north and the south, however, are no more striking than the variations between north Wales towns themselves.

Wrexham, a relatively large industrial town in the north east of Wales, is the most important place to start. Its population grew from 23,295 in 1921 to 30,967 in 1951, and by the end of the 1950s it was officially the largest town in north Wales. Although smaller than some of the industrialized towns in the south, its social structure was broadly similar to theirs. In Wrexham 17 per cent of workers were in professional or intermediate positions (compared with 15 per cent in Swansea and 18 per cent in Cardiff); 30 per cent were either unskilled or partly skilled (the corresponding figures for Cardiff and Swansea were 34 and 28 per cent respectively).[85] Similarities are also evident in terms of cinema development.

In 1918 Wrexham had four cinemas (or at least four venues at which pictures were shown); by 1939 the number was five. As with the towns in the south, however, it was the nature, rather than the number, of cinemas which altered in the inter-war years. All four of the 1918 cinemas survived into the 1950s, three of them largely unchanged. The Glynn, which had been erected as a temporary cinema in 1910, underwent some alterations in 1919, and did remarkably well to survive until 1960. The Hippodrome, which had been the Public Hall, lasted until 1959; the Empire, originally a music hall, was used for film from 1911 to 1956. The other venue open in 1918 was the Majestic. Originally built in 1910 as a skating rink, it was known in its early days as a cinema before the First World War as the Rink and Pavillion. The name changed in 1922 and in the 1930s it underwent major renovations, giving the 1,770-seat auditorium a modern, art deco, design.[86] The inter-war modernization of Wrexham's cinemas was completed in March 1937 with the 1,246 seat Odeon. Built on a site recently cleared of poor-quality housing, the new cinema was indeed a welcome addition 'in a district which needed a first class entertainment hall'. During the opening ceremony, architect Harry Weedon was congratulated on designing and building a theatre which 'could not be improved upon anywhere.'[87]

By the end of the 1930s Wrexham's two premier picture houses could claim to reflect the latest practices in cinema design, and although there were three others which could not, the combined seating capacity of the Majestic and Odeon outnumbered that of the other venues. Thus, as with many other towns in south Wales, Wrexham supported a balance of cinema venues, some modern, others with a longer history in the local community.

A similar balance is to be found in other north Wales towns. In Bangor, for instance, there were three cinemas in 1939, the 1,500-seat Plaza 'super-cinema' (opened in 1934), the New City Picture House (seating 900 and erected in 1919) and the County Theatre (originally a chapel, but used for film shows since around 1918). Bangor's oldest picture house, known variously as the Picturedrome, the Electric Pavillion and the Cosy, never installed sound equipment and had closed by 1931. The situation in Caernarfon, also with three cinemas by the Second World War, was broadly similar. The 1,178-seat Majestic, built in 1934, was a relatively large, modern building, equipped with a café which claimed to be 'worthy of the finest traditions of the cinematograph world'.[88] The Guildhall was a much smaller and older building: seating 500, it was converted to full time cinema use in the 1920s. The Empire, which also seated 500, was a purpose-built cinema dating from 1915.[89] What we see, then, is a variety of types of cinema, some reflective of the recent developments in British cinema design, others part of a local architectural tradition dating from a period before the cinema had begun to develop its own distinctive style.

While such a balance is evident in most Welsh towns, Rhyl provides an exceptional case. This popular north Wales seaside resort had five cinemas by 1939: of these, four had been built since 1920 and the other had received a new interior in 1933. The town's unusually generous provision of modern cinemas was acknowledged by the chairman of the local council on opening the Plaza in 1931. 'It was', he claimed, 'a great thing in such depressing times that there were men in Rhyl who had such confidence in the future that they could embark upon such an ambitious enterprise.'[90] Such confidence, and ambition, was not in such abundance in most parts of north Wales, although it does seem that in some of the more affluent areas the number of cinema venues, if not new buildings, increased considerably during the inter-war period. In Llandudno the number of cinemas leapt from two to five between the wars: one of the new venues was a 1930s 'super-cinema'; one was opened in 1920 (although probably planned before the First World War); the other, the old Princess Theatre, was converted to cinema use in the 1920s. In Colwyn Bay too a rapid growth of cinema venues occurred after 1918. Three new cinemas, the Arcadia, the Princess and the Supreme, were built between 1920 and 1923. To these were added the Odeon in April 1936.[91]

In parts of north Wales, then, it appears that the early 1920s saw as much, if not more, cinema construction than the years leading up to the First World War. The small size of many mid and north Wales towns, combined with their lack of prosperity, meant that it was not until the 1920s (by which time cinemas were firmly established as the most popular sites of public enter-tainment) that they came to be built throughout this region. Many communities here had continued to rely on travelling cinemas for access to the silver screen up until the 1920s. The result was that the picture houses in north Wales towns had a more modern feel to them than those in the rest of Wales. In a sample of six north Wales towns, 52 per cent of cinemas open in 1939 had been built since 1918; the corresponding figure in a similar sample of south Wales towns was 32 per cent.[92] This may help to explain why Dafydd Roberts, in his study of the slate quarrying communities of north-west Wales, found that it was only 'from the early twenties on' that 'the cinema became an intrinsic part of social life within every town and larger village in the quarrying areas'.[93]

Across Wales, films continued to be shown even into the 1950s in buildings that had been constructed before the cinematograph was invented. Architecturally, many cinemas were incorporated into a town's existing facil-ities as others imposed a new modernist style on the high street. Further, it was local conditions which determined the extent to which this process of modernization could actually take place. Social and economic circumstances clearly came into play in this respect, but so did specific indigenous factors. The work of firms such as Rhyl Entertainments Ltd in the north Wales town, and the Splott Cinema Company around Cardiff and Penarth, meant that cinema-goers in these localities were particularly well served in terms of modern cinemas.

Another way in which local conditions influenced cinema design was in terms of the relatively small size of north Wales towns. The modern cinemas erected here in the 1930s tended to be smaller than those elsewhere in the UK. The seating capacity was usually between 1,000 and 1,500, seldom any more, and there were certainly no cinemas to compare with the Plaza in Swansea or the Capitol in Cardiff in terms of sheer size. Outside of the main towns, however, a number of small modern cinemas were to be found. A large proportion of the population of north Wales lived in fairly small towns or villages of 8,000 or less inhabitants, which could not support large cin-emas. It was the lack of major urban centres, rather than a lack of recent cinema building, that provides the best explanation as to why north Wales picture houses were, on average, smaller than those in the rest of Britain. New cinemas were, it seems, being erected in small north Wales towns, to a much greater extent than was evident in the south Wales Valleys. In very few communities did there appear to be no change at all in the provision of cin-emas between the wars. Further, it seems that the new cinemas here bore many of the hallmarks of modern design. Captain Pritchard, who was responsible for the construction of buildings like the Majestic in Caernarfon, also opened cinemas in Pwllheli, Porthmadog and Blaenau Ffestiniog. Sidney Colwyn Foulkes, a north Wales architect, who had designed cinemas such as the Plaza and the interior of the Queens Theatre in Rhyl, was also responsible for the Plazas at Queensferry and Flint. Other new cinemas were built in the 1930s in Conwy, Llanrwst, Penmaenmawr, Broughton and Bagillt. With names such as the Luxor, Regent and Palace these cinemas had many of the comforts of the modern 'super-cinema', but an average seating capacity of only around 625.[94]

Again, however, it is questionable whether these halls should be categorized as 'dream palaces'. Many of the cinemas built in mid and north Wales in the inter-war years had more in common with the modern halls erected by the Splott Cinema Company in Cardiff than with the largest showpiece cinemas. As well as being small, these cinemas were usually built by local firms, and they tended to be situated in areas where there was no other cinema. In other words, they provided the local public with a cheap and convenient means of going to the pictures; they did not seek to provide a more glamorous alternative to existing halls.

Summary

The three categories of cinema discussed in this chapter – the newly constructed cinemas, the converted theatres and music halls, and the pre-war 'fleapits' – could be found across Wales (and indeed Britain) throughout this period. One of the most notable features of cinema architecture in Wales, however, was the scarcity of newly constructed 'dream palaces'. Most medium-sized Welsh towns could boast at least one cinema with around 2,000 seats that offered the latest pictures in surroundings which were comfortable, if not luxurious. 'Dream palaces' *were* to be found in Wales but, for the most part, they were not newly built cinemas. There were a handful of new Odeons across Wales, and the odd cinema like Swansea's Plaza, which combined imposing exteriors with plush decoration inside. It was much more common, however, for the most prestigious cinemas to be converted theatres or variety halls. Such buildings were able to keep abreast of the latest developments in interior design – without significantly altering their exterior appearance. The Lyric in Carmarthen was typical of many old theatres converted to cinema use in the 1920s and 30s. Patrons were promised 'a place of entertainment second to none in west Wales' with 'comfort and convenience far beyond one's usual expectations' and the decoration 'designed entirely on modern lines'. It was also pointed out, however, that '[t]he dignified facade in King Street has not been disturbed.'[95]

Most modern cinemas built in Wales in this period were not found in the high streets of major towns, but in outlying districts, suburbs and small towns. Though influenced by modern developments in cinema architecture, these halls were usually fairly small (often under 1,000 seats). Most of these cinemas were well designed with care having been taken to provide the latest interior designs. Their purpose, however, was not to target custom from existing halls, or to attract a more upmarket clientele. These halls were built in areas where no cinemas previously existed, and they served to facilitate the development of cinema-going as a habitual and locally based experience.

The success of local cinemas in attracting a regular audience (almost irrespective of the particular film on offer) is most clearly evident in the survival of so many 'fleapits'. Many such cinemas, built before the First World War and offering little by way of comfort or refinement, were able to survive because they were cheap and they had a regular local customer base. Their presence was most evident in the south Wales Valleys, but the inhabitants of most Welsh towns would have been able to identify at least one local fleapit.

The nature of cinema provision in Wales between the 1920s and 50s reflected a pattern of consumption based around the habitual weekly attendance of mainly working-class film-goers. Cinema buildings in Wales did undergo significant changes during the period, but continuity was equally in evidence. Some new cinemas were built, others were renovated, but many remained largely unchanged throughout the period. The large modern 'super-cinema' remained the exception rather than the rule, and the majority of audiences continued to watch films in venues that could best be described as local institutions. These cinemas were 'locals' not only because they drew their customers from the surrounding area, but also because the employees, managers and indeed owners of these halls also came from the local community. The following chapter explores the extent to which the exhibition side of the film industry in Wales was locally controlled.

3

COMPANIES AND EMPLOYEES

Business and economic historians have, until recently, paid little attention to the British film industry. Accounts of the film industry's development in Britain have often been provided by historians more interested in the cultural value of films than in the economics of the industry.[1] As such there has been a tendency to measure the performance of the British industry by the level of critical acclaim for its films, rather than their popular appeal or commercial success.[2] When viewed in terms of their popularity among audiences, rather than critics, British films (particularly of the 1930s) have been shown to be much more successful than was once thought (and government intervention to promote British film production has also been seen in a more positive light).[3] While British films have been the subject of much scholarly attention, however, our knowledge of British cinema companies remains patchy. Some attempts have been made to explore the strategies employed by film companies in the twentieth century,[4] but much less is known about such business enterprises in Britain than in the USA.[5] This reflects the greater degree of interest shown in film production compared to distribution and exhibition. American companies, of course, produced more films than British studios, and throughout the period covered here the majority of films screened in British cinemas were made by US firms. The process of film exhibition in Britain, however, was controlled almost entirely by British firms, but business and economic historians have, to date, paid little attention to their activities.

Examinations of the film industry in Britain have almost inevitably been written from the perspective of film-makers – or at least those with an interest in promoting films. If exhibitors are considered at all it is in the context of their role as outlets for films, rather than as sites of consumption. Attention, therefore, has been focused almost exclusively on the major cinema chains of Gaumont, Associated British Cinemas (ABC), and from the mid-1930s, Odeon.[6] These circuits were undoubtedly highly influential within the British film industry. As the Plant Report into the British film industry pointed out: 'a booking with one of the three main circuits is indispensable if the producer of a British film is to have any prospect of recouping his production cost.'[7] A booking with a major circuit was equally important for US films released in the British market.[8] By 1951 the three major circuits controlled a fifth of all British cinemas, and a third of all seats – a considerable proportion of the industry in the hands of just three companies. The remaining exhibitors were far too small to exert any real influence over film producers, and cinema historians have tended to view them as peripheral to the industry:

> As for the independent showman with one or more theatres, he is at the far end of the queue and must bide his time until the crumbs fall from the rich man's table. He has in fact no independence but must console himself by digesting the various reports on the tendencies to monopoly in the film industry.[9]

Viewed from the perspective of the producer, the role of the major circuits within the film industry was absolutely central. From the consumers' viewpoint, however, the position of the smaller exhibitor was more important. Not only were the majority of cinemas (and cinema seats) controlled by small circuits or independent exhibitors, most cinema admissions were also to halls that were not part of large circuits.[10] The small film exhibitor must play a prominent role in any consumer-oriented history of film-going in Britain, but in Wales their importance was particularly striking.

Film companies in Wales

It was argued in the previous chapter that film-going in Wales, more than in other parts of Britain, was centred on small, local cinemas that had been constructed before the 1920s. Table 15 indicates that the majority of these cinemas were not part of a circuit at all (singleton cinemas), and of those that were, almost all were in chains of less than fifty halls. The degree to which film exhibition was concentrated in the hands of a few major companies varied considerably within Britain. In London and the south-east major chains were much more prominent than in the north. Nowhere, though, was the penetration of the large circuits so limited as in Wales.

The cinemas operated by the major chains tended to be larger than other halls, which is why the large circuits accounted for a greater proportion of cinema seating than of cinemas themselves. The large-circuit cinemas also attracted a disproportionate share of cinema admissions, which meant that even though only a quarter of British cinemas belonged to a large chain, these halls accounted for over two-fifths of ticket sales. In Wales, however, fewer than one in six cinema visits was to a hall that formed part of a large chain (see table 16).

Of the cinemas in Wales that were part of large circuits the majority belonged to the Odeon chain. This circuit was established by Oscar Deutsch, a Birmingham entrepreneur who became involved in the cinema industry in the 1920s. The first Odeon cinema was built in 1930, and over the next decade

Table 15
Cinemas and cinema seats in circuits, 1951 (%)[11]

Region	Singleton		Small		Medium		Large	
	halls	seats	halls	seats	halls	seats	halls	seats
North and Scotland	35.6	27.6	29.7	27.8	14.9	15.9	19.7	28.7
South and Midlands	28.2	18.7	25.2	18.2	12.7	12.7	33.9	50.5
Wales	55.5	45.6	17.0	16.7	21.6	26.0	6.0	11.7
Britain	33.8	24.5	26.8	22.7	14.4	15.0	25.0	37.8

Source: Browning and Sorrell, 'Cinemas and cinema-going in Britain'.

Table 16
Admissions to singleton and circuit cinemas, 1951 (%)

Region	Singleton	Small	Medium	Large
North and Scotland	25	27	16	32
South and Midlands	18	17	15	50
Wales	39	18	27	16
Britain	21	22	16	41

Source: Browning and Sorrell, 'Cinemas and cinema-going in Britain'.

Deutsch pursued a strategy of building new cinemas in suburbs and new towns across Britain.[12] Almost 300 cinemas belonged to the Odeon chain by the end of the 1930s, although only six were in Wales.[13] Odeons were constructed in the north Wales towns of Colwyn Bay, Llandudno and Wrexham.[14] In the south, only Newport and Llanelli gained new Odeon cinemas in the 1930s, though Cardiff's Imperial cinema was acquired by the chain in 1936.[15] After Deutsch's death in 1941 control of the circuit had passed into the hands of J. Arthur Rank. The policy of new cinema building could not be continued in the war years although Odeon did expand its presence in Wales through acquisition of existing halls, such as the Maxime in Sketty and the Majestic in Port Talbot. By the end of the 1940s there were nine Odeon cinemas in Wales, of which only five had actually been built by the company itself. The Odeons in Wales, like those in the rest of Britain, were not necessarily the most prestigious cinemas in the largest towns. They were certainly much larger than the average Welsh cinema, and as such achieved much higher weekly takings than most Welsh halls. In terms of takings per seat, however, Odeon cinemas were much closer to the Welsh average than to the figures achieved by Gaumont, whose halls were typically the premiere cinemas in their localities (see table 17).

Table 17
Size and weekly takings of cinemas in Wales, *c.*1947

	No. of Cinemas	Average Seating	Average Weekly Takings (£)	Takings per seat (£)
Gaumont	4	1067	565	0.53
Odeon	9	1645	592	0.36
Wales Total*	352	727	287	0.39

* The figures for Wales as a whole are for 1951.

Source: United Artists Archive, Sears Papers, box 10, file 5; Browning and Sorrell, 'Cinemas and cinema-going in Britain'.

The Gaumont and ABC circuits had even fewer cinemas in Wales, and all of these were acquired rather than built by the firms themselves. Gaumont gained control of the Coliseum in Newport and the Hippodrome in Cardiff in 1927, the latter city's Empire was also acquired in 1931. As well as these large halls, Gaumont also found itself in control of much smaller cinemas in Chepstow and Monmouth, that had been part of the Provincial Cinematograph Theatres (PCT) chain acquired by Gaumont British in 1929.[16] ABC, meanwhile, acquired the Queen's and the Olympia cinemas in Cardiff in 1927 and 1936 respectively (both kept their original names). ABC also gained control of Newport's Olympia in 1929 and Merthyr's Castle in 1932.[17] These were mostly first-run halls – the first to screen the latest new releases in their area. By no means all such cinemas, however, were controlled by the major chains at this time. The Park Hall in Cardiff, and Swansea's Plaza remained outside circuits altogether.

The great multitude of Wales's less prestigious cinemas were of no interest to the major circuits. Indeed, it was not unknown for smaller cinemas taken over by these companies to revert back to independent control. Gaumont, for example, acquired the Palace in Treharris as well as the cinemas in Monmouth and Chepstow when they took over PCT in 1929. Whereas

Table 18
Average weekly takings of Gaumont and Odeon cinemas, *c.*1947

	Gaumont		Odeon	
	Cinemas	Takings (£)	Cinemas	Takings (£)
London	48	729	80	563
Provincial	149	574	177	546
Wales	4	565	9	592
Total	197	612	257	551

Source: United Artists Collection, Sears Papers, box 10, file 5.

Gaumont chose to keep and renovate the latter two halls, they quickly got rid of the valleys' cinema, which was taken over and reopened by an independent company in 1930. Swansea's Albert Hall and Carlton cinemas also became part of the ABC circuit in 1937 but were taken back by the local firm South Wales Cinemas two years later.

The cinemas controlled by the major circuits were not typical of those found in most parts of Wales. As well as being much larger in terms of seating capacity, the circuit cinemas also generated greater weekly box office receipts. Even at the end of the 1940s, when economic conditions in Wales were relatively strong, the weekly takings of the average Welsh cinema was only half the amount the generated by a Gaumont or Odeon hall. The prevalence of small cinemas in Wales, with limited revenue earning potential, must explain why the major circuits were reluctant to invest there.

Of the Welsh cinemas which were in circuits at this time (45 per cent in 1951), the vast majority were in small chains of less than fifteen cinemas. These were often locally run, in many cases as a family business. A browse through the *Kinematograph Year Books* of the inter-war period reveals the limited geographical area to which most of these circuits were confined, in some cases to a single town.[18] As with the major companies, the development of smaller cinema chains within Wales owed as much to the economy and geography of the area, as it did to the state of the British film industry. Given the lack of any major transport links between north and south Wales it comes as little surprise that the largest of these circuits, (those with between ten and fifteen cinemas which might be described as regional, rather than local, in character), tended to expand along a west–east axis rather than a north–south one.[19] Thus, the Wrexham-based Cambria and Borders circuit, as its name suggests, ran cinemas in places such as Market Drayton and Ellesmere as well as Colwyn Bay and Llanidloes. There were very few circuits which operated cinemas in both north and south Wales.

The total number of Welsh-based circuits altered very little in the inter-war period; the figure was usually around ten according to the *Kinematograph Year Book*. What did change, however, was the area in which the majority of circuits were located. Companies based in the south Wales valleys such as Amman Alpha, Rowland Williams and Welsh Hills, were listed in the 1920s but all had disappeared by 1935. Interestingly, this did not mean that the cinemas themselves had closed. Many of the halls run by these chains, such as the Picturedrome in Tonypandy and the New Theatre in Maesteg, continued independently into the 1950s. The new circuits which emerged in this period were usually based in areas without such severe economic problems. Cardiff and Hereford[20] both housed newly formed cinema companies in the 1930s. It is also noticeable by the end of the 1930s that more south Wales circuits were beginning to set up headquarters in Cardiff. The 1922 *Kinematograph Year Book* mentions only one circuit based in Cardiff: by 1939 there were five.

There is some evidence that Welsh circuits became larger in the inter-war years, but they started from a very small base and there was nothing spectacular in their rate of growth.[21] The only Welsh circuit containing more than ten cinemas in the 1920s, Cambria and Borders, vanished from the trade directories as quickly as it had appeared. The W. E. Willis circuit, which first appeared in 1936 with fourteen cinemas, had added just one to this total a decade later. The only Welsh circuit that appears to have maintained steady growth throughout the period was the Splott Cinema Company. Formed in 1913 in order to build the Splott cinema, the company continued to construct cinemas and purchase others throughout Cardiff in the 1920s and 30s. By 1939 the company owned thirteen halls in Cardiff and Penarth. One episode in the company's history, however, suggests that this development of steady growth was not as smooth as might first appear.

In 1925 the company won a court action against its own managing director, one William J. C. Thomas. Mr Thomas had apparently led his fellow directors (who were also his cousins) and his bank to believe that he was negotiating the purchase of the Canton Cinema from Mr Samuel Instone on behalf of the company. After the deal had been struck, however, he claimed to have bought the property for himself with the intention of setting up his own company. After a protracted court case the Canton cinema did eventually become part of the Splott circuit, but it is noticeable that from this date on the company built its own cinemas rather than acquire existing ones.[22] This case may not have been typical of the difficulties incurred by cinema companies in this period, but it serves to demonstrate that in small businesses personal differences, as well as the general economic outlook, could affect the prospects for expansion.[23] The Splott Cinema Company clearly had ambitious plans, but not all Welsh circuits were so intent on expansion. Companies such as South Wales Cinemas (with four halls), Castle and Central (with three), and Will Stone (five), seemed content with small circuits and made little effort to add to them. Perhaps more significantly, they were able to survive throughout the period without being absorbed into a larger concern.

The largest cinema circuit to develop within Wales did not emerge until cinema audiences had gone into decline. The early post-war years saw a continuation of the trends of the 1930s. In north Wales the Paramount company (a Welshpool-based circuit run by Mr Guy Baxter) continued to grow, with twenty halls by 1950. It was joined by Deeside Entertainments, which ran twelve cinemas in 1955. In the south the larger circuits of Splott and W. E. Willis continued to operate in the early post-war years alongside the likes of South Wales Cinemas and new circuits such as Bridgend Cinemas. As audiences began to fall away in the 1950s these companies clearly encountered increasing problems. Rather than entering a prolonged period of terminal decline, however, it seems that many south Wales companies sold their cinemas to a single chain. By 1963 there were only two south Wales circuits listed in the *Kine Year Book*: Bridgend Cinemas, with six halls; and Jackson

Withers, with thirty-five. The smaller circuits had been able to continue operating for as long as the cinema business was profitable, only selling up when
the film-going habit fell into decline.

Whatever the circumstances shaping its development, the cinema industry
in Wales between the 1920s and 50s remained closely rooted in local communities. Of the cinemas that were in circuits most were in small,
locally-based chains. The overall majority of cinemas in Wales, however,
were not part of a circuit at all. These were the independently managed, so-
called singleton cinemas.

As well as being much smaller than many of the cinemas attached to large
chains, these small independent halls were also managed in a quite distinct
way. In many singleton cinemas, for instance, the proprietor and the manager were the same person. His (and most cinema managers were men)
primary responsibility was, necessarily, to ensure that the cinema operated at
a profit. Even in cinema's heyday, however, this was not something small
independent exhibitors could take for granted. For one thing non-circuit cinemas were in a very weak position when it came to booking films. They were
mostly second- or third-run halls, unable to screen major releases until after
the premier cinemas. The earning potential of these small independent halls
was further reduced by their small size in comparison to major circuit cinemas. Proprietors of second- or third-run cinemas did pay a lower flat rate
for film hire, but because these halls generated much less in weekly takings,
the proportion of their revenue going to the film distributor was often higher
than in the main first-run halls. The regions of Britain where the proportion
of net takings spent on film hire were highest were those with the greatest
proportion of small singleton cinemas: Wales and the south-west. The most
obvious way in which independent cinema owners could attempt to increase
profitability was by raising admission prices. In Wales, however, ticket prices
were below the national average, and the exhibitors' share of net takings was
lower (per seat) in Wales than any other part of Britain. In the south-west by
contrast, where cinema admissions were relatively expensive, the amount of
revenue generated by exhibitors per seat was well above the national
average (despite the high proportion of takings going on film hire).[24]

Why did cinema exhibitors in Wales not follow their counterparts across
the border in setting higher prices? The most plausible explanation must
simply be that exhibitors were constrained in this regard by what their regular working-class audience was prepared to pay. There would have been
little purpose in raising prices if the result was that a larger proportion of
customers chose to sit in the cheaper seats. One attempt to increase prices at
Cardiff's Park Hall for the screening of *Gone With the Wind* certainly met with
a hostile response. The manager recalled 'people picketing outside with
notices telling the public to boycott the film because of the prices'.[25] The Park
Hall, as a large, city-centre hall, at least had the advantage of a large auditorium which if filled to capacity could bring in a large revenue. For the

smallest cinemas with under five hundred seats, however, there was less opportunity to take advantage of particularly popular films.

The independent cinema manager, while presiding over the home of the most popular form of mass entertainment, faced a number of constraints and could expect only modest profit margins, even when attendances were booming. In the face of all the difficulties confronting them, small independent exhibitors were able to survive by providing programmes of entertainment which were, as far as possible, tailored to the demands of the local cinema-going public.[26]

Cinema managers were usually very public figures in the local community. According to Stephen Ridgwell, 'the prominent public role of the manager ... was of no small significance in [the] process of binding the cinema to its locality'.[27] One way in which this occurred was through advertising. The major US film distributors did allocate significant resources toward the marketing of their films, but these efforts were designed to encourage people to watch the latest new releases in the largest first-run cinemas.[28] The managers of the smaller local cinemas, therefore, needed to take responsibility themselves for bringing their programmes of entertainment to the attention of the public. They could seldom afford to take out half-page advertisements in the local papers, as the film distributors did,[29] and resorted, instead, to other forms of publicity. One cinema-goer from the south Wales Valleys recalled how '[a] religious epic was advertised the week before its screening by the appearance on the stage at the cinema concerned of massed chapel choirs of the area. They sang suitably sacred anthems, then a discreet announcement was made about the film and its content.'[30] Such advertising stunts were not confined to the auditorium. A 1971 article in the *South Wales Echo* recalling the heyday of the Park Hall cinema, described the manager as 'a great believer in publicity stunts':

> ... for years the Park staged elaborate campaigns to get people to queue for its films. Efforts ranged from simple uniform displays accompanying military pictures to the parading through Cardiff of a stuffed Bengal tiger in a cage to advertise a film involving a one-man big game hunt, *Harry Black*.[31]

Cinema proprietors were also able to use the popularity of their halls to the immediate benefit of local communities. This was most evident in the case of the miners' cinemas, which were housed in the institutes owned and run by local workmen.[32] In numerous communities, such as Ton Pentre, Ynisher, Ynysybwl, Mardy and Pontcymmer, the Workmens' Institute was home to the only cinema throughout the inter-war period. Historians of the south Wales coalfield have attached considerable importance to these institutes in the creation of an active and distinct working-class culture.[33] Furthermore, Bert Hogenkamp has pointed out that '[f]ilm exhibition guaranteed the survival of the halls and institutes, which otherwise would have had difficulties making ends meet due to high unemployment among miners.'[34] In the Tredegar Institute, for example, the rent paid by the Spanish Aid Committee for the hire of the cinema in 1937–8 'was refunded as a matter of routine without discussion'. The cinema committee here even managed to persuade British Lion 'to supply a film free of charge for the Spanish Aid Committee'. What is more, the cinemas 'opened the Institutes, those bastions of typically male activities, to women, to children (special children's matinees) and to the unemployed'.[35]

The owners of small circuits were known to play an active role in the running of their cinemas, and frequently displayed an acute awareness of their role within the local community. Will Stone, who owned a small chain of Valleys cinemas, 'organised a sort of free lottery based on seat numbers', according to one of his employees. Many a poor family got prizes of new shoes or parcels of food from that little scheme, just by going to the cinema.'[36] Another cinema owner, W. E. Willis, promoted the young Tommy Farr in his first fight, on the stage of the Empire, Tonypandy.[37]

Local social and economic conditions clearly influenced the structure of the cinema industry in Wales. The major cinema circuits of Odeon, Gaumont and ABC were reluctant to invest heavily in film exhibition, which left the vast majority of Welsh cinemas under the ownership and control of local businesses. In terms both of their ownership and management, these halls were tied closely to their local communities. As well as being local meeting places or institutions, however, cinemas were also local employers, and much needed ones at that.

Employment in the cinema industry in Wales

Precise figures for the number of people employed in the cinema industry in Wales are not easy to obtain. According to the 1921 census, there were 1,834 people in south Wales employed in theatres, music halls and picture palaces. The number working in film production and film studios was a mere twenty-eight. By 1931, the number employed in theatres, music halls and picture palaces had increased to 2,422 in south Wales, the figure for Wales as a whole was 3,011.[38] The total employed in film producing and film studios at this time was ninety-four. The 1951 census provides slightly more precise information. The total number of people in Wales working in theatres, music halls and cinemas stood at 4,988. Of this number, 3,577 (nearly three-quarters) were working in cinemas. In England and Wales as a whole, the equivalent proportion was 57 per cent. These figures clearly demonstrate that within Wales, as far as employment is concerned, the exhibition side of the industry was far more significant than film production or distribution. Further, if the 1951 figures are anything to go by, it appears that within Wales cinemas employed a much greater proportion of those in the entertainment industry than was the case in Britain as a whole.

The three-and-a-half thousand jobs available in the cinema industry in Wales by 1951 made it quite a significant feature of the economy. It was only a minor employer when compared to the heavy industries or agriculture, but in the inter-war years it was one of the few areas where new jobs were being created. This is not to say that unemployment was not a worry for cinema workers. The late 1920s saw hundreds of musicians thrown out of work as the technique of presenting sound films was perfected.[39] The 1931 census shows that in parts of Wales unemployment among those employed in theatres, music halls and picture palaces was very high indeed, reaching 45 per cent in the Rhondda, and standing at 26 per cent for Wales as a whole. It is unknown what proportion of these were recently unemployed musicians, indeed, it is far from clear exactly how many were cinema workers. What is apparent, however, is that unemployment in the cinema industry was not as widespread as in the Welsh economy as a whole, and that the absolute number of jobs available in this industry was increasing throughout the period, despite the drop in the number of musicians. The cinema offered employment opportunities for women, and in some parts of Wales female cinema workers outnumbered males. Women, however, were most likely to be employed in the least skilled jobs which offered the lowest rates of pay.

The most senior member of any cinema staff was the manager. Some non-circuit cinemas were managed by the proprietor, but for the most part managers were salaried employees of a cinema company. As well as advertising (see above) their primary responsibility was to oversee the day-to-day running of their halls: to ensure that the buildings and their facilities were in good working order; to see that the accounts were properly kept; and to deal with any queries from the public. Managers of independent halls also had to book the films, though most circuits had a separate booking manager.

A less visible, but equally important member of the cinema staff was the projectionist. In the earliest days of the cinematograph operators were highly skilled technicians whose role included more than simply operating the machinery. As the cinema industry developed, and new technologies became available, however, individual expertise became less important:

> Many a proprietor saved money on new machinery by relying on his operator's skills as a *bricoleur*, a technical wizard of home-made improvements (even, according to projectionists' folklore, as late as the introduction of sound). But these skills lost much of their importance when music halls, and then proper cinemas, installed permanent equipment. Basically all that was needed was for someone to turn the handle. This was still a skilled job, since it needed quite a lot of expertise to turn the handle smoothly, and keep the flicker on the screen down to a minimum. But the old school of operators chided the new school for being *mere* handle turners.[40]

The development of electrical projection equipment, although frequently problematic in its early days, eventually reduced the need even for 'handle turners'.[41] Cinema projectionists, in the period under consideration here, clearly did not require the same skills as their predecessors. This is not to say that they were unskilled. Extensive knowledge of the machines they operated was required in order that any difficulties could be resolved without interrupting the film. Audiences, from the 1920s onwards, were increasingly intolerant of stoppages in the programme of entertainment. As one former projectionist remembers of working during the First World War: 'It was a fairly difficult job in those days, but films were so new that the audience didn't seem to mind if anything went wrong. For instance there was no shouting or slow handclapping when the screen blacked out while reels were changed.'[42] The development of new projection equipment may have reduced the skill levels of operators in the 1920s, but the coming of talkies required projectionists to develop new skills.[43] Throughout the period, however, their job remained a critical one. A loss of concentration on the projectionist's part had implications not just for the smooth running of the film, but also for the safety of the audience. The highly flammable properties of film stock were well known, and fire regulations were strictly enforced by local authorities (see chapter 6). One could not expect to become a projectionist, therefore, without first having served an apprenticeship as an assistant. Whereas the role of the cinema manager was to get enough people through the door of the cinema to make it financially viable, the projectionist bore much of the responsibility for the smooth, and safe, running of the entertainment on offer inside. It is worth noting, perhaps, that as well as the films themselves, the lighting, music and any sound effects within the cinema were controlled from the projection room. While such duties would have been taken for granted by audiences, it was also possible for the projectionist to make a much more direct impression. Mac Smith, who worked as a projectionist for fifty years, recalls that for the screening of *All Quiet on the Western Front* (the original silent version) he 'got some cordite bombs which could be detonated electronically at suitable moments'. This apparently was not an isolated incident, on another occasion he experimented with sound effects in an attempt to boost the popularity of the film *San Francisco*.[44] Not all of these innovations were successful, and he admitted that after the incident with the cordite bombs, 'I nearly lost my job and the audience were terrified'. These examples, from one of Cardiff's largest cinemas, may overstate the level of influence which most projectionists exerted over the audience, but their role was certainly important in shaping the atmosphere in which films were viewed. As these incidents suggest, the job of cinema projectionist was not without its interesting moments, but it also involved a multitude of less memorable duties, and long, unsocial hours.[45]

Another group of workers who played an important role in creating an appropriate atmosphere within the halls were musicians. Prior to the coming of sound a small orchestra was employed by many of the larger cinemas, while in the smaller halls a single pianist often provided the appropriate musical background. To perform suitably dramatic music for each film screened demanded a particular talent. The films themselves usually changed twice a week, leaving the musicians with little or no time to rehearse. A certain amount of improvisation was usually demanded – the wife of one cinema pianist in the 1920s recalls that her husband

> would read the synopsis when each film arrived and once he had the idea he could fit in the right accompaniment for any situation . . . I doubt if he ever played the same tune twice. And of course, the fact that he never used sheet music meant that he could watch the film as he played.[46]

With two or three screenings a day, the musicians, like all cinema employees, worked long and anti-social hours. The working day of the above pianist apparently lasted from 1 p.m. until midnight, and occasionally it would be even longer. As his wife regretfully remembered: 'By the time he'd come home and looked at the papers and had something to eat it was about three in the morning . . . so he stayed in bed late. It was a lonely life for me.'[47]

On the positive side this particular pianist was able to earn as much as £8 in a busy week, which was more than many managers took home. Another cinema musician, a drummer who worked at Will Stone's Empire in Tonypandy, remembers that '[i]t was hard work but enjoyable and the musical standard was remarkable'. He also went on to praise Mr Stone himself: 'All of us got a week's paid holiday a year – quite something in those days[48] – and an evening off once a month. Mr Stone even paid for our substitutes on those evenings.'[49]

It is doubtful that all cinema workers would have seen their employers in such positive a light, and nor were cinema owners themselves so sanguine about the rate at which they paid their musicians. The head of the Castle and Central chain of cinemas in south Wales made enquiries as early as 1922 about purchasing a pipe organ or orchestrelle that 'would completely take the place of an orchestra of seven of eight'.[50] This particular plan to do away with musicians came to nothing, and the orchestra at Swansea's Castle cinema remained in (well paid) employment in 1926 (see table 19). The coming of the sound film a couple of years later finally did eliminate the need for live music in the cinema, at least during performances. Not even the benevolent Will Stone could avoid making his musicians redundant after the coming of talkies.[51]

There was still employment for a few musicians in some of the largest and most prestigious halls. In the café at Cardiff's Capitol Theatre, for example, 'Falkman's Syncopated Five entertained customers daily' in the 1930s.[52] There was also a need for gifted organists, capable of mastering the huge and increasingly elaborate Wurlitzer or Hammond organs. At the opening of

Table 19
Staff earning £160 per annum or more in Swansea's Castle Cinema, 1926

Surname	First Name(s)	Occupation	Weekly Wage		
			£	s	d
Gambold	A. R.	Manager	6	–	–
Millard	Wm James	Asst manager	3	10	–
Illingworth	William	Operator	3	10	–
Hawkins	Edward	Relief operator	3	5	–
Arnold	John Wm	Orchestra leader	5	–	–
Williams	Arthur	Organist	4	10	–
Selly	John Sydney	Violinist	4	–	–
Williams	Edgar David	Cellist	3	10	–
Payne	Katherine	Pianist	4	5	–

Source: GRO, Andrews Collection, D/D A/B 18/6/25.

Swansea's Plaza cinema, it was pointed out that the organist, Frank Matthew, was classically trained, having 'played all the principal cathedral organs during his travels both in England and France'.[53] In Wales only a small proportion of cinemas actually contained such instruments, but their appeal extended well beyond the auditorium. The organist at the Plaza for much of the 1930s was Tom Jenkins, but his reputation extended far beyond Swansea thanks to his regular broadcasts for the BBC Empire programme. The broadcasts went out live from the cinema and apparently won Jenkins admirers in many parts of the globe.[54] Organists such as these were clearly well respected figures in their own right, and it is perhaps significant that Jenkins was manager at the Plaza as well as organist.

The majority of jobs on offer in cinemas, however, were low-skill, low-pay positions which promised little by way of career opportunities. The most prominent such position was that of commissionaire, a feature of many cinemas of the period. Dressed in their immaculate uniforms, these important looking officials were intended to provide a form of customer service, as well as providing the cinema with an air of respectability. Much of their job, however, involved ensuring that the audience had paid for their seats and that they behaved in a civilized manner, both inside and out of the auditorium. A prominent figure at the cinema entrance, the commissionaire was not a skilled worker, and as a result was not as well paid as the musicians of the 1920s. The general secretary of the National Association of Theatrical and Kine Employees (NATKE) made the point forcefully in 1934: 'Arrayed like brigadiers while on duty, yet unable to feed like the officer's charger when off duty – that is the position of many commissionaires outside cinemas today.'[55]

The position of commissionaire, however, was far from being the most lowly in the cinema business, and rates of pay were not as low as union leaders sometimes claimed. In the largest 'super-cinemas' he[56] was supported by a small army of page-boys and usherettes, also smartly dressed, and much less well paid. Smaller cinemas also employed usherettes, but not in such large numbers. The tasks carried out by these employees were a far cry from the glamour and romance which their places of work had come to symbolize. A cinema usherette was expected to do far more than simply show people to their seats. As a former employee of Ely's Regent cinema remembered:

> I was 15 at the time in 1943 when I started as an usherette and cleaner. There were eight of us in all and our day started at 7.30 a.m. when we scrubbed eight rows of seats on each side for two hours with other duties. Then we went home for dinner and prepared for the matinee and evening performances, when we were the usherettes.[57]

The extent of the cleaning duties varied, no doubt, from cinema to cinema, but they were often taken extremely seriously by the management. An employee of Will Stone's recalled that

> His wife was fanatically concerned about cleanliness. She paid the cinema cleaning women the best wages in the Rhondda. But woe betide them if they skimped on the job. After they had cleaned the cinema Mrs Stone used to come in wearing a pair of white gloves. She would run her fingers over any surfaces such as seat backs or mouldings that caught the dust and if the gloves came away marked someone was in trouble.[58]

After spending their mornings scrubbing, polishing and clearing litter, the page-boys and usherettes were expected to present an immaculate appearance when the cinemas opened to the public. A page-boy at Cardiff's Capitol Theatre who recalled worked twelve-hour days, six days a week for 10s a week, spent his mornings polishing the building's many brass railings, then at 1.30 p.m.: 'The whole 21 of us on the staff had to parade in a straight line each day, and woe betide us if there was as much as a speck of dirt on our shirt fronts or uniforms.'[59]

Once the cinemas had opened, these employees performed various duties such as handing out programmes, tearing tickets, guarding cloakrooms, selling ice cream and directing people to their seats. They were also expected to offer whatever advice or assistance was required by the patrons. The page-boys at the Capitol were also ordered not to accept tips, but instead to reply 'Capitol service, sir'. Given the wages they were paid, however, it would not be a surprise if staff occasionally failed to adhere to this regulation.

The pay of cinema workers was notoriously low. Under the heading 'Scandalous Cinema Conditions', *The Daily Herald* in 1934 reported that in larger circuits girls were working between fifty and sixty hours a week for

25s, while in other halls the hours were from fifty-five to seventy with wages in the range of 12s 6d to 18s. Men, it claimed, were marginally better off, earning between 40s and 55s for similar hours in larger halls, and from 30s to 40s in other houses.[60] In Wales, where the vast majority of cinemas were not run by large circuits, low wages were commonplace. The manager of one Porth cinema was clearly aware that his main cleaner (who earned 14s 6d a week) was 'worth more than she receives'.[61] The working conditions of these employees is seldom referred to by cinema historians. Yet as John Clarke and Chas Critcher have astutely observed, the service and leisure industries were becoming 'the new sweated trades'. 'The cinema usherette, working unsocial hours for low wages, suffering from boredom and sore feet, was a sympto-matic figure – the invisible support of the glittering world of the "dream palace" '.[62]

Trade unionists had regularly complained about the pay and conditions of cinema workers and the lot of the 'girls who are employed in the cinemas' even pricked the conscience of a Conservative MP who, exaggerating, felt that they amounted to 'slave conditions'.[63] The rates of pay for all employees at one of Cardiff's largest cinemas is given in table 20.

Table 20
Cardiff Olympia wages list, September 1936

Position	Number of Employees	Weekly Pay		
		£	s	d
Manager	1	7	0	0
Assistant manager	1	4	15	0
Chief operator	1	4	0	0
Assistant operator	1	3	0	0
3rd operator	1	2	10	0
4th operator	1	2	5	0
Cashier	1	1	10	0
Assistant cashier	1	1	0	0
Kiosk attendant	1	1	5	0
Usherette	5	1	0	0
Usherette	9	–	16	0
Usherette	1	–	10	0
Commissionaire	2	3	5	0
Night watchman	1	2	5	0
Attendant & boilerman	1	2	7	6
Page-boy	2	–	10	0
Forewoman	1	1	5	0
Cleaner	4	–	15	0
Cleaner	1	–	10	0
Cloakroom attendant & cleaner	1	1	5	0

Source: GRO, Andrews Collection, D/D A/B 20/27/31.

As workplaces cinemas were divided clearly along gender lines. In Cardiff's Olympia, for example, all employees earning £2 a week or more were men, while all of the usherettes and cleaning staff were female. When complaints about the working conditions of cinema employees were voiced, the plight of the 'girls' usually attracted most attention. It should be pointed out, however, that the cinema industry was one of the few sectors of the economy that offered employment opportunities for Welsh women. The inter-war years saw an exodus of young women leaving Wales to work as domestic servants in more prosperous areas such as London, the Midlands and the south-east of England. A job at the local cinema was no more arduous than the lot of a domestic servant, and it at least enabled the women employed there to remain close to their families. By 1951, 60 per cent of those working in Welsh cinemas were women.

The range of job opportunities provided by cinemas was far more limited for women than for men. The more senior positions of manager and chief projectionist were dominated by men. The 1921 census shows that of 260 managers of theatres, music halls and picture palaces, only 19 (7 per cent) were female. Similarly, of those classed as 'stage hands, cinema and limelight operators', there were 193 males to just 18 females. Women did make up 30 per cent of musicians, but the category which they dominated was that of 'money takers, programme sellers, attendants'. Here, females outnumbered males by 404 to 63; almost half the women employed in the entertainment industry worked in this sector. The 1931 census does not give as detailed a breakdown of those employed in theatres, music halls and picture palaces; it does, however, show that of the 1,393 women working in this area only 27 (2 per cent) held positions that were described as managerial. The number of men employed in such positions was 355 (22 per cent).

Whereas men who entered the cinema industry, even at the lowest level, had some opportunities for promotion, the female employees tended to remain in the same low-paid jobs until they stopped work. Equality of opportunity, at this time, was a principle held by few, and practised by even fewer. The period covered here saw little sustained feminist activity, and were more noted for supporting a 'cult of domesticity'.[64] Marriage bars remained in operation for women teachers and civil servants until the 1940s, while a range of influential sources, from leading psychiatrists to popular magazines, argued in no uncertain terms that a mother's rightful place was at home with her children. The view that 'saw the mother–child relationship as the key to the healthy development of the child' was frequently expressed. 'Women's work outside the home therefore stood condemned as likely to produce juvenile delinquents.'[65] While the number of women in employment did increase in inter-war Britain, they remained in a small minority. In Wales, it should be added, the rates of female employment were considerably lower than in England.[66] It was not until the 1960s that rates of female employment in Wales caught up with, and went on to overtake, the national average.

Working Welsh women in the inter-war years were 'breadwinners of the last resort'.[67] The general pattern of female employment at this time was for young women to work to help support themselves and their families until they married and had children. The Second World War did little to alter this. Both Penny Summerfield and Harold Smith have stressed continuity rather than change in womens' attitude to work in the 1940s.[68] To the majority of women, either side of the war, it seems that marriage and domesticity were considered more liberating than the workplace. This is the context in which the position of female cinemas workers must be seen. The cinema did not provide career opportunities for females, it offered young women the chance to earn some extra money by carrying out mundane, and at times arduous tasks.

The largest 'super-cinemas', which prided themselves on comfort, service and cleanliness, were the ones that employed the highest proportion of female staff. The size of the buildings, and the number of patrons they attracted, meant that a fairly large team of cleaners and usherettes were required for their smooth running. The smaller houses, on the other hand, while still employing a manager, projectionist (plus assistant) and perhaps a commissionaire might only require one or two female staff. It is noticeable that in the south Wales valleys and much of rural Wales, where the vast majority of cinemas were small, the proportion of women employed in the industry was considerably less than in the larger south Wales towns. In the urban district of Rhondda and the counties of Cardiganshire and Anglesey in 1931, the proportion of females working in theatres, music halls and picture palaces were 36, 29 and 41 per cent respectively. The corresponding figures for Cardiff, Swansea and Newport were 48, 55 and 51 per cent.[69]

Trade unions and the cinema industry in Wales

Given the long hours of work and low rates of pay available to many groups of workers in the cinema industry, it is perhaps surprising that it was seldom affected by industrial relations problems. There is little evidence of antagonism between the staff and management in most cinemas. Indeed, some cinema workers from this period have fond recollections of how they were treated: the drummer at Will Stone's Empire cinema described his boss as 'a marvellous employer and a philanthropist'.[70] This can be partly explained by the fact that cinemas were modern institutions that provided employment, for mainly unskilled workers, at a time of severe economic depression. Furthermore, most cinema workers did not have traditions to maintain: they were not a historically skilled group of workers, whose control over working practices had been steadily eroded by new technologies or increasingly intrusive management techniques. Where such arguments did apply – as in the case of projectionists or musicians – some evidence of industrial militancy did exist, as we shall see. The union that represented the vast majority of cinema workers in this period, however, the NATKE sought, wherever possible, to avoid confrontation with employers.

NATE, (the 'K' was added in 1936), did have a history of militant action. It had been closely involved in the music hall strike of 1906,[71] and considered itself to be at the forefront of the 'new union' movement, whereby workers were organized, irrespective of their skill levels, into 'industrial', as opposed to 'craft' unions. The right to represent all workers in the cinema industry was jealously defended by the NATE leadership throughout this period, and at times they seemed more willing to fight for this than for improving the conditions of their members. Any traces of militancy had certainly disappeared by the 1920s. Their main priorities in this decade were to broaden the membership, to gain national recognition by the Cinematograph Exhibitors' Association (CEA), and to avoid direct confrontation with employers.[72] Not surprisingly, then, NATE held few fears for cinema exhibitors in Wales. Even the miners' cinemas of the south Wales valleys, run by the workmen of various collieries dotted across the coalfield, had little inclination even to permit union organization. Certain institutes, such as Cwmllynfell, did sign agreements with the union,

> but the overall picture was so disappointing that in 1939 NATKE general secretary Tom O'Brien took the unusual step of arranging a meeting with Oliver Harris, general secretary of the South Wales Miners' Federation, hoping 'that the influence of the Federation would be helpful in securing any improvements necessary'.[73]

(Those in charge of the miners' institutes, such bastions of working-class culture and collective spirit, were apparently far less enamoured with the concept of industrial democracy when they found themselves in the position of employer.) Many other cinema managers felt equally uncomfortable at the prospect of having to deal with unions. The cautious and conciliatory approach taken by NATE must, therefore, have been quite a relief to them.

Even though it was accepted by the TUC that NATE was the official union for cinema employees, some of those who worked in the industry were members of different unions. NATE objected strongly to what they saw as the intrusion of rival unions on to its territory. However, workers belonging to these other unions usually received much stronger representation. In Swansea, due to peculiar local circumstances, a number of cinema workers belonged to the Dock, Wharf and General Workers Union.[74] This union had threatened strike action against Swansea exhibitors in 1920,[75] and there was a marked contrast in the attitude of local cinema managers in their dealings with the Dockers' Union compared with NATE. Referring to a meeting of local exhibitors with the Dockers' Union representative, the manager of Swansea's Castle cinema, A. R. Gambold, reported that

The secretary is one of these bullying, blustering sort of men who tries to force his views down your throat, does a lot of thumping on the table and makes all sorts of terrible threats . . . I have taken no part in the wrangle as to what we shall pay cinema employees, this has been left to Mr. Dix and Mr. Gwynn mostly, and whatever the result will be we shall agree to no doubt.[76]

Given the forceful approach taken by the Dockers' Union representative, it is understandable that Arthur Andrews, who controlled the Castle and Central circuit, suggested to Gambold that 'it might have been better if we had re-cognised the NATE when they approached us some time ago'. The response was revealing: 'It slipped my memory for the moment, but as a matter of fact, we did recognise them and met a deputation and spent the whole afternoon with them, but could do nothing but decide to ignore them as they would not give way on any point.'[77] The fact that Gambold had not only been able to ignore NATE, but forgot that he had even met with them at all, suggests that while the union would not modify its demands it had no intention of forcing them upon anybody. The Dockers' Union, in contrast, was willing to be both forceful and flexible in its negotiations.[78]

It was not only in Swansea that groups of cinema workers were able to find representation outside NATE. In the 1920s the Musicians' Union (MU), whose members were both highly skilled and in considerable demand, used some innovative methods to defend their interests. When five Rhondda cin-emas applied to the local Urban Council to have their licences renewed in 1920, the MU objected to the renewal on the ground that clause 12 of the licence was not being complied with by the proprietors. The clause reads: 'that the kinema management should engage only Trade Unionists and to pay them only the recognised Trade Union Rates'.[79] It is unclear whether this strategy was effective, but it at least demonstrates that the MU was active in the south Wales cinema industry in the 1920s. Further evidence for this comes from Swansea, where A. R. Gambold (still manager of the Castle in 1927) was becoming exasperated at the MU's insistence that musicians should be paid extra for performances that were broadcast on the BBC.[80] As cinemas across Wales were wired for sound from 1928 onwards, however, hundreds of musicians were thrown out of work, and the role of the MU, in the cinema industry at least, became likewise redundant.

The other skilled group of workers able to find representation outside NATE were projectionists. They had, in fact, been the first group of cinema employees to organize, forming the National Association of Cinematograph Operators (NACO) as early as 1896. NACO was affiliated to NATE, and by the 1920s it had been established by the TUC that NATE was the official union for cinema operators. A number of projectionists had traditionally belonged to the Electricians' Union (ETU), however, and this period wit-nessed an ongoing dispute between NATE and the ETU regarding the representation of projectionists.[81] The ETU were, strictly speaking, not supposed to entice cinema projectionists away from NATE, but the ETU's willingness to trade on the skill levels of its members to force the hand of employers attracted many cinema operators. In 1920, for instance, the ETU used the threat of strike action against exhibitors in Cardiff, Newport and the Rhondda Valley.[82] It was the ETU that organized the cinema operators' strike of 1938 – the most militant action taken by any group of cinema workers in this period. The strike did not effect south Wales, however, which suggests that the ETU had lost whatever foothold it once had in this area by the end of the 1930s.

Action such as the 1938 projectionists strike was never contemplated by the NATKE leadership. Indeed, to Michael Chanan: 'It was all too clear that while the ETU was striking against the employers, the NATKE leadership was only interested in seeing their rivals' backs broken.'[83] NATKE, however, had considerably strengthened their position in south Wales as a result of a membership drive in 1936–7.[84] As well as increasing their membership, NATKE was also successful in securing the recognition of the south Wales branch of the CEA. It was in their fight for recognition by employees that NATKE took their most forceful stance. They wrote to all members of the CEA in south Wales, stressing that they represented the majority of cinema employees ('with 100 per cent membership in some areas'), and threatened to use strike action against those exhibitors who failed to recognize the union.[85] This threat was apparently effective: all but a handful of south Wales exhibitors agreed to recognize NATKE without much objection; the few that did hold out, among them the 'benevolent' Will Stone, eventually gave in under further pressure from both the NATKE leadership and local activists.[86]

Once NATKE had established itself in south Wales, the local membership were quick to demonstrate their willingness to confront their employers directly. In the Rhondda, the local membership threatened the CEA with strike action in April 1938;[87] and in west Wales, NATKE members fought (a successful) battle against a company called Union Cinemas.[88] In neither case did stoppages actually occur (the leadership much preferred conciliation to direct action), but on both occasions the cinema workers were able to secure improvements in their pay and conditions.

Cinema workers in Wales quite clearly were prepared to join trade unions in order to secure improvements in their pay and conditions. Militant action, however, was never carried out and seldom even threatened. This can partly be attributed to the conservative stance adopted by NATKE, but it also makes sense given the nature of the cinema industry in Wales. The very size of the vast majority of cinemas meant it was inevitable that the cinema manager, and maybe the proprietor, would know each of their employees personally. Such personal relations might have made the threat of industrial action much less likely. Further, the proprietors of the smallest independent cinemas were in a far from powerful position themselves, being as dependent on major production and distribution companies as their employees were on them. They were also in competition with much larger and newer halls, sometimes part of a circuit, which had far greater financial resources behind them. Were it not for the commitment and cooperation of management and staff, it is uncertain whether such cinemas could have survived for as long as they did.

The gender composition of the cinema workforce may also have played a role in limiting the influence of trade unions within the cinema industry. The various institutions of the labour movement have traditionally been male dominated in both membership and outlook. While willing to accept female members, most trade unions were, at this time, reluctant to campaign on their behalf for rights such as equal pay for equal work. With the traditional instruments of working-class protest somewhat less than welcoming to women workers, the cinema employees with the strongest claim to an improvement in pay and conditions were in the weakest position to go about making such demands. Yet while the unions could have done more in support of female cinema workers, it is less than clear whether the usherettes and cleaners were themselves committed to the idea of collective protest. Alternative forms of employment for young females in this period were often less appealing than the cinema. Domestic service, for instance, would usually have involved longer hours, less freedom and little, if any, extra pay. For many young women in inter-war Wales, a job at the local picture house would not only have provided much needed cash, but also enabled them to remain at home – a possibility most would have been loath to jeopardize. As well as having its advantages for many Welsh women, a job at the local cinema, like most forms of female employment, was usually regarded as a short-term measure. If the long-term plans of the majority of female cinema workers involved getting married and bringing up children, then immediate concerns about pay and conditions at work took on rather less significance. The growth of the cinema industry in this period clearly was not entirely detrimental to the position of female workers in Wales, but neither did it offer an improvement in employment opportunities for women. Rather, it served to reinforce existing patterns of female employment.

Summary

Film exhibition, in contrast to distribution or production, was shaped more by regional social and economic conditions than by the strategies of a few companies based in Hollywood or Wardour Street. In Wales, the economic depression, combined with the small size and geographical isolation of many communities, hindered the development of the major circuits. However, the absence of major cinema companies from so many Welsh towns meant that the ownership and control of the industry in Wales remained, to a much larger extent than in Britain as a whole, in local hands. The social function that the cinema performed in local communities was, arguably, more pronounced in Wales than in many other parts of Britain.

This examination of smaller circuits and independent halls has drawn attention to the strong local character which cinemas expressed – even though they showed films with an international appeal. This local identity was further reinforced by those who worked in the industry. Managers may have had relatively little influence over the entertainment they were able to screen, but the popularity of the films lay in the fact that they offered audiences a temporary escape from the realities of their local environment. The significance of the manager, and his staff, was that they could help create a familiar environment in which audiences could feel comfortable, if not exactly 'at home'. If we regard cinemas 'as a kind of community centre or "club"',[89] rather than purely as an arena for viewing films, then their ability to reflect local conditions becomes more apparent. Whether it was by organizing lottery schemes for patrons, providing live entertainment to accompany the films, or simply by force of their personality – cinema managers were able to provide even the smallest of cinemas with a distinctive character. Similarly, the atmosphere in which films were viewed was influenced, in the 1920s particularly, by projectionists and musicians working at the cinemas.

The cinema staff who helped create such a viewing environment could not expect to be handsomely rewarded in their pay packets. Cinema may have been a form of mass entertainment to which men and women had equal access, but when it came to employing people to provide this entertainment, there was little sign of equality. All cinema employees had to work similarly long and unsocial hours, but while the more senior and well-paid positions were dominated by men, female usherettes and cleaners were expected to carry out the most mundane, and at times arduous tasks, for very low rates of pay. Some improvements in working conditions were won by trade unions representing cinema employees in this period. The cautious leadership of the main cinema workers' union, however, allied to the precarious economic environment in Wales, meant that this was not a period of tense industrial relations. The low pay and difficult conditions faced by cinema workers in this period were a feature of the Welsh economy as a whole, not just the cinema industry.

II

Film-Going as Popular Culture

The opening part of this book has established that cinema-going was a popular (indeed habitual) activity for many people in Wales, and that cinemas themselves performed an important social and economic role in their local communities. The following part examines what it was these local institutions had to offer. In analysing and explaining the cinema's appeal, chapter 4 makes an argument that is applicable to any part of Britain, not just Wales. The argument is illustrated, however, with examples from Wales, and it should be stressed that the particular appeal of small local cinemas was more central to film-going in Wales than other parts of Britain. Chapter 5 focuses more specifically on the entertainment provided in Welsh cinemas. Again, there were more similarities than differences between the types of films shown in Wales and the rest of Britain. The lack of large showpiece cinemas in Wales, however, meant that the introduction of live variety entertainment into cinema programmes was rarely seen in Wales. Throughout the period covered here the most popular films with Welsh audiences were made by American companies, and while screen depictions of the Welsh (in British and American pictures) did attract considerable interest, there are grounds for believing that British films were not as popular with Welsh audiences as they were in the rest of Britain, even in the 1940s. The Welsh, it seems, were attracted to the cinema for much the same reasons as audiences in the rest of Britain, though the films they most enjoyed were not necessarily the same as those with the greatest appeal elsewhere in Britain.

4

CINEMA'S APPEAL

Chapter 1 of this book examined the level of film attendance in Wales, and compared patterns of cinema consumption there with the rest of Britain. We know how many people went to the cinema in Wales and how often they did so. The question to be addressed in this chapter is: why? Which social groups were the most avid film-goers, and what was it that attracted them to picture halls on a weekly (or more frequent) basis?

The chapter is divided into three sections: the first looks at who went to the cinema and the next two examine why they went. The opening section provides an analysis of the social make-up of cinema audiences, identifying those social groups for whom the cinema held the greatest appeal. The second section examines the appeal of the cinema as a social institution: it looks at the communal experience of film-going and the social function performed by these public sites of entertainment in their local communities. The third section explores the cinema's appeal in terms of the cultural experience of film-going. This section will not explore in detail the nature of the entertainment provided for Welsh audiences (this is the focus of chapter 5), but instead asks: What was it about the projection of moving images onto a screen that held so powerful an appeal for so many people?

The social composition of audiences: to whom did cinema appeal?

The film audience is Everybody ... At one end of the scale is Tommy who cadges threepence from a harassed mother glad to be rid of him for the Saturday morning matinee; at the other end is the Duke of Blankshire who pays ten guineas for his seat at a London charity premiere. In between lie the mothers and fathers, the youths and lasses of every walk and station of life. In the main, however, the cinema audience is a young audience, and (because the prices are cheap) predominantly a working-class audience. Furthermore, as has been intimated, the cinema flourishes most successfully in the industrial areas.[1]

Ernest Lindgren's analysis of the typical 1940s cinema audience is not one that most historians writing about film-going in this period would now accept. Most would agree that the cinema was particularly popular among working-class youngsters in industrial areas, but few would now argue that film-going was for 'everybody'. The idea that 'once upon a time everyone went to the cinema' has been dismissed by the authors of one study as 'the myth of the universal audience'.[2] Others have been equally keen to emphasize that even at the peak of the cinema's popularity there remained a large contingent of the British population (around one-third) who never went to the pictures at all.[3] Yet Lindgren's observation should not be dismissed out of hand. Not everybody in the country actually went to the cinema, but neither were any social groups actually excluded from this form of entertainment. The cinema, though more popular among some groups than others, *was* enjoyed by men and women of all ages and from different social backgrounds right across the country. This was reflected in the way that film production companies approached their market. While recent scholarship has demonstrated that film producers were acutely aware of the composition of cinema audiences, and that they tailored the content of their pictures accordingly,[4] the practice of making films targeted at specific market segments only became common practice once cinema attendance went into decline.[5] For the period between the 1920s and the early 1950s, film studios were careful to ensure that their major releases would appeal to as wide a range of social groups as possible.[6] The cinema audience was not a 'universal' one in the sense that not every person went to the pictures, but nor was cinema's appeal restricted to any particular section of society.

The group least likely to be film-goers were those aged over sixty-five. A study conducted for the Wartime Social Survey in 1943 (see table 21) found that 69 per cent of this group never went to the cinema while only 5 per cent were regular attenders. The comparison with those aged between fourteen and seventeen is striking. Among this younger age group almost 80 per cent went to the cinema at least once a week (over half of whom attended twice a week or more), while only 2 per cent claimed not to go at all. It seems certain that adolescents and young adults were the most avid films fans in this period, although in all age groups up to forty-five a clear majority (over 70 per cent) were at least occasional cinema-goers.[7] A similar picture emerges from another survey conducted in 1946, though this later survey found that 11 per cent of those aged sixty and over were regular film-goers.[8] For the generation who had grown up with the cinema, whether in fairground booths or the earliest purpose-designed buildings, the habit of movie-going died hard. Clearly, as this generation grew older and faced up to parental responsibilities their visits to the cinema became much less frequent, but they did not stop altogether. For those who had reached adulthood by the time the first film shows were beginning to attract public attention, cinema-going seems not to have held such an appeal.

As well as being a pastime more popular with younger audiences than old, cinema-going was also, in the main, an urban phenomena. This is not to say that people in rural areas did not go to the pictures – many clearly did, often

Table 21
Frequency of film-going by age, 1943 (%)

Frequency	14–17	18–40	41–45	46–65	Over 65
More than twice a week	20	6	1	1	–
Twice a week	23	12	6	3	1
Once a week	36	25	20	13	4
Once a fortnight	6	8	6	5	2
Once a month	5	7	6	5	2
Occasionally	7	24	34	31	22
Don't go now	1	8	9	10	9
Never go	1	10	18	31	60
No information	1	–	–	–	–
Sample	304	2368	714	1692	454

Source: Moss and Box, 'The Cinema Audience'.

to travelling cinemas. It is also probable that attendances would have been higher in these areas had there been a greater choice of picture houses and a more regular supply of films.[9] However, only two of the twelve categories of employment defined in the 1943 survey had an attendence that did not exceed 50 per cent: the 'retired and unoccupied' and 'agriculture'. The essentially urban nature of the cinema-going habit is confirmed in a regional analysis. Whereas the highest proportion of regular movie-goers, and the lowest percentage of non-attenders, were to be found in London, the north and north-west, cinema-going was least common in areas such as the southwest and East Anglia.[10] Some mention of a cinema-going habit is made in most of the social surveys of British towns and cities conducted in this period.[11] Furthermore, since picture houses arrived later in rural districts,[12] there would have been a higher proportion of the population in these areas who had not grown up with the silver screen, and for whom the cinemagoing habit was less well established.

The elderly, and those in rural areas, were the only groups of whom it could be said that only a minority were film-goers. Those belonging to the middle and upper-middle classes tended not to go to the cinema as regularly as those lower down the social scale, but they were more likely to be at least occasional film-goers. According to the Wartime Social Survey it was the lower social groups, whether identified by income or education, that contained the highest proportion of both regular cinema-goers *and* of those who never went.[13] Another survey of film-going, using different criteria to categorize income groups, found that those on middle incomes were the most frequent filmgoers.[14] Taking the two surveys together, it appears that while the cinema-going habit was more common among the working classes than the middle classes, the highest earning section of the working class were the most regular film-goers of all. The middle classes, it seems, while avoiding the regular screen fare presented in cinemas on a weekly or twice-weekly basis, were less inclined to shun film-going altogether. For this social group the cinema was just one of a range of leisure pursuits that might take up an evening. Other options, such as a visit to the theatre or a meal at a restaurant, would seldom have been undertaken by those lower down the social scale. (Alternative working-class leisure activities, such as the pub, dog track or football match were essentially male preserves.) Further, the prospect of spending the evening at home would have been considerably more appealing for those who lived in warm, spacious and comfortable houses than for working-class families living in rather more cramped accommodation.

Among the working classes the amount of money available for leisure activities, and also the range of options, were more limited. Whether cinema-going was a habit (as it was for many young people) or an occasional evening out (as for married couples with young children) it was not one of a wide range of possible options. One argument put forward to explain the level of the cinema's popularity, especially among the working class, is that the picture houses themselves performed an important social role. This argument, which is considered in more detail below, posits that when going to the cinema one would be in familiar surroundings with people one knew: the sense of community, as much as the films themselves, appealed to regular cinema-goers. If this was indeed so, then for those working-class people who were not usually film fans, and therefore not part of the 'cinema-going community', occasional visits to the local cinema would have been a less attractive prospect. Non-cinema-goers, perhaps, found a sense of community and belonging in the pub, and were happy to ignore the pictures altogether.

As the mass popularity of the cinema began to decline from the 1950s onwards, the social make-up of the cinema audience also changed. The emergence of a discernible post-war 'youth culture' presented a wider range of leisure interests to the groups that had formed the backbone of the cinema

Table 22
Frequency of film-going by economic group, 1943 (%)

	Lower	Middle	Higher
More than twice a week	5	2	1
Twice a week	9	6	3
Once a week	21	17	15
Once a fortnight	6	7	7
Once a month	5	8	6
Occasionally	23	35	40
Don't go now	9	9	10
Never go	23	16	17
Sample	4185	1121	282

Source: Moss and Box, 'The cinema audience'.

audience. As young people began to show more interest in rock and roll music, and spent more time in espresso coffee bars, the proportion of working-class *regular* attenders dropped, becoming comparable with those from other social groups. By the 1970s a transformation had occurred, with those in the higher social groups showing a higher propensity to attend the cinema than those in the lower categories.[15]

The presence of women in cinema audiences during the first half of this century has frequently been commented upon, both by contemporaries and historians. As Roger Manvell put it: 'The old fairground showman who put a notice outside his little travelling cinema saying that his films were "refined and pleasing to ladies" obviously had the right idea: soon the ladies were eating and drinking dainty teas when they met their friends at the picture palace.'[16] In a much more recent study of cinema-going in south Wales Stephen Ridgwell has argued that 'it was working-class women, housewives and young single girls who probably formed the backbone of the cinema audience'.[17] This, it has further been suggested, was reflected in the nature of the British films being made. The films most popular with British audiences during and immediately after the Second World War, for example, were costume dramas such as *Madonna of the Seven Moons* (1944) and *The Wicked Lady* (1946), which are often described as 'womens' pictures'.[18] From the 1950s, interestingly, this trend was apparently reversed as films targeted at male audiences such as *The Dam Busters* (1955) and *The Bridge on the River Kwai* (1957) became ever more prominent. Richard Maltby identifies the 1950s as the period during which Hollywood's target viewer 'changed gender', and argues that this was 'the key change in Hollywood cinema, the real marker of the shift between Classical and post-Classical Hollywood.'[19]

That women formed the majority in most cinema audiences from the 1920s to the 1950s is certainly one of the more significant features of cinema's development. Yet there has arguably been a tendency for the popularity of the cinema with females to be over-emphasized. One social survey carried out in the 1930s estimated 'that 70 per cent of the weekly audience consists of girls and women. Men tend to go only when they have nothing better to do, or when they have a girl friend to take out.'[20] Stephen Ridgwell argued that 'cinema was equally popular among the women of industrial South Wales'.[21] In their broad survey of modern Britain, historians S. Glynn and A. Booth casually assert that cinema attendance was 'mainly female'.[22] Such sweeping claims, though not completely without foundation, do require a certain amount of qualification.

Evidence from the Wartime Social Survey confirms that women were more likely to be film-goers than men, but the gender difference was not great (see table 23). Men and women were equally likely to be among the most committed film addicts who went to the pictures more than twice a week. More women than men went to the cinema once or twice a week, while men were more likely than women to be occasional film-goers. For both men and

Table 23
Frequency of film-going by gender, 1943 (%)

	Men	Women
More than twice a week	4	4
Twice a week	7	9
Once a week	17	21
Once a fortnight	6	6
Once a month	6	6
Occasionally	28	25
Don't go now	9	9
Never go	23	20
Sample	2491	3148

Source: Moss and Box, 'The cinema audience'.

women the proportion who never attended the cinema were in a distinct minority.[23] The same pattern was revealed by the 1946 survey of film-going in Britain.[24]

While film-going was more frequent among adult females than males, the same did not hold true for children – who were also regular cinema-goers.[25] Docherty, Morrison and Tracey have claimed that children demonstrated a 'quite extraordinary level of engagement and involvement' with the cinema. The clearest reflection of this was to be found in the cinema clubs (which were particularly popular in the 1940s), and which 'tied the cinema to every aspect of a child's life'.[26] These clubs, however, were significantly more pop-ular with boys than girls. One study of children's leisure activities found that in the age group of eleven to fourteen, only 26 per cent of girls were mem-bers of a cinema club, compared with 39 per cent of boys.[27] Part of the reason for this may have been that the clubs screened films that appealed particu-larly to boys, such as Westerns and adventure pictures, as opposed to romance.[28] Yet it was not necessarily just the cinema clubs which were more popular with boys than with girls. The same study found that 78 per cent of boys and 74 per cent of girls aged fourteen years and over went to the cinema once or more a week.[29] The 1946 film-going survey also found boys of school age more likely to be regular film-goers than girls.[30] Among children, it seems that boys were more likely to be cinema enthusiasts than girls. It was in adolescence and young adulthood that girls' cinema attendance began to outstrip that of boys. When children are taken into account, and there is no reason why they should not be, estimates of female cinema domination ought to be revised.

Cinema-going, for adults and children alike, was very largely a social activity, often involving families and couples. The fact that cinemas were the first public places of entertainment to which women had equal access must have made females more conspicuous to contemporary observers – particularly since single young women were the most regular attenders. The overall gender balance of cinema audiences does seem to have been weighted in favour of females, but it is unlikely that they formed as much as 70 per cent of the total audience. There is no reliable evidence for the gender distribution of cinema audiences in Wales, but there are grounds for doubting whether the image of the typical female cinema-goer in inter-war Britain can be applied to Wales. All of the evidence considered so far has suggested that young, working-class women were the most regular cinema attenders. This is borne out by the distribution of cinema-goers into occupational groups by the Wartime Social Survey. The two groups that contained the highest proportion of regular cinema-devotees were 'clerical/secretarial' and 'light manufacturing inc. munitions workers'. These were groups containing a high proportion of young female labour. Housewives contained a far lower proportion of frequent cinema-goers. Yet in Wales the levels of female employment were considerably below the national average throughout this period.[31]

A multitude of young Welsh women had no option but to leave home in order to find work between the wars, often in the Midlands or the south-east of England. The popular image of Welsh women in this period was that of devoted mother and scrupulous housewife – the 'Welsh Mam' in fact. This was precisely the opposite image of womanhood to the young working women, with no commitments to house and home, money to spend and time to enjoy themselves. It was such women as these, with make-up and hairstyles modelled on those of the stars, the 'factory girls looking like actresses' to borrow J. B. Priestley's phrase,[32] who were most associated with cinema-going in this period.

This is not to say, of course, that cinema was not popular with Welsh women, it clearly was – a point which ought to force us to see beyond the myth of the 'Welsh Mam'. The difference between the popular stereotype and the lived experience of Welsh women is hinted at in the recollection of one regular cinema-goer from Pen-y-graig: 'Mind, my parents didn't allow any make-up, not before the age of eighteen: it was strictly forbidden. So you would put it on after leaving the house and then wipe it all off before you got back home again.'[33] It still needs to be recognized, however, that the opportunities for, and experience of women in Wales in this period was in many respects quite different from that of women in the more affluent areas of the country. There simply could not have been so many 'factory girls looking like actresses' in Wales: there were not as many factories. Young working women may not have formed as large a proportion of the total cinema audience in Wales as in the rest of the country. What does seem apparent is that while certain groups were more regular attenders, the broad appeal of the cinema, especially for those in urban areas, was remarkably wide, cutting across divisions of class, gender, and for the most part, age.

The social experience of film-going: cinemas as public places

> Rather than individual films, the cinema sold a *habit* – a place to go out to . . .
> To 'go to the local', meant in the language not only a visit to the pub but,
> equally, a visit to the cinema.[34]

Nicholas Hiley has argued that during the First World War 'for many
working-class patrons the cinema was not so much a place for watching
films as a comfortable venue in which they were greeted warmly by the proprietor and enjoyed the novel experience of being in a public space which
they could both dominate and control'.[35] The degree to which cinema auditoria were 'controlled' by working-class audiences declined, according to
Hiley, in the 1930s as 'management' played a more active role in monitoring
film reception.[36] As chapter 2 demonstrated, however, the types of cinemas
that employed commissionaires and a score or more usherettes to watch over
audiences remained a rarity in most parts of Wales throughout our period.
Whether working-class audiences were really able to 'dominate and control'
cinema auditoria in Wales in the 1930s and 40s is open to debate. What seems
certain is that for many working-class film-goers, the cinema appealed
because it provided popular entertainment, at very little cost, in a local environment that was both familiar and informal.

Cinema's informality, in contrast to the theatre, was often commented on
by contemporary middle-class observers. To P. Morton Shand, the cinema
was 'a sort of public lounge . . . one can drop in and out at will . . . on any old
pretext, at any old time and in any old clothes'.[37] Similarly Iris Barry found
that 'you can walk into a picture-palace as easily as into your own kitchen . . .
the place becomes a sort of informal club'.[38] For poorer sections of the community, however, the cinema's informality was one of its most important
features, and this appears to have been a key reason for its mass-appeal in
Wales.

A survey of young people in south Wales, published in 1941, sought to
ascertain '[i]n what lies the special appeal of the cinema?' One of the
responses received was that '[b]ecause of the darkness, it is possible to go to
the cinema after "slipping on your coat" '. Cinema was not only cheap, it was
available to those who avoid other activities on the grounds that 'I haven't
got the clothes to go in'.[39] This point was made explicitly by one gentleman
recalling his youth in Abertillery, where even the local dance could be pro-
hibitively expensive: 'The posh one was the Hospital Dance when it came
round, at two shillings a ticket – but we didn't have the right clothes for it
anyway. We would go to the pictures and see stars like Rudolph Valentino
and Ronald Coleman.'[40] The fact that cinema entertainment could be enjoyed
at such little expense and without formality was clearly a significant feature
of its appeal. It also meant that the cinemas themselves could act as focal
points for their communities. One historian of the cinema in south Wales has

argued that the picture hall operated 'as a kind of community centre or "club" '. 'Old and uncomfortable as they may have been, for relatively little cost the valley cinemas provided warmth, hours of entertainment, and above all a sense of common interest and togetherness.'[41]

Cheapness, convenience and informality were central to the mass appeal of the cinema, but it must also be acknowledged that certain halls provided audiences with an experience that was considered quite extraordinary. The attraction of cinema for those wishing to mark a special occasion was acknowledged by the head of one leading chain of modern halls in 1937.

> As a social institution, the local cinema represents to a section of the population the peak of glamour. Warmth and colour are to be had there; there are comfort, richness, variety. The cinema is so often the poor man's sole contact with luxury, the only place where he is made to feel a sense of self-importance ... Not only the film programme, but the deep carpets, the bright lights, the attention 'fit for a king', are the weekly delights of the majority of picture-goers.[42]

Roger Manvell made the same point in the 1940s:

> There is more to cinema-going than seeing films. There is going out at night, the sense of fun and excitement. Wise to this, the builders of cinemas have designed the majority of them like palaces, picture palaces, with many advantages over the live theatres and music-halls, especially cheapness and accessibility.[43]

There were occasions when a visit to the cinema could be a special event, but these did not constitute the majority of attendances. In Wales, where 'dream palaces' were relatively few and far between, there is even less reason to suppose that the cinema's appeal lay in the fact that it provided something out of the ordinary. The distinction between the cinema 'habit', and cinema-going as a special event is closely related to the distinctions between the cinemas themselves. The cinemas which were a 'sort of public lounge' or 'community centre' to which millions flocked twice a week (or more) were usually local second-run halls, their main attractions being price, familiarity and for the most part, relative comfort. The large, first-run, town-centre halls were the favoured venues of middle or higher income groups and those seeking a venue for a more special social occasion. It was here that people had the opportunity to dress up, although as one female cinema-goer put it, she dressed 'for the boyfriend, not for the cinema'.[44]

The cinema may have attracted audiences from a range of social backgrounds, but not all film-goers went to the pictures for the same reason, and nor did they attend the same types of cinema. Even within the same hall important distinctions existed, and people from diverse backgrounds generally did not sit alongside one another enjoying a common leisure interest. What, then, were the key differences between, and within, cinemas in terms of audience appeal?

Differences between the halls

The most prestigious cinemas – the large first-run halls – such as Cardiff's Capitol and the Plaza in Swansea were the ones that most consciously sought to attract a better class of patron. One of the ways in which they did this was to offer a range of facilities other than just the films themselves. These were places where one could go to eat (or at least have afternoon tea); where live musical (and sometimes variety) entertainment was provided; and where a host of page-boys and usherettes attended to the customer's every need. The interior design of most first-run halls, both in terms of comfort and cleanliness, and the notable feature of the balcony, were clearly supposed to appeal to the more affluent sections of the community. Indeed, the prices of admission charged by these large, town-centre halls also helped to set them apart from the smaller fleapits or suburban halls. Cinemas such as the Odeon, Park Hall and Capitol in Cardiff charged between 9d and 2s for admission by the end of the 1930s. This was hardly extortionate, and the majority of seats were of the cheaper variety. Yet at two and a half times the price of the cheapest, the most expensive balcony seats were beyond the means of the working-class cinema-goer, at least on a regular basis. Cinemas such as these made little effort to appeal to the very poorest sections of the community. The cheapest seats at Cardiff's Capitol were more than double the price of those at the City's Central cinema.[45] This is not to say that the more prestigious halls were inaccessible to working-class cinema-goers altogether. Certainly, it would have been beyond the means of the average teenager to pay 1s 6d (or even 1s) to go to the cinema twice a week or more, but as somewhere to go for a date, or a special occasion, such cinemas were ideal.

The largest, and most well-known of these halls were in the biggest towns or cities, but most of the smaller Welsh towns also had a 'leading cinema'. The Odeons in Wrexham, Colwyn Bay and Llanelli, the Majestic in Port Talbot (later to become an Odeon), and the Castle in Merthyr are a few examples. As shown in chapter 2, however, in some parts of Wales such prestige halls simply did not exist. One cinema-goer from Treorchy recalled that

> It was a great treat to go to Cardiff to the Pictures and see the Organist rise out of the floor before the screen playing the cinema organ. We did not have this luxury in the Rhondda, although one of the cinemas in Aberdare had such an organ and all the local girls fell for the handsome organist.[46]

Another cinema enthusiast, from Anglesey, has recalled occasions when she would take the Saturday train to Bangor to visit the Plaza cinema.[47] Such outings were clearly regarded as being very different from a visit to the local 'fleapit'.

This brings us to the type of cinema buildings placed in the third category of chapter 2. In popular reminiscences of the cinema, and cinema-going, terms like 'fleapit' and 'bug-house' recur over and over again. They are as much a part of cinema's social history as the 'dream palaces'. The so-called 'fleapits' were almost inevitably survivors from pre-war days. They were not necessarily the oldest buildings used for showing films, but were often early examples of purpose-built cinemas erected to meet a working-class demand for moving pictures in an era before film-going was considered 'respectable'. In south Wales particularly, a considerable proportion of these were able to survive, with minimal alterations, into and beyond the inter-war period. They did so by providing a very different service from the larger, more prestigious halls.

The minor luxuries which cinema audiences had come to expect in the newly-built or refurbished halls were unlikely to be found in pre-war buildings. The terms 'fleapit' and 'bug house' – often used as terms of endearment – did not originate by accident. One Swansea cinema-goer recalled a particularly notorious hall: 'The Rialto was bad. The fleas used to live in the upholstery . . . on the odd occasion when you got home you found you "had company".'[48] In Holyhead, the Cybi cinema was apparently known to locals as the 'sit and scratch'.[49] Regular patrons of such cinemas were even known to turn a hall's reputation to their advantage. 'My father had a good technique for getting a seat in those crowded days when you couldn't get in', recalled one gentleman, 'he and his brother would start scratching themselves; in ten minutes they'd have seats.'[50]

Dating from a period when cinema-going was an almost exclusively working-class leisure pursuit, these cinemas made little attempt to broaden their appeal. Those people who would willingly pay 1s 6d or 2s to watch a film in opulent surroundings were not catered for. The fleapits appealed to a quite different market. By charging just a few pence for the cheapest seats, these cinemas cost significantly less to attend than the more prestigious halls. They were also second- or third-run halls, which meant that they did not show the latest new releases. That such cinemas did not offer the latest screen entertainment only served to strengthen their local identity. These halls seldom showed films that attracted visitors from outside their immediate area. Rather, they catered for a regular, working-class audience who demanded a regular diet of Hollywood entertainment, not simply the latest new release.

The appeal of these cinemas can be explained largely by the fact that they cost so little to enter. For those on very low incomes, or the unemployed, the local fleapit would have been the only cinema cheap enough to visit regularly. It comes as little surprise that Wales, which was one of the most depressed regions of Britain throughout the inter-war period, should have a high proportion of such cinemas. It was in the south Wales Valleys – the worst affected area within Wales – however, that their presence was most noticeable.[51] Whereas many Valleys towns saw virtually nothing in the way of modern cinema provision between the wars, in the majority of Welsh towns elsewhere the old halls had to compete with a number of new rivals. Had the popularity of the cinema been determined entirely by peoples' desire to see the latest big release, such halls would not have survived. But survive they did, in their hundreds, across the whole of Wales. The existence of the fleapit halls throughout the inter-war years and into the 1950s ensured that those from economically deprived backgrounds were able to continue going to the pictures, even in times of real hardship. The fact that so many survived into the 1950s, long after the depression had passed, demonstrates their importance to local communities.

The prestigious first-run halls and the ageing fleapits represent, in terms of cinema provision, extremes of splendour and squalor. During the inter-war years, however, a number of halls were constructed that fell somewhere between these extremes: the halls placed in the second category in chapter 2. These modern 'super-cinemas', usually situated in suburban areas or small towns, were far more impressively designed and decorated than the older fleapits, but they served a broadly similar function. Their significance lay in the fact that they improved the conditions in which films were seen by many working-class audiences, not that they attracted a new, more sophisticated public. Their admission prices of between 6d and 1s 3d by the end of the 1930s were more comparable with the local fleapit than the main first-run halls. The modern suburban cinemas, such as those run by the Splott circuit in Cardiff were second-run halls; their twice-weekly programmes of old, or low-budget films, however, could hardly be considered as entertainment designed to appeal to the middle-classes. In terms of design and marketing these 'super-cinemas' may have appeared to be buildings which could appeal to the more respectable film-goer. Beneath the cosmetics, however, such details as the price of admission and the selection of films offered, mark them out as essentially working-class institutions. By the end of the 1940s a number of these modern 1930s cinema buildings had become part of the Odeon circuit. As the previous chapter showed (see Table 17), average takings per seat in these cinemas were no higher than the Welsh average, suggesting that even the Odeons kept prices low to cater for the same type of working-class audience as the Splott cinemas.

The difference between the Splott cinemas and their city-centre rivals is clearly demonstrated by their respective advertisements in the local press. Adverts for the first-run halls were more eye-catching, usually featuring a picture of the leading star(s) in the main feature – which generally stayed for a whole week. An advert for five Splott cinemas, by contrast, took up approximately one third as much space as one for, say, the Capitol. Within this limited space were the names of all the films showing in each cinema –

a considerable number given that they all screened double features and had a twice weekly change of programme. Whereas the Capitol and other first-run halls heavily advertised their films (and the stars they featured), adverts for the Splott circuit, like those of the Olympia, Globe, Coliseum and Central cinemas, merely provided information. It seems unlikely that many people would have been attracted to these cinemas on the strength of the adverts alone, though regular patrons of these halls would no doubt have found the information useful.

Differences within the halls

Social distinctions were just as likely to be marked by where one sat in a particular cinema, as by the type of cinema one attended. In smaller towns particularly, where the choice of cinemas was more limited, there was a greater likelihood that a range of social groups would be gathered under one roof. This did not mean, however, that they enjoyed a shared experience.

There was a discernible difference in terms of comfort and convenience between the cheapest and most expensive seats within most Welsh cinemas. The cheapest seats were usually situated at the front of the hall, with those occupying them forced to look up at the screen from an awkward angle. For those unfortunate enough to be seated at the sides of the auditorium the problems must have been even worse. In some of the older cinemas and converted theatres there were also restricted viewing seats available. In a number of these older theatres the cheapest seats were not to be found in the front stalls, but in 'the gods'. The Coliseum in Aberystwyth, built in 1906, is one such example. Its layout was recalled by a former patron:

> There were the stalls, and an upper and lower circle. The upper circle, affectionately known as 'The Gods' didn't have any seats, just a bench which ran around the horseshoe shape of the circle, and if you sat up there, for the princely sum of one shilling you got a nasty crick in your neck from trying to see the whole of the screen.[52]

As this account implies, the discomfort incurred by sitting in such seats was not only a result of straining to see the screen, but also of the nature of the seating itself. Long wooden benches were a feature of many cinemas throughout this period. As well as being uncomfortable to sit on, these benches had the added disadvantage (or benefit for unscrupulous managers) of being able to accommodate a high density of people. Gwyn Thomas has described, in his typical style, the extreme overcrowding that could, and almost certainly did at times ensue.

> There was also a strange but profitable system of 'stacking' members of the audience. At the back of the cinema were a few rows of benches. Unsuspecting

people would be shown to a seat at one end of the bench and room would be made either by pushing the person at the other end off his seat or by squashing up the row until it bulged visibly in the middle.[53]

For many people, clearly, visits to the cinema were not an opportunity to experience luxuries unavailable at home. Others were more determined to sit in the more comfortable seats, whether they could afford it or not. In Treorchy, apparently, '[i]t was common for boys to pay a penny for the seats at the front of the Pavilion cinema and then crawl further back to the tuppennies when the lights were lowered.'[54] Similar anecdotes are told about other valleys cinemas. The Saturday morning 'penny rush' at Merthyr's Oddfellows Hall, for example, was remembered thus: 'we'd be shepherded into the perfumed, smoke laden and urine impregnated atmosphere of the Hall where, after being allocated seats, we'd set off in search of better ones.'[55] Gwyn Thomas observed such behaviour from his position in the balcony with some incredulity: 'Downstairs a lot of the audience seemed to have something akin to a lemming instinct. Given half a chance they'd get down on the floor and crawl away under the seats, emerging through a forest of legs in a completely different section of the cinema.'[56]

For those wishing to avoid discomfort and inconvenience by more legitimate means the rear of the stalls usually contained moderately priced seats (not benches) which were more comfortable and afforded a better view. The difference in price between these seats and the cheapest ones, although perhaps only two or three pence, was clearly significant for many people, particularly if they were regular cinema-goers. The best view of all, and the most comfortable seating, was to be found in the balcony – with the front balcony seats the most expensive of all. The difference in price of seats from one section of the cinema to another, however, cannot wholly be explained by their relative level of comfort or convenience. Even in the suburban halls of the Splott circuit – which prided themselves on providing good seats *throughout* the hall – the most expensive seats were almost three times the price of the cheapest.

The reason why some people were willing to pay up to three or four times more for their seat was not just a matter of sight-lines or comfort, but also social status. The only reason people would have chosen to sit in the cheapest seats of all, particularly in older cinemas, was because they could not afford to sit elsewhere. These seats were therefore filled almost exclusively by people from the lowest socio-economic groups. This, in itself, would have deterred some others from wanting to sit there in order to save money. When visiting the cinema with family or friends on a weekday evening, there may have been no second thought before opting to sit in the cheap seats. When going on a date with a partner, however (and cinemas were usually the most popular venues for courting couples in Wales), the situation would probably be very different. A young man hoping to impress a new girlfriend would certainly be reluctant to take her to the cheapest seats. The infamous double seats for courting couples, of course, were situated toward the rear of most halls.

Even in cinemas where the cheapest seats were not that uncomfortable there could still be some form of stigma attached to them. One regular patron of Pwllheli's Palladium cinema, ('which was considered quite classy as there was a café in the building'), has recalled that 'the price then was either one shilling or one and three pence. We never liked to sit in the shilling seats as that was lowering the tone.'[57] A similar sentiment was expressed by a Porth man who recalled being taken by his father,

> to the Central, a better and higher form of theatre. It cost 2d. [*sic*] and we usually sat upstairs in the first row of the balcony. The show fare was as much up-to-date as possible and we were quite interested in the more sophisticated products of Hollywood ... It was quite nice to go into a comfortable, good smelling building, without the crowds of noisy street urchins. Also, the manager had a daughter in my class in school and I was quite attracted by her.[58]

The new friends he could now associate with in the more expensive sections of the hall was clearly as important a consideration for this youngster as the social group he was leaving behind.

The balcony provided the most obvious and visible sign of the social division within cinemas. A middle-class couple with a comfortable income would probably never consider sitting in the front stalls, just as a working-class family with much less money could seldom afford to 'go upstairs'. These two groups were physically separated and they formed quite distinct audiences, albeit of the same film. J. B. Priestley's assertion in 1934 that cinemas, along with the wireless and other 'very modern things' were 'absolutely democratic, making no distinctions whatever between their patrons',[59] along with P. Morton Shand's claim that the cinema was 'an essentially democratic institution'[60] must clearly be called into question.

To the manager of Porth's Central cinema the social and cultural distinction between the balcony patrons and those who sat in the rest of the auditorium was at times all too evident. The visit of a touring opera company to neighbouring Tonypandy, for instance, provided a significant counter-attraction – but only for a certain section of the audience:

> I am afraid that our circle patrons have absented us this week. The reason is, I think, the visit of the Carl Rosa Co. to 'Pandy. Opera has a distinct appeal here and as it is changed every evening it looks as though we will be very badly 'let down'. It was quite an unnatural thing to see the circle almost empty on a Monday evening while the other part was full.[61]

Prices varied not just between different sections of the hall, but also from one showing to another. Saturday matinée programmes were almost inevitably cheaper than evening ones, and usually attracted a very different (younger) audience. The atmosphere within a cinema could change significantly from afternoon to evening. Even in cinemas where commissionaires and ush- erettes patrolled the aisles vigilantly in the evenings, youngsters were able to voice their excitement more freely earlier in the day. A former Treorchy cinema-goer made the point succinctly: 'On the whole, the behaviour in the evening performances was quite good, it was at the penny rush which all the kids attended on a Saturday morning that we could make our feelings felt.'[62] The Odeon Saturday Morning Club, for example, was remembered by Leslie Thomas as 'a hell-on-earth of screaming, rampaging kids where I relished every moment.'[63] As well as being quieter, some cinemas were also much cleaner during evening performances – as one lady has recalled:

> The picture-house in Tonypandy wasn't very grand. For the matinée you would go to your seat to the crunch, crunch of shells: monkey-nuts – peanuts – eaten, with the shells thrown down on the floor. Every Saturday afternoon children would be admitted without their parents, but not in the evening when it was more sedate. You had to be with your parents in the evening, so the place was quieter – they had cleaned up the nut shells too – so it wasn't crunch, crunch, as you moved your feet.[64]

The distinctions between matinée and evening performances, between dif- ferent types of cinema, and the varieties of seating provision within the halls themselves all point to the diverse function performed by the cinema for dif- ferent people. A broad range of social groups were drawn to the cinema, and they were entertained in contrasting environments, even within the same building. It remains now to consider what united these various groups of film-goers: the appeal of the pictures themselves.

The cultural experience of film-going: *the appeal of films and stars*

In explaining the cultural appeal of the cinema, a distinction should be drawn between feature films and moving images. Films are only one specific type of moving image: they are cultural artefacts which relatively few people feel the need to see on a weekly or twice weekly basis. Moving pictures, on the other hand, have an appeal which might be regarded as much more deep seated. The desire to watch pictures that moved existed long before the cinema was invented. Attempts to project moving images can be traced back to the seventeenth century with the development of the magic lantern. Throughout the nineteenth century numerous innovators strove to design machines that could more convincingly create an illusion of living pictures. The phenakistoscope (1820s), the zoetrope (1860s) and the kinetoscope

(1890s) were among the many devices developed for this purpose.[65] The goal of perfecting the recording and presentation of moving images was regarded by those involved as a scientific endeavour, not an artistic or commercial opportunity. Yet the public attention given to the many precursors of the cinema, and the huge audiences that flocked to early Kinetoscope and cinematograph shows, suggest that the demand for moving pictures was highly developed before the 1890s. Michael Chanan draws attention to 'the baffling fact that, like the primary, basic material needs of human existence – for food, clothing, a dwelling and warmth – the demand for the cinema seemed to anticipate the particular means of satisfying it. This is an undeniable fact of social history.'[66]

As well as pre-dating the invention of the cinematograph, the desire to see moving pictures showed no signs of abating when the cinema's appeal went into decline. The latter half of the twentieth century actually saw the development of a plethora of new techniques and (virtual) technologies which were intended to make the images presented on television screen or computer monitors appear more *real* than ever. The extent to which moving pictures became a feature of everyday life in twentieth century society, suggests that the cinema's role as a provider of moving images may have been more important than just the films themselves in explaining its popularity. According to this line of argument the remarkable mass-appeal of the medium up to the 1950s was due to the fact that the cinema was the only provider of moving pictures in the period. Yet why should the experience of watching moving images in a cinema environment have held such an extraordinary appeal?

One reason, frequently commented upon by contemporaries and occasionally mentioned by historians, was that the cinema heightened the psychological effect of watching motion pictures. The darkened surroundings, huge screen and (often) comfortable seats were considered to have enhanced both the influence and the appeal of the cinema. Within this viewing environment the experience of watching a film was considered to be almost like a day-dream. For Iris Barry, this dream-like quality was what made the cinema so much more popular than the theatre:

> To go to the pictures is to purchase a dream. To go to the theatre is to buy an experience, and between experience and dream there is a vast difference . . . we come out of the pictures soothed and drugged like sleepers wakened having half forgotten our own existence, hardly knowing our names.[67]

The association of the pictures with day-dreaming was quickly established in the film-goers vocabulary. The increasingly grand and luxurious halls were commonly referred to as 'dream palaces', and the American anthropologist Hortense Powdermaker coined the phrase 'dream factory' to describe the Hollywood studios.[68]

The dream-like quality of cinema entertainment helps to explain not only its popularity, but also some of the opposition it aroused. There was certainly concern in some quarters that people were going to the pictures just to see moving images rather than to enjoy the artistic quality of films. Roger Manvell, in the passage below, expresses a sentiment which was frequently voiced by highbrow critics of the period:

> A person in control of his film-going will, if the queuing system at his cinema allows it, go in to view the picture he wants to see, and then leave the cinema unless the rest of the programme promises to be of sufficient interest to warrant his staying on. Merely to sit through any film for the sake of watching images passing over the screen is a habit which is more universal than we may imagine. The mental outlook it indicates is certainly rather a dull one . . . There should be special cinemas for the dull-eyed with a blank screen where they may be taught not to watch but to sleep.[69]

It was not just the lack of serious criticism being applied to *films* which was of concern, but the psychological effect which moving pictures could have on individuals, particularly children, when they were in the cinema. One contributor to the *Penguin Film Review* felt that

> The conditions of mass film showing bear a strong resemblance to those utilised when putting a subject under hypnosis. The warmth, the comfortable seats, the darkness and the fixation of moving objects upon a lighted screen: add to these the feeling of communication with other members of the audience and you have all the features which increase suggestibility, diminish logical thought and criticism, and enable opinions, sentiments and attitudes in the film to be accepted more easily by the audience.[70]

The thought that children could be easily influenced by the cinema was of particular concern. Writing of the serials, which were one of the highlights of the Saturday morning children's cinema clubs in the 1940s, the sociologist J. P. Mayer wrote: '[t]hey are pernicious in their psychological effects, leaving the children at a high pitch of expectation for the next week's show, poisoning their day-dreams and, by an utterly artificial unreality, influencing their play.'[71] Mayer went on to suggest that the cinema clubs should be closed, and that young children should only be allowed to watch films made especially for their age group. The psychological effect of the cinema has remained a subject for debate throughout this century, and is closely linked to the issue of censorship.[72]

Since the 1950s, the argument that the cinema entertainment satisfied a deeply felt need has been advanced less often. This, no doubt, is because the argument does very little to explain the rapid decline in cinema admissions in the 1950s and 60s. The large screen, darkened surroundings and comfortable seats may have heightened the psychological impact of the movies, but this alone did not account for their fundamental appeal. It is interesting that historians of the early years of the cinema, such as Michael Chanan, have been willing to accept that the cinema satisfied an important human (psychological) need, those who have studied the period of declining audiences do not. As the authors of one study put it: 'In the 1940s habitual cinema-going was a social experience rather than the product or expression of a deep-seated psychological or cultural need.'[73] For the period covered here the cinema was the sole provider of a form of publicly consumed entertainment (in the form of motion pictures) which was popular, affordable and accessible to all. In this sense it did satisfy a 'deep seated' need, which was both social and cultural. As one south Wales film-goer bluntly put it: 'If it wasn't for the wireless, and a penn'orth of pictures once in a while, it's off our heads us women would have gone long ago.'[74] When other forms of entertainment became available which served a similar function, however, the cinema's role changed and its social significance declined.

Feature films and their stars

The social experience of film-going, and the psychological effects of watching pictures that move, must have contributed to the enormous popularity of film-going between the 1920s and the 1950s, but no examination of the cinema's appeal in this period can ignore the role of the films themselves. As Roger Manvell put it: '[t]hough they both depend on each other for their main welfare, the film could, in the end, exist without the cinema, but nobody supposes that the cinema could exist without the film.'[75]

The cinema has been described as the last invention of a machine age and as the first art form of the twentieth century.[76] The importance of technology in its creation and development is signified by the fact that it was the mechanical device of the cinematograph that gave its name to the industry which developed in the wake of its invention. A device to project moving images, however, had not been developed with feature films in mind. Early pioneers such as Janssen, Muybridge and Marey, were more interested in science than in story-telling or entertainment.[77] Once perfected, the greatest potentialities of the new invention were felt to be its ability to record important events for posterity, and its role as an aid to education. The early uses to which the cinematograph was put certainly bear little resemblance to the production of modern feature films – with which it has now almost become synonymous. The earliest films, lasting little more than a minute, featured such events as a train pulling out of a station. The sheer novelty value of seeing pictures move attracted the earliest audiences to the showman's booth. What prevented this novelty from wearing off were developments in film-making. Not only did films become longer, but they evolved beyond a mere recording of events and developed a narrative structure. Perhaps the most important development in this respect was the use of editing, which arguably did more than anything else to establish the film as an art form. It both opened up new possibilities for film-makers, and provided them with a much more powerful means of expressing their ideas. The point has been made by, among others, the great Russian director Vsevolod Pudovkin:

> Editing is the language of the film director. Just as in living speech, so, one may say, in editing: there is a word – the piece of exposed film, the image; a phrase – the combination of these pieces. Only by his editing methods can one judge a director's individuality.[78]

The work of directors such as D. W. Griffith in America and Sergei Eisenstein in the Soviet Union is widely felt to have extended the possibilities of the film to a new level. The importance of such developments was not simply that they helped to attract larger audiences (although the films of Griffith and Eisenstein were remarkably popular within their own countries), but that they also attracted a new type of audience. Prior to 1914 the cinema had generally been regarded by educated minds as merely another form of idle amusement for the masses – a fad that would soon pass. By the end of the 1920s it had become clear to a body of 'highbrow' critics that cinema was, in fact, a genuine art form. The Film Society had been formed in London in 1925, counting among its members such notables as H. G. Wells, George Bernard Shaw and Ivor Montagu;[79] serious publications dealing with the cinema and its history began to emerge;[80] this was also the period in which serious film criticism began to flourish.[81] Thanks largely to developments in film-making, cinema's place in mainstream society was established. As Roger Manvell confidently asserted in 1951: 'To this day the social status of our cinemas varies widely with the districts in which they operate, but the social respectability of the cinema as a whole is as assured in this country as that of the popular press.'[82]

While developments in film technique (new editing styles and principles of documentary film-making) were providing the medium with artistic credibility among highbrow critics; new technical developments (sound films and colour stock) helped to reinforce its popular appeal. The first films to make effective use of these new technologies, such as *The Jazz Singer* (1927) with sound, and *Gone With the Wind* (1939) with colour, were enormously popular. Yet while technological developments played a significant role in determining the popularity of individual films, they do not appear to have fundamentally altered the cinema's appeal. After the coming of sound films, attendance levels remained much the same as they had been during the First World War; the routine use of colour stock in feature film production actually coincided with a sharp fall in film-going.

The decline in attendance levels in the 1950s reminds us that the quality of the films themselves was not the only determinant of the cinema's appeal. As one 1952 report, in explaining the drop in film-going since 1946, put it:

No one can seriously contend that the entertainment value of films changed so suddenly as to be entirely responsible for so considerable a decrease. It seems probable that the re-opening of other forms of popular entertainment, and the beginning of a return to peacetime living conditions, reduced the extraordinary dependence on the cinema as a form of recreation which was an undoubted feature of the war years.[83]

Far from mass-producing films of a diminishing technical or artistic standard which the public were no longer prepared to pay to see, the Hollywood studios tackled the problem of declining audiences in the 1950s by producing ever more colourful and expensive films, and by developing new technical innovations. This was the period of the classic Technicolor Hollywood musical. Films such as *Singin' in the Rain* (1952) and *White Christmas* (1954) are fondly remembered now as if they dated from the 'golden age' of the Hollywood studios: in fact they were part of a deliberate response by film producers to the decline in cinema attendance, which emphasized the advantages of the big screen over television.[84] Other aspects of that response included the development of Cinemascope, Widescreen and 3-D films – all of which date from the 1950s. Hollywood studios actually concentrated a far greater proportion of their resources on the production of big-budget 'event' films in the 1950s and 60s than they had in earlier decades, because these were the only pictures that could still make a profit in a period when film-going has ceased to be a habit.[85]

It is not enough to say that that cinema's appeal was based on the popularity of the films shown, but nor can we properly understand the cultural role of the cinema without recognizing the appeal of the films themselves. One of the key features of this appeal, and the main device used by major studios to market their products, was the presence of stars.[86] In most recollections of cinema-going the names of actors and actresses recur much more frequently than those of films. It was the stars with whom audiences felt they could identify, not just the characters they played or the situations in which they found themselves on screen. This comes across not just from oral testimony – it becomes plainly apparent when browsing through any of the movie magazines which were sold in their thousands throughout this period.

'Stars', as Richard Dyer has pointed out, 'represent typical ways of behaving, feeling and thinking in contemporary society, ways that have been socially, culturally, historically constructed.'[87] They have a particularly important role to play in industrial, capitalist society by highlighting the individual in a world of 'mass' production and consumption. The phenomena of international entertainment stars, however, was something rarely heard of before the era of cinema. Theatre and music-hall favourites had an appeal which was usually geographically limited. Film stars, because they did not need to appear physically before an audience, could be watched simultaneously by millions of cinema-goers in any part of the world. These stars were clearly more than just actors or actresses, they were cultural icons. Their hairstyles, dress and use of language were imitated by fans who seemed to have an insatiable appetite for stories and gossip about every aspect of their lives.[88] Their enormous appeal helps to explain why the cinema has been such a popular medium of entertainment, but it does not explain why it was *particularly* popular from the 1920s to the early 1950s. More significant in this respect is that for the generations who grew up in this period, the cinema was virtually the sole provider of stars. This was not so in the later 1950s and 60s when the likes of Bill Haley, Buddy Holly and, of course, Elvis Presley,[89] came to rival the older generation of screen idols, which included Humphrey Bogart, James Stewart, Norma Shearer, Ingrid Bergman, and for specifically British audiences, James Mason, Stewart Granger and Margaret Lockwood. As Docherty, Morrison and Tracey point out: 'the symbolism of teenagers ripping up cinema seats when Bill Haley played *Rock Around the Clock* was pregnant with meaning'.[90]

Summary

For the majority of British cinema audiences between the 1920s and the 1950s film-going was a habit conducted on at least a weekly basis. Some people were more likely to be film addicts than others. Most regular film-goers were young people, they were usually working-class, and they were more often female than male. Habitual film-going, particularly in Wales, most often took place in small, local cinemas that shared little in common, architecturally, with the more prestigious dream palaces. Large modern cinemas were fairly scarce in Wales, and for most working-class film-goers a visit to one of these halls was an 'event' quite unlike a routine visit to their 'local'. If the largest town centre halls were 'dream palaces' or 'pleasure domes', the smaller local halls performed a function more akin to a community centre or club.

The environment in which film-going took place may have been firmly rooted in the local community, but the films which audiences flocked to see certainly were not. Films, and more particularly their stars, held an appeal which crossed national, as well as social, boundaries. Audiences in Wales may not typically have shared the same social experience as cinema-goers in many other parts of Britain, but they did get to see the same films. The nature of the entertainment these audiences consumed provides the focus of the next chapter.

5

CINEMA ENTERTAINMENT

Throughout the period covered by this book the majority of films screened in British (and Welsh) cinemas were American in origin. This had not always been the case. In the years prior to the First World War the majority of films shown in Britain were made in Europe, and at least half of these were British. Indeed, in some years European films outnumbered American ones even in the US itself. The film industry, however, entered a crucial phase of growth, innovation and market concentration during the period of the First World War. European firms, unable to participate in these developments, found it impossible to compete against the major US companies that had been created by the end of the war, and remained in their shadow thereafter.[1] By the mid-1920s only 5 per cent of films screened in the UK were actually British, and even after legislation was introduced to protect the British film industry in 1927, around three-quarters of all films shown in British cinemas continued to be American.[2]

The dominance of US-made films on British screens troubled those who believed that the cinema was acting as an agent of Americanization – of whom there were many. This was a belief US film executives themselves were only too happy to promote,[3] and which journalists and politicians in Europe were quick to accept.[4] By the time the British Parliament introduced legislation to restrict the amount of foreign films that could be shown in its cinemas, the *Daily Express* felt that several million people were already 'temporary American citizens'.[5] Responses to this perceived cultural threat, in Britain and in Wales, are examined in the final two chapters. This chapter will examine the nature of the entertainment provided in Welsh cinemas in closer detail. The focus will not just be on the main feature films themselves, but also the rest of the supporting programme, including live acts and the provision of live musical entertainment. Taken as a whole, were these programmes of cinema entertainment really dominated by American product? Were there significant variations in the types of programmes provided by different types of hall? Were American films really much more popular than British ones, and did attitudes to British films change during this period?

The chapter tackles these questions in four separate sections. The first examines the emergence of cinema entertainment in Britain. It argues that even though the cinematograph was a modern technical invention and many of the films shown were foreign, this form of public entertainment can in fact be seen as a continuation of much older traditions of British popular culture. The second section provides an analysis of the type of entertainment which made up the supporting programme in most cinemas. This mixture of short films, cartoons, newsreels and 'B' pictures was just as important a part of the diet of regular film-goers as the main feature itself. The third section explores the nature of the live entertainment provided in certain cinemas in the 1920s and 30s, arguing that this was an important factor shaping the type of film-going experience provided by different types of hall. The final section addresses the main feature films themselves, and questions whether Welsh audiences were any different to those in the rest of Britain in their preferences for British or American films.

High art or popular culture?

The previous chapter argued that the cinema appealed to a range of social groups, and that the nature of its appeal varied for different audiences in different types of hall. Historical accounts of the emergence of cinema entertainment in the early twentieth century have also provided contrasting interpretations of the medium's cultural origins. For those wishing to champion the idea that cinema constituted a new art form, a narrative was constructed in which man had continually striven to perfect a technique for producing moving images. In such accounts the artistic ideal of the moving image was held to be permanent, but this goal was only finally achieved with the invention of the cinematograph in the 1890s. In one of the earliest such histories Terry Ramsaye claimed that 'Critics and forecasters, academic, professional and commercial, are continually committing themselves to error, and to the swift exposures of those errors, because of their failure to see the screen as one of the strands in the yarn of life, with an infinity behind and ahead.'[6] He went on to provide a detailed account of the development of the cinematograph, taking into account the work of men such as Marey, Muybridge, Friese-Greene, Paul, Edison and the Lumière brothers.

Ramsaye's monumental study, first published in 1926, was an important part of the process, taking place in the 1920s, by which cinema became accepted as an art form and won a measure of intellectual credibility. In the process of investing the cinema with a new cultural respectability, however, its intellectual supporters overlooked, or chose to ignore, the commercial forces that had helped shape the provision of cinema entertainment in the previous two decades. For Ramsaye, the obstacles preventing the emergence of this new art form were technical ones, which gradually came to be removed. A similar interpretation was provided by the critic Andre Bazin in the 1960s. To Bazin, the concept of the cinema had existed 'fully armed in men's minds' long before it was technically perfected: 'If cinema in its cradle lacked all the attributes of the cinema to come, it was with reluctance and because its fairy guardians were unable to provide them however much they would have liked to.'[7]

An alternative interpretation of cinema's early development has been provided by those who see its primary function as a form of popular entertainment and as an industry. Michael Chanan, for example, points out that the prominent figures in the pre-history of the cinema, 'weren't trying to invent cinematography: they were involved in a search for quite different discoveries, in the fields of astronomy or the investigation of animal locomotion; they used rapid series photography as an instrument or tool of scientific research.'[8] In order to understand the way in which the cinema developed, either as an art form or as a medium of mass entertainment, it is necessary to examine its broader social, economic and cultural context.

Far from being hailed as a new medium for creative expression, cinema, in its early years, was shunned by the respectable classes. Even those 'Bohemians and other refugees from the middle-class' who had delighted in the music hall saw little merit in the cinema. 'They thought of the movies as a mechanical novelty, a meaningless and trivial craze which might be allowed to provide a moment's distraction at a music hall or vaudeville show but which normally belonged to the amusement arcade or fairground.'[9] This was precisely the point. Despite later attempts to suggest that the invention of cinema marked the birth of a new art form, contemporaries recognized that its roots lay in working-class culture which, as E. P. Thompson memorably pointed out, had 'its more robust and rowdy features'. Thompson's description of the traditions associated with popular amusements in the eighteenth century remains relevant for cinema historians of the twentieth:

> We must also remember the 'underground' of the ballad-singer and the fairground which handed on traditions to the nineteenth century (to the music-hall, or Dickens' circus folk, or Hardy's pedlars and showmen); for in these ways the 'inarticulate' conserved certain values – a spontaneity and capacity for enjoyment and mutual loyalties – despite the inhibiting pressures of magistrates, mill-owners, and Methodists.[10]

It was out of this 'underground' tradition, through fairground showmen and music hall proprietors, that moving pictures found their way to the public. Only later did businessmen, governments, censors, and the likes of J. Arthur Rank (mill-owner and Methodist), seek to regulate and commercialize this form of entertainment: to rid it of its more 'rowdy element' and appeal to a middle-class audience. As Rachael Low and Roger Manvell have argued: 'It is to the fairground showmen that cinema owes its ultimate success . . . It was they who bridged the gap between the music hall days and the later, more respectable picture palaces, and they disappeared only with the First World War – long after the coming of the regular cinema.'[11] A further indication of the cinema's origins is provided by Michael Chanan, who explains that

Around 1905 some of the cinematograph operators thought of joining the Variety Artistes. This is not as strange as it sounds, since many of them were originally theatrical illusionists and magicians who had adopted the cinematograph because it extended their range of trick devices; or else they belonged to the tradition of magic lantern lecturers. At any rate, many of them thought of themselves as performers of some kind.[12]

The growth of the cinema industry in the first half of the twentieth century meant that by the 1920s film-makers had little left in common with fairground showmen or entertainers. Some cinema exhibitors, however, continued to regard themselves as 'showmen' for much longer, and certainly recognized that they remained in competition with more traditional forms of entertainment. Letters written by cinema managers from the Castle and Central circuit in south Wales indicate the sort of competition these picture houses faced. G. W. Robinson, who ran the Central Cinema in Porth wrote the following to his employer in June 1920:

> I am afraid that this week will prove one of the worst in the year for us. We have the annual fair here, which I had previously been warned would play havoc with our business, I did not believe that this could possibly interfere with trade until I paid a personal visit. I really think the whole population of Porth remain there from afternoon till 11 p.m.[13]

A. R. Gambold, manager of Swansea's Castle Cinema in the 1920s, expressed similar concerns:

> I hope I am wrong, but I am rather afraid somehow that we shall experience a slump during the summer months. Swansea, as you know, has great outdoor attractions during the season and this summer Campbell's will be running a regular service of pleasure boats, they have secured a good site for embarking etc. almost within a stone's throw of the bottom of Wind Street and judging by the preparations, they evidently mean doing the thing well.[14]

Such counter-attractions were unable to rival the cinema's appeal on a national level, or for a prolonged period. Indeed, the existence of alternative forms of popular culture could on occasions benefit the local cinema industry:

> The large influx of Saturday trippers to Cardiff and other parts of South Wales to witness football games is a big advantage to the kinemas, which do a huge week-end business. This was particularly the case during last Saturday's International encounter at Swansea, for in the evening the picture palaces were literally crowded.[15]

The popular appeal of cinema entertainment may have grown out of a long tradition of working-class amusement, but the sheer commercial value of the industry inevitably began to shape both the nature of the entertainment itself and the way it was consumed. The Cinematograph Act of 1909 (much like the Suitability Act of 1878)[16] was ostensibly intended to improve safety within cinemas but rapidly became exploited by local authorities to influence the content of the filmed entertainment itself. If the authorities were anxious to regulate this new form of entertainment, however, the industry itself was equally keen to broaden its appeal. As Rachael Low puts it: 'The showman, not satisfied with a penny-gaff public, sought a more dignified position in society.'[17] Jeffrey Richards has pointed to a similarity between music hall and cinema in this respect:

> Moralists had consistently attacked the music halls for their association with drunkenness, sexuality and rowdiness. But reform came at the behest of music hall proprietors and theatrical entrepreneurs, anxious to broaden their appeal and make yet more money up-market . . . In the process they created a bastard form of music hall called 'variety' to which the working class continued to flock, though now joined by middle- and upper-class audiences. The same pattern developed in the cinema industry, where the control of film content and improvement of cinema facilities were instigated by the commercial interests themselves.[18]

Accepting that a similar process of commercialization took place in each case, Peter Stead has argued that whereas music hall and vaudeville were forms of entertainment that were transitional 'between the genuine folk culture of an earlier age and the mass commercialisation of the twentieth century', the 'movies had broken through to a vast new public and everything was on a different scale'. For the showmen, therefore, '[t]o attract bigger audiences was not just a bonus, it was part of the whole logic of the industry'.[19] Commercial opportunism led showmen to take their picture shows out of fairgrounds, penny-gaffs and music halls into more permanent accommodation. In a passage already alluded to in chapter 2, Rachael Low has described how this process worked:

> More and more effort was spent in impressing the audience with comfort and elegance, and proving the pictures worthy of better-class audiences. Red plush and marble, ferns in brass pots and plenty of electric light were guaranteed to give that 'air of cosy refinement' which was wistfully sought by a trade anxious to disclaim its low birth . . . In the matter of names, too, was reflected the search for class – Olympia, Bijou, Empire, Jewel, Gem and Mirror were favourites, and endless variants such as Electroscope, Picturedrome, Pallasino and even Palaceadium. Such inept efforts to be dignified may have made a more favourable impression on the working-class public than on the classes for whom they were intended.[20]

The earliest attempts on the part of showmen to broaden the cinema's appeal, then, consisted largely of changes to the environment in which the pictures were viewed. 'Only gradually' according to Peter Stead, 'did the commercial preoccupation with the projector and the venue shift to a greater interest in the films themselves.'[21] Yet, just as developments in cinema architecture did not prevent old skating rinks or public halls from being used as cinemas until at least the 1950s, the emergence of the feature film did not entirely displace shorts and newsreels from programmes of cinema entertainment.

Cinema programmes

The influence of existing forms of popular culture on feature films has been explored by a number of film historians. We know, for instance, that some of the most celebrated exponents of Hollywood film comedy, such as Charlie Chaplin and Stan Laurel, learned their trade in travelling variety troupes. Music hall traditions remained alive in British cinema in the 1930s and 40s in the work of, among others, George Formby, Gracie Fields and Will Hay. Victorian melodrama was also evident in the films of Tod Slaughter and much of the output of Gainsborough Studios in the 1940s.[22] Of the cultural significance of cinema *programmes*, however, as opposed to individual films, much less is written.

That part of the cinema programme which came before the main feature is easily (and often) overlooked. The items contained therein (one- or two-reel comedies, serials and newsreels), were of much shorter duration than the main film, they did not feature the most popular stars, and much less effort went into advertising them. This element of the cinema programme did not provide the central attraction for cinema-goers, but it was, nonetheless, an important feature of the cinema-going experience, and both managers and audiences treated it as such. A. R. Gambold, for instance, was at pains to explain to his employer that 'our patrons seem to expect all the items in our usual programme even when we are showing an extra long picture, I believe I mentioned this to you when we had "The Only Way", some of the patrons appeared to be disappointed that there was no second feature.'[23]

In some cinemas programmes were run continuously, so one could arrive at any point and remain in the auditorium until the programme had come full circle. As such the main feature did not necessarily conclude an evening's (or afternoon's) entertainment. In other cinemas, usually the smaller working-class halls where programmes were run separately, it is significant that the time of the main film's screening was seldom advertised. There was simply a choice between attending the 'first house' or 'second house'. A visit to the cinema, then, entailed much more than the viewing of a feature film. In his reminiscences of cinema-going in the 1950s Peter Stead referred to his time spent 'in the cinemas of the Llynfi Valley where relations in Maesteg, Nantyfyllon and Caerau were always encouraging us to join them at what they called "a show" '.[24] While patrons had come to expect two or three hours cinema entertainment, not just a single film, managers were concerned to ensure programmes were suitably balanced and appealing. G. W. Robinson certainly took the shorter films into account when considering how best to attract the Porth public to his cinema:

> May I suggest that programmes be balanced thus. Where we have a two reel *serial* booked, the second big feature should be a comedy drama the remaining comedy element being supplied by a one reel comedy. The other half of the week we could perhaps have a two reel comedy with two dramas as I know one cannot always obtain a good Comedy Drama in four or five reels. In any case I reckon it is bad business to book two one reel comedies on the same programme they are not appreciated by the audience. A comedy must be good to be well received, and I am sure the majority would dispense with some willing provided the main pictures were good. Then again we must consider the younger patrons, who delight in a good comedy.[25] (Original punctuation maintained.)

Gambold was equally sceptical of the appeal of one reel comedies for his patrons in Swansea:

> With regard to Sybil Thorndike single reel dramas I do not see how we can do with these unless we could have single reel comedies to go with them, and of course this would mean cutting out the two reel comedy, I am not in favour of this unless we can be certain of getting good one reel comedies.[26]

In terms of the way in which programmes of entertainment were structured, providing an assortment of shorter features as well a main film, there is clearly an element of continuity between the cinema and older traditions of music hall and variety. It is the content of these supporting programmes to which attention will now be turned.

Much the longest of the supporting items on cinema bills were second features or 'B' pictures. These were usually low-budget American pictures lasting about an hour. The types of films shown as supporting features fell into a number of different categories. Hugh Louden, in recalling his movie-going experiences of the 1930s and 40s describes them variously as 'the western', 'the murder mystery', 'the actioneer featuring working guys in tough situations', 'college romps' and 'domestic comedies'.[27] Although lacking the sort of meticulous production values that would characterize a studio's premier releases, these films could at times express a crude authenticity which appealed to working-class audiences. Peter Stead, recalling his early cinema-going days, claimed that '[i]t was those B movies, which we rarely comprehended as we had always joined the story during a lengthy flashback, that fascinated us most and left us in no doubt that we lived in an unsophisticated town that was behind the times.'[28] Similarly, Louden asserted that '[i]n my early days I enjoyed the B movies almost as much as those with grander pretensions.'[29]

Although these films seldom featured established stars, they often contained characters who were familiar and formats that followed a tried and tested formula. Fictional personalities who proved popular with cinema audiences were regularly used to form the basis of a whole series of low-budget films. While it would be easy to criticize such movies for their unimaginative direction or repetitive storylines, they undoubtedly held a strong appeal – particularly for younger audiences. As Louden remembers it: 'Fans liked the regular feel of Charlie Chan, Mr Moto, the Cisco Kid, Sherlock Holmes, Blondie, Michael Shayne, Boston Blackie, the Jones Family, the Saint, the Falcon, Hopalong Cassidy and Mr Wong.' Such films appear to have been most appreciated by the habitual working-class film-goers in small local cinemas. Indeed, these halls were often the only ones prepared to screen them: 'Many B films never found their way into the bigger and better cinemas, inferior product being given a showing only in the meanest of halls.'[30] Even the films that larger cinemas would probably have shunned, however, were regarded as an important feature in lesser halls. This was illustrated rather well in a letter written by the head of a small chain of picture houses in south Wales to his local MP regarding the proposals for the 1938 Films Act:

> It is proposed that British films, to count for Quota, should cost a minimum of £15,000: one result of this will be that the import of foreign films will be restricted, as it is obvious that it will not pay to import a foreign film of moderate earning power, under these conditions. This will have a serious effect, (1) On industrial districts especially, where films of the Western type are popular, and (2) On cinemas owned by small independent proprietors, as the circuits will have preference for the smaller number of films available. In our case we shall be penalised both ways, and the outlook for an adequate supply of films is very black, if these proposals become law in the form now proposed.[31]

Formulaic B movies were not the only films of 'moderate earning power'. Serials fell into the same category and their appeal was likewise limited to an almost exclusively working-class audience. The manager of Porth's Central Cinema provides a striking example of how attitudes to serials differed markedly between different social groups. In the early 1920s he felt his cinema was attracting the highest-class patrons in the town, even suggesting that 'We are in a position to work on different prices to other Porth halls because we have a balcony';[32] this consideration influenced his attitude to serials:

> I am not at all particular about starting them again, and am of the opinion that they are badly overdone. There are four different ones showing in Porth at

present, and we have been congratulated upon the absence of such from our programme, by many circle patrons. Of course, this may not represent the views of the cheapest seats, but taking all things into consideration I feel sure we have reached a stage when we may dispense with this item altogether.[33]

The appeal of serials depended not just on the quality of their plots or production but also the cinema-going habits of the audience. To follow a serial from beginning to end one needed to attend the same cinema for perhaps twelve consecutive weeks, regardless of the main feature in the programme. Those who were at all selective about the films they chose to see were simply not prepared to do this. For such patrons, viewing a single episode of an ongoing serial each time they went to the cinema would probably have been more irritating than entertaining. For those who did follow the serials throughout, however, each episode was eagerly awaited. The recollections of south Wales cinema-goers would suggest not only that serials were a popular feature in this area, but also that their leading characters achieved star-like status in certain communities. The name which crops up more often than any other in peoples' reminiscences of serials is that of Pearl White.[34] According to a Tonypandy projectionist: 'Pearl White was idolised . . . There was even a popular song about her which the audience used to sing before she appeared on the screen. It was called *Pearl, Pearl, you're a wonderful girl.*'[35]

The environment in which serials were most often appreciated, free from the derision of circle patrons, was in the children's matinee or 'penny rush'. The likes of Roy Rogers, the Lone Ranger and Zorro held huge appeal for younger audiences, and it was in the form of serials that their adventures were most often followed. As Hugh Louden remembers:

The penny rush was nothing without the serial . . . we relished each episode avidly and after twelve episodes felt a real rapport with the characters. The heroes and the villains – mostly played by actors who never appeared in a major film – were well known to young audiences. It was film watching on a different level.[36]

Similar experiences have been recalled by a Caernarfon cinema-goer: 'The Guildhall was our mecca on a Saturday afternoon. This was our picture 'ouse and for two pence were a variety of films for an hour and a half: cowboys and Indians, comics, drama and a serial. Pearl White was my idol, plus Charlie Chaplin.'[37] These children's performances only made up a small proportion of total cinema programmes, but their role was an important one. Children were a significant part the cinema audience, and it was in the Saturday matinées that their cinema-going habit was often forged. The appeal of particular serials may have worn thin with the passing of years, but the routine of attending the pictures at least once a week took much longer to die out.

Serials were less likely to form part of evening cinema programmes in the later 1920s and 30s, but there would almost inevitably have been at least one short film in addition to the two longer features on the bill. The form that these short films took varied from week to week and depended upon the nature of the main attractions (as noted above). Short dramas and comedies (in either one or two reels) were frequently booked and, despite occasional complaints about single-reel comedies, generally seem to have been well received. These short entertainment films, along with topicals (pictures of actual events) were survivors from the earliest days of the cinema. Such films had certainly become less prominent by the 1920s, but they had not disappeared completely. Some managers continued to make their own films for local audiences in the inter-war period, much as the early pioneers had decades before. George Townsend, who managed the Central in Porth from the late 1920s until the 1940s, felt that such films still held a strong appeal for audiences in the 1930s:

> This late afternoon and evening I took pictures of a local Gala. I can assure you quite definitely that providing I have had some success in taking these pictures . . . the interest taken by the local people was very keen and we can rest assured, that when we advertise the showing, the response will be good.[38]

Similar initiative was shown by J. Leo Rippen, manager of Cardiff's Pavilion: when providing two free tickets for a flying demonstration in conjunction with the film *The Dawn Patrol*, he took the opportunity to film the event, and show it to audiences the following week.[39]

It is possible to trace the proportion of short films in the programmes of the Central Cinema in Porth from surviving cash books. A typical programme of entertainment from 1919 consisted of one five-reel film, one two-reeler and three or four single-reelers. By the mid- to late 1920s, however, it was usual to screen two of the longer five- or six-reel films, with only one or two shorter films making up the rest of the programme – a pattern which continued until after the Second World War. This development was not to the satisfaction of some of the more traditional showmen. According to a 1925 edition of *Kine Weekly*, Thomas Orminston, then president of the CEA, claimed that in his experience 'patrons demanded variety in the kinema programme, and he deplored that the market in short features was not so large as it was in the earlier days, when the industry owed its present development to this class of picture.'[40]

If, in some respects, short films were a remnant from an earlier age of cinema history, in others they provided opportunities for innovative film-makers to develop new ideas and stretch cinematic boundaries. Animated films provide an example of how this process could take place. Cartoons had proved equally popular with audiences and critics throughout the 1920s. In 1925, for instance, Harold Tilney felt confident enough to book a series of

Felix the Cat for his cinemas in Cardiff and Newport lasting a whole year. He was apparently one of thirty exhibitors who had made such a booking in the space of a week.[41] In his monumental *The Film Till Now*, Paul Rotha quoted a film magnate as saying '[y]ou spend a million dollars on a super-spectacle and they sit through it just to see Mickey Mouse.' Indeed it was the work of Disney that seemed to attract the broadest range of admirers. When the middle-class protagonists in the film *Brief Encounter* went to the cinema, Donald Duck was the only feature that they really seemed to appreciate. They were not alone: Paul Rotha (writing in 1929) claimed that for 'many writers at the moment, the Disney cartoons are the most witty and satisfying productions of modern cinema'.[42]

Disney was one of the only film-makers in this period to appeal equally to critical and popular opinion. Many critics were dismissive of the sort of pictures that the majority of cinema-goers watched on a weekly basis. Indeed, the practice of sitting through an entire cinema programme was something those who prided themselves on possessing a critical faculty often derided. Yet this is what most of the cinema audience frequently did.

The one aspect of the cinema programme other than the feature film which has been rigorously examined by historians is the newsreel. This item was usually featured between the two main films, so only those arriving very late in the programme would miss it. As with other short items on the bill, newsreels were not the main attraction for most cinema audiences; however, they were much more than simply a means of filling out the programme. By examining the content and appeal of the newsreel, one can detect trends which apply the cinema more generally. Indeed, 'Newsreels are not an extraneous branch of cinematographic work, grafted on to the essential business of film production. On the contrary, the cinema itself developed out of the presentation of topical events.'[43]

Short actuality films had been the staple diet of the earliest cinema audiences. In Wales pioneers such as Arthur Cheetham had filmed local events to attract audiences to his fairground shows around the turn of the century.[44] The demand for moving pictures soon led to the development of companies in the US, Britain and France, eager to sell films of current events to growing audiences. The first newsreel companies were established in the first decade of the twentieth century, but the likes of Pathe and Gaumont had never been in the business of attempting to present an objective view of current events: they sought, primarily, to provide entertainment.

As in all small leisure-business, whether pubs, fairs or 'pics', the first rule was that you must please the regulars, for on them depended the business. Therefore, working-men and their wives, from adolescence to about middle-age, were better placed to get the kind of product which they actually wanted in the local cinema than anywhere else. For once it was they who paid the pipers and were seen to be paying them too.[45]

In its very earliest form the very novelty of the moving image meant that the actual events depicted did not need to be 'newsworthy' in order to attract an audience. This did not last long, however, and soon the showmen were competing to screen actuality footage of all sorts of weird and wonderful events. Sir Arthur Elton's evaluation in 1955 of early newsreels is revealing:

> For at least the first thirty years the content of the newsreels was determined mainly by the passing fads and fancies of the time . . . Of scenes of one-legged men pushing turnips with their noses from Paris to Rome there is much; of boat races, crowned heads, bathing belles, railway smashes, the glossier phases of war, fashion parades, fires, murders and dance marathons more . . . Taking a parallel from written sources, it is as if the historian of the early twentieth century had little more to guide him than the *Daily Mirror, Old Moore's Almanac, Tit-Bits* and a run of Nelson's Sevenpenny Novels.[46]

This was precisely the sort of popular working-class culture out of which the early newsreels grew: as did the cinema itself. As Terry Ramsaye remarked in 1934: 'The newsreel is not a purveyor of news and is never likely to become one . . . Whether they know it or not, the newsreels, as they call them, are just in the show business.'[47] In pinpointing one of the essential characteristics of the newsreels, Elton and Ramsaye rejected the idea that such films could be of any interest to historians. Unlike the documentary film-makers inspired by John Grierson, whose main concern was the portrayal of 'reality',[48] newsreels projected a light-hearted and populist view of the world.

When newsreels did concern themselves with the serious issues of the day they could find themselves under attack from audiences, which was potentially far more damaging than critical derision. The reporting of the 1931 general election (in a manner entirely sympathetic to the newly elected National Government) evidently proved too much for many south Wales cinema patrons. After numerous complaints from cinema managers that audiences had 'got up and booed', the south Wales branch of the CEA protested to the newsreel companies about the propaganda content of their films. Replies were apparently drawn from Fox, Gaumont and Pathe 'in which it was pointed out that it was not the practice to include speeches of a controversial nature, and that the items were only included in consequence of the importance of the recent General Election'. This was not enough for the south Wales CEA who passed a further resolution 'expressing the opinion that items of controversial politics should be rigidly excluded from the news as being detrimental to the exhibitor's business, and further calling on the General Council to press this matter home'.[49] Similarly, Anthony Aldgate has argued that 'the newsreels suffered a sharp decline in credibility' when the events they reported were ones that audiences were experiencing themselves. This was most apparent during the Second World War, when audiences were 'able to evaluate their own response in comparison with the portrayal of events as depicted in the cinema'.[50]

Audiences were clearly highly sensitive to being served what they recognized as propaganda. For the most part newsreel companies concentrated on safe events which were easily filmed, had popular appeal and generated little controversy. Football matches, ship launchings and royal visits are typical examples of the sort of items regularly featured. Newsreels were not subject to the scrutiny of the British Board of Film Censors (BBFC), yet the companies' policy of avoiding contentious issues was absolutely in keeping with that of the BBFC. Jeffrey Richards describes the aims of British film censorship in the 1930s as being '[t]he maintenance on the one hand of moral standards, and, on the other, the avoidance of all political, religious and indeed social controversy.'[51] In summarizing the influence of newsreels in the 1930s Nicholas Pronay suggests that

> In real and practical terms the Newsreels served well their regulars who wanted to hang on to what they believed were the basic decencies of their situation: a belief in the good intentions of their rulers, the belief that things would get better without violence in Britain, and that they should bravely meet their present plight with a laugh. In all they felt, and the Newsreels helped them to feel it, that they must avoid despair.[52]

In this regard newsreels performed a similar function to the films of Gracie Fields or George Formby.[53] They continued to be an important part of cinema programmes for as long as the medium itself remained a regular part of peoples' weekly routines. As cinema attendance went into decline in the late 1950s and 60s, so the newsreels became less significant, and eventually died out altogether. The type of material once covered by newsreels found a new home on television as habitual patterns of viewing moved from the big screen to the small. When television first arrived, however, there was much scepticism as to whether it would ever be able to screen the kind of events covered by newsreels:

> Advanced as television is, remember its limitations . . . these pictures are being reproduced on a small screen no more than a foot square. Reduce the Wembley Stadium to this size and imagine how large the individual players would appear. More important still, imagine the size of the ball. It would be so small as to make it almost impossible for a televiewer to watch its progress.[54]

Such a failure to appreciate the future possibilities of television is entirely understandable in south Wales in 1936. Television, at that time was a novelty available only to a very limited audience in the London area; its technical quality was poor; and while cinemas remained such popular social institutions and centres of entertainment it seemed to serve little obvious purpose. As long as people attended the cinema once a week or more, these places remained social institutions that provided their regular patrons with a range of entertainment extending well beyond feature films.

It would be stretching a point to claim that cinema achieved the appeal it did *because* the programmes of entertainment were so varied. However, as long as the cinema maintained its position as the dominant form of public mass entertainment, it made every effort to provide as broad a mixture of entertainment as possible. This did not only mean that older traditions of popular culture survived in cinema programmes; managers also sought to incorporate new forms of entertainment into the bill.

In 1923 the management of Swansea's Castle cinema decided to launch an experiment as to the feasibility of incorporating radio broadcasts into their programmes. The manager reported:

> From what I can gather, the wireless has drawn a few patrons over and above what we should have had in the usual way, but I did not expect to do much during the experimental stages, what I had in mind was that in the event of anything special being transmitted at any time we could make a feature of it.[55]

These experiments were abandoned when it became apparent that even if a 'state of perfection necessary to include Wireless as part of the programme' was achieved, there was 'a clause in the license which stipulates that the set must not be used during broadcasting hours'.[56] It was licensing regulations, not a lack of ambition on the management's part, which prevented this innovation from reaching fruition. No such regulatory difficulties, however, stood in the way of live entertainment being performed in picture houses.

Live entertainment

The live element of cinema entertainment was an essential feature of just about all programmes in the 1920s, prior to the coming of sound films. Even the smallest fleapit would at least have employed a pianist to provide some musical accompaniment to the images on the screen. In some of the larger halls a small orchestra was considered necessary to provide a suitable atmosphere and their influence on a film's reception was certainly recognized by managers. (The now familiar) G. W. Robinson at Porth held his musicians at least partly responsible for the success of *Madame X* in 1921:

> Never in my experience have I known a picture with such universal appeal as 'Madame X'. To see hundreds of people leaving a hall some openly crying, and

the majority of men and women dabbing their eyes, (in the case of the ladies) very red ones at that, is a most remarkable sight. I have had showers of personal congratulations and thanks for having screened such a picture, and with such beautiful music. Curiously enough I had most of the trade show music myself and I must give every credit to the orchestra for the way they performed it, as a bad setting would have spoiled the effect.[57]

Attempts to provide an effective accompaniment to silent films often went beyond just instrumental support. For a film such as *The Volga Boatman* it was considered necessary for a choir to provide the necessary vocal support. When this film was shown at the Castle in Swansea in 1927, for example, it was accompanied by the Gwent Glee Singers.[58] Though relatively unusual for managers to book choirs in order to enhance a film's appeal, they were encouraged by sections of the trade press to be innovative in terms of providing audiences with 'special effects'.

The finest film may be greatly enhanced if accompanied by the right and appropriate sound; the poorest film may also be saved from failure by the same means . . . The aim of the theatre manager should be gradually to acquire such a collection of instruments that no demand upon it – from the raising of a ship's anchor to a cork pop – need remain unsatisfied.[59]

Fletcher Clayton, writing in *Kine Weekly*, made a similar point, though rather more cautiously:

The exhibitor, with his instinct for showmanship, should always seek 'stunts' likely to attract and delight his patrons. This does not mean that he must engage freaks, or indulge in eccentricities; but that, knowing what pictures he is showing each week, he should try and devise some special 'effects'. The pictures are, of course, *the* attraction; 'effects' are only intended to heighten their impressiveness.[60]

The use of such effects had its critics. Gilbert Stevens, writing in the same edition of *Kine Weekly*, argued that in those halls employing an orchestra of a dozen or more instruments there was no need for crude effects. 'Why', he questioned, 'should the ear be offended by the noise of stones rattling on a drum as a crude imitation of the sound of waves beating upon the shore when so much music interpretive of the noises of the sea has been written? . . . Let us have good music, not good music spoiled by crude imitations.'[61] Most cinema managers, particularly in Wales, had nowhere near twelve instrumentalists in their employment, though such comments do suggest that a good orchestra was able to influence not just the reception of films, but also the reputation of cinemas. In recommending price increases for admission to the *circle* of Porth's Central Cinema, the manager stressed that 'the little over and above the other halls we well deserve, considering the comfort, cleanliness and service generally given, not to mention the orchestra which stands alone here'. Nevertheless, he still maintained that 'I should like if possible to improve our music if we carry out these changes.'[62]

Live entertainment in cinema programmes was developed to its greatest extent in the larger first-run halls which sought to attract a middle-class patronage. This took the form not only of bigger and better orchestras, but also live variety stage acts. There was nothing new in the notion of showing films and live variety entertainment on the same bill. Music halls, along with fairground booths, had been important outlets for the screening of early cinematograph pictures. But whereas earlier music hall proprietors had sought to exploit the craze for moving images in order to boost their audiences, by the 1920s cinemas were using live acts to win over the custom of music hall and variety patrons. *Kine Weekly* offered advice to managers as to how best to achieve this:

> Undoubtedly the introduction of variety acts has brought into the picture houses any number of entirely new patrons who have developed, and are still developing, a taste for pictures as apart from their original preference for variety. This educational work would certainly be much more effectively carried on if the 'alternating' form of programme . . . was adopted. For where the variety part of the entertainment is a self-contained section, the chances are that these new patrons who have been music-hall 'fans' hitherto will time their visit to coincide with the appearance of the variety acts. The 'alternating' programme would prevent this. In order to see the variety acts this new audience would be obliged to see the pictures as well, and in due course be numbered among the picture 'fans'.[63]

The desire for respectability, as well as profitability, encouraged cinema proprietors to appeal to this market. The introduction of variety acts into cinema programmes, therefore, was part of a more general phase in cinema's development which also witnessed improvements to the design, comfort and cleanliness of the buildings themselves. The halls which provided variety entertainment were usually those which also boasted 'the last word in luxury'. In Cardiff, for example, the Capitol and the Olympia, both first-run halls, featured variety acts regularly in this period. The latter advertised itself as providing 'Always the Latest and Best Pictures & High Class Variety Turns'.[64]

As for smaller towns, the Grand Pavilion in Llandrindod Wells is a good example of the sort of hall which provided live entertainment. The proprietor described the hall as the 'Llandrindod Wells Super Cinema and Rendezvous', pointed out that 'in addition to cinema performances, stage plays are held' and boasted that 'the free car park is usually lined with vehicles'.[65] Evidence of variety entertainment in cinema programmes is also to be found in some of the more prosperous north and west Wales tourist resorts. The Coliseum in Aberystwyth, for instance, featured acts ranging from

'Musical Dawsons (Real Live Educated Birds)' (1933) to the Aberystwyth Madrigal Singers (1932) as part of their programmes.[66] The Rialto in Colwyn Bay even employed its own variety troupe, known as The Rialto Sparks.[67] In the south Wales valleys, however, cinemas could seldom afford to provide live, as well as screened entertainment. An attempt to introduce variety at the Central in Porth in 1923 'did not pay off'.[68] The contrast between the sort of entertainment provided in valleys cinemas, as opposed to those in more prosperous areas was vividly described by Gwyn Thomas. Having experienced the 'great novelty' of seeing a dancer at a London cinema, he went on to explain that

> Back home, ancillary turns at the cinema were rare. One cinema in Cardiff, a Babylonian palace visited specifically as a treat, had an organist who rose from the basement to a height of about ten feet above the heads of the front row, riding his organ and playing as he rose. In the valley we would sometimes have reciters, failed actors who contributed to the theme of the film being shown . . . But girls wearing only an ounce of beads and moving their bodies in ways that breathed soft bordello notes with every ripple, we never got as far as that, and even when we had a film about Salome the reciter stayed fully clothed.[69]

Even in the age of silent films there was a discernible difference in the sort of entertainment being provided in different classes of hall. After the coming of sound films around 1928–30 this distinction became increasingly pronounced. Smaller halls, having invested heavily in sound apparatus, were in no position to retain well-paid musicians whose role had become superfluous. Even if a good orchestra did attract more custom, the extra income generated in small halls would have been modest and a significant share of it would have disappeared in tax and film hire. In Wales, where small independent cinemas were so prominent, musicians were in a particularly precarious position, partly because the small capacity of most halls meant there was relatively little scope for improving takings, but also because it was here that the renters' share of total income was highest.[70]

While the majority of small exhibitors dispensed with live entertainment in the 1930s, in the more prestigious larger cinemas it was being expanded. Looking ahead to the year 1931, *Kine Weekly* pointed out that although '[w]hen 1930 came in, the musicians' only note was one of extreme pessimism', before the year was out 'super kinemas were rapidly reaching completion . . . and it was noted by musicians that nearly every one which opened started with an orchestra and a modern unit organ, in addition to artistic ballet and variety stage presentations.' This article, stressing that in the large circuit halls 'the size of the orchestras will be very much greater than in the days of the silent film', went on to suggest that 'musicians can safely regard the worst phase of kinema history as passing away and normal conditions of kinema employment returning.'[71]

Perhaps the clearest symbol of the growing importance of live entertainment in the largest and most prestigious halls was the cinema organ. Names such as Wurlitzer, Hammond and Christie had been around in the 1920s, yet it was not until after the coming of sound, when they were no longer a practical necessity, that they took on their greatest significance. Rather than doing anything to enhance the actual exhibition of films, they came to be regarded as a symbol of the class and prestige of a particular hall, and as such they were in great demand. According to *Kine Weekly* the John Compton Organ Co. had installed cinema organs at the rate of one a week in 1930, 'an achievement which is without parallel in the history of British organ construction'. The following year it was pointed out that 'one of the principal British organ builders has already extended their works, and another is doing so at the present time'.[72] The newly built or renovated super-cinemas created this demand, however, and these were in a distinct minority in Wales. Most Welsh cinemagoers, like those elsewhere in Britain, would at some point have had occasion to visit a 'Babylonian palace', even if it was only on rare occasions. As such the image of the organist rising up from under the stage became as established a cinema cliché in Wales as anywhere else. As well as creating a striking visual effect the organs did, of course, provide an important musical attraction, as well as enhancing a cinema's local reputation.

If the organs were symbols of splendour and prestige, the orchestras were intended to provide additional entertainment for the higher class of patron these cinemas were aiming to attract. At Swansea's Plaza, for instance, the management introduced 'a series of weekly, Thursday afternoon, tea-dances, on the floor at the top of the building'.[73] In the café of Cardiff's Capitol, 'Falkman's Syncopated Five entertained customers daily'.[74] As well as musicians variety acts were also maintained, and in some cases became more prominent, in the talkie era. Judging by advertisements in the local press, variety certainly seemed to be a more significant feature of the Capitol's programme in the 1930s than it had been a decade earlier. On occasions it even took priority over the films themselves – as in April 1938, when a ninety-minute stage show called *The Show's the Thing* took top billing for one week.[75]

The increasing prominence of live entertainment within the programmes of leading cinemas was matched, in the 1930s, by the conversion of some of the remaining theatres and variety halls into picture houses. Swansea's Grand Theatre, for instance, faced direct competition after the opening of the Plaza in 1931. As Stephen Ridgwell observed: 'This high-class family cinema was able to attract many of the Grand's traditional patrons who might otherwise have overlooked the less "respectable" cinemas of the town.' As a means of retaining its audience between 1934 and 1947 the Grand took to showing films.[76] Similarly, Cardiff's New Theatre installed talkie equipment in 1931.[77] This was not in response to any direct threat posed by a particular cinema, but it came at a time when the leading halls were extending their efforts to attract middle-class patrons. Outside the major Welsh towns similar developments occurred. Aberystwyth's Coliseum, for example, was a variety theatre which converted to a cinema in February 1932.[78] In their competition to attract a particular class of patronage, many leading picture houses and more traditional theatres had become virtually indistinguishable during the 1930s.

The distinction between the most prestigious cinemas and the smaller working-class halls increasingly lay not just in the type of patrons they attracted or the quality of their interior decoration, but also their programmes of entertainment. That these different types of hall were able to attract such a large and reliable patronage suggests that their audiences had genuinely differing demands and expectations. A *Kine Weekly* feature headed 'Variety in the Kinema' made the point succinctly: 'A working-class audience prefers quite a different sort of programme to that acceptable to a more "West-Endy" audience, just as their tastes in pictures differ.'[79]

This in itself was no great surprise. Variety was introduced at the leading cinemas in order to attract a new, higher class of patronage. Yet while other innovations intended to appeal to middle-class audiences proved equally popular with those lower down the social scale, such as improved seating and interior decoration, the lure of variety entertainment was less appealing to working-class audiences. The failure of variety at Porth's Central Cinema has already been noted, but even a first-run hall such as the Olympia in Cardiff, when faced with competition from the likes of the Capitol and the New Theatre, was forced to drop live entertainment from its programmes in 1932. This decision did provoke a small number of complaints from disappointed patrons who had greatly enjoyed not just the variety turns but also 'the musical items given by Mr Wheeler's Olympians'. One 'annoyed' gentleman took the step of informing the management that he and his family would now go elsewhere 'as your show has gone down 100 per cent & this is not only my opinion'.[80] More interesting than this complaint, however, was the reply it received, which is quoted in full:

We thank you for your letter, and are pleased that you have given us an opportunity of replying to your criticism. For our part, we tried hard to retain the Orchestra and, as you are aware, we recently introduced extra Musicians, to form a Jazz band, which seemed to be what modern taste called for. Unfortunately, the public did not support us, and we think we can say, without any exaggeration, that our receipts at the Pay-Box did not seem to improve at all, as a result of the extra Band. It has been a great disappointment to us, but we feel we have not had the support we should have had in our effort to keep an Orchestra, and we cannot afford to bear all this extra expense, without support. It is something like the public's attitude to British films: they say they want British films, but when we show one, as a rule, we do bad business.

There are probably a small proportion of people, like yourself, who are prepared to support British entertainment, but it would appear that the vast majority of the public prefer the American variety: it is a matter for regret.[81]

As well as demonstrating the lack of interest shown by the majority of cinema-goers in such live entertainment, the comparison drawn with the public's attitude to the films themselves (also touched on in the *Kine Weekly* article) is an extremely interesting one. What evidence there is certainly suggests that the groups least inclined to favour variety turns within cinema programmes were precisely those with whom American films were most popular.

British or American Films?

There was no survey of attitudes to British and American films carried out in Wales in this period. However, some indication of the relative popularity of such films in a predominantly working-class industrial district is provided by a Mass-Observation questionnaire issued in Bolton in March 1938. A clear majority of respondents (63 per cent) said they preferred American films, only 18 per cent preferred British, with the remainder holding no preference. Further, the questionnaire was issued at three cinemas in the town, and it was in the Palladium, described as 'a down-market cinema, frankly a "fleapit"' where the Hollywood product was most popular. Here, three-quarters of respondents preferred American films, compared to just over one-in-ten who would rather have seen British ones.[82] In Wales, where so many cinemas were of a 'down-market' type, the pattern seems to have been the same.

While it is not possible to say with any certainty which films were the most popular with audiences across Wales, some indication of the preferences of south Wales film-goers are provided by the surviving records from Porth's Central Cinema. This valleys picture house was one of the larger and more prominent cinemas in its area, though it catered mostly for a local, working-class audience. It was neither a 'dream palace' nor one of the most down-market 'fleapits', and its audience would have been representative of many south Wales film-goers in this period. Table 24 identifies the films that provided the greatest box-office draw between 1924 and 1946. Where two films are listed for the same year, these were the two main featured attractions for the week in which most money was taken. In some years the biggest week at the box-office came when the same feature film played for six days, and in most other cases it has been possible to identify one film which proved a more popular attraction than any other. This one cinema did not screen all the main films released in any given year, so the list is not a definitive guide to the most popular films of the period (*Gone With the Wind*, for example, does not appear). It does, however, provide a good indication of the *types* of film most popular with cinema audiences in the south Wales valleys at this time.

The dominance of American films in this table for the 1920s and 30s is consistent with what we know of film-going preferences across Britain in this period, but the limited impression made by British films in the 1940s is perhaps more of a surprise. The Second World War and the years immediately after marked a high point in British film production, when directors such as David Lean, Anthony Asquith, Powell and Pressburger and the production studios at Ealing and Gainsborough made pictures that, for the most part, achieved both critical and popular acclaim. British studios could not compete with American ones in terms of the number of films made, but according to the available data for box-office receipts, as well as polls conducted by the *Daily Mail*, the best British pictures were at least as popular with British audiences as the best American ones.[83] In his survey of the cinema and the English, Ross McKibbin argued that throughout the 1940s 'the English showed no particular preference for American films, and the most popular actors and actresses of the decade were nearly always English'.[84] The evidence from Porth, however, suggests that Welsh audiences may have differed from English ones in this respect.

Many British films did play, with some success, at the Central in the 1940s. There is certainly no evidence of any particular hostility towards British-

Table 24
Most popular films at Porth's Central Cinema, 1924–1946

Year	Film	Nationality
1924	The Law of the Lawless	US
1925	Self-Made Failure/His Forgotten Wife	US/US
1926	The Lost World	US
1927	The Volga Boatman	US
1928	Ben Hur	US
1929	The Singing Fool	US
1930	Hollywood Revue	US
1931	New Moon	US
1932	Jailbirds	US
1933	42nd Street/White Sister	US/US
1934	King Kong	US
1935	David Copperfield	US
1936	Mutiny on the Bounty	US
1937	San Francisco	US
1938	Snow White and the Seven Dwarves	US
1939	The Citadel	US company in UK
1940	Swanee River	US
1941	Little Nelly Kelly/Comrade X	US/US
1942	Blossoms in the Dust	US
1943	Stolen Life/Wuthering Heights	US/US
1944	The Lodger/Sweet Rosie O'Grady	US/US
1945	When Irish Eyes are Smiling	US
1946	The Wicked Lady	UK

Source: GRO, Andrews Collection, D/D, A/B, box 41.

made films at this time, and every reason to believe that British pictures were much more popular than they had been in the 1920s and 30s. Yet only one British film, *The Wicked Lady*, was able to match the appeal of the leading American pictures. This film, a historical costume drama featuring Margaret Lockwood as the wife of a magistrate who leads a secret life as a highway robber, topped box-office ratings in Britain but did not achieve widespread critical acclaim. The films that British critics celebrated as marking the emergence of a new 'national cinema'[85] continued to hold less appeal for film-goers in south Wales than those of Hollywood studios.

Confessions of a Nazi Spy, for example, was conspicuously unsuccessful when it reached Porth in 1940. Following, perhaps, the call of Graham Greene to 'give as whole-hearted a welcome as we can to this magnificently constructed engine-of-war',[86] it was one of the few films of that (or any) year booked to play for a full six days at the Central. Yet the cinema's takings that week were barely half the amount netted in the week that *Swanee River* was shown.[87] The collected film criticism of Graham Greene does not contain a review of *Swanee River*, nor of many of the films which topped the box office takings at this cinema.

Perhaps the clearest example of cinema-goers in this south Wales town bucking the national trend, however, is provided by the case of *The Young Mr. Pitt* (Carol Reed, 1942). Here was a film which, as Jeffrey Richards has shown, was 'extremely well received. With a few exceptions, the critics were unanimous in praising the film, Donat and Carol Reed.' Publications as diverse as the *News Chronicle, Sight and Sound, Kinematograph Weekly*, the *Daily Express* and the *Daily Mirror* awarded it a ringing endorsement. The British public, apparently, concurred: the film was one of the most successful of its year at the box office and featured among the top twenty British films of the war years in the *Daily Mail* readers poll of 1946. Reassessing the picture in the 1980s, Richards rated it 'among Britain's finest film works'.[88]

The response to the film back in Porth, however, could not have been more different. The manager of the Central Cinema, conscious of the hype which had been generated by this picture in both the trade and 'lay' press, had enough confidence in its potential appeal to agree to pay a higher booking fee than was usual. It proved to be a costly mistake, and led him to make the following complaint to the distributors:

> We have just completed our run on the above film, and we would draw your attention to the returns which we have sent you. You will observe that this film has failed completely to match our usual standard of business with Twentieth Century Fox Films and in view of the high percentage we have contracted to pay you for this subject, we shall, without doubt, lose considerably on the booking.
>
> In view of this, I have been instructed by my Head Office, to ask that you meet us in some way, either by a substantial reduction in percentage, or by some concession on a future booking.[89]

No record exists of a response to this request, but the very fact that it was made at all serves as a reminder of the diverse tastes of cinema audiences. It could be that south Wales audiences simply refused to accept the aristocratic, Tory Pitt as a national hero, and identified more closely with the radical Charles James Fox, who was made to look rather foolish in Reed's film. While the film draws obvious parallels between Pitt and Churchill, Jeffrey Richards suggests that Fox, too, had a contemporary equivalent in Aneurin Bevan.[90] If this point got through to cinema audiences, then it may explain why the film was received so poorly in this Rhondda community. The *alleged* willingness of Churchill to deploy armed forces against striking miners in Tonypandy in 1911 has never been forgotten, or forgiven, in this part of south Wales. Bevan, by contrast, had learned his politics in the Tredegar Workman's Institute and 'went to Westminster fully formed and informed by the society which had sent him there'.[91] His quickly acquired reputation for haranguing Tory politicians in the Commons made him far more of a heroic figure than Churchill for many in these communities.

If films projecting a national British 'consensus' were not always popular in Wales, those which attempted to portray the Welsh themselves did attract large audiences. In Porth, *Proud Valley* achieved considerable success when it was shown in September 1940. It was not one of the highest grossing films of the year, in part because it played in the first half of the week and so was not screened on Saturday – the most popular film-going night. Only two other films that year, however, took more money playing Monday to Wednesday.[92] *How Green Was My Valley* was given a more favourable booking at this cinema, playing for four days (Tuesday to Saturday) in October 1942. It certainly justified its longer than usual booking, and proved to be the second highest grossing film of the year at the Central behind *Blossoms in the Dust*. Much of the appeal of *The Citadel* at this cinema (booked for a whole six days in May 1939), can also be attributed to the film's Welsh setting (although the Welsh themselves are not portrayed in a positive light).[93]

Evidence for the popularity within Wales of films with a Welsh theme also comes from the Coliseum cinema in Aberystwyth. If we measure the pulling power of individual films by the amount of business they were able to generate on a single night, we see that two of the four most successful films screened at this cinema between 1932 and 1955 had a Welsh setting.[94] One of these was *How Green Was My Valley*, an internationally successful film that won the 1942 Academy Award for best picture; the other was *Valley of Song*, an Associated British picture, directed by Gilbert Gunn, which has all but been forgotten by British film historians.[95] The latter film, an Ealing-style comedy about the rift caused in small Welsh community by a dispute within the local choir, was neither a critical nor a commercial success in Britain.[96] It was certainly a big hit in Aberystwyth, however, where it played for six days in June 1953, and then returned for another three in October (the film returned yet again in 1956 and once more in 1958). *Proud Valley* did not achieve the level of success enjoyed by *How Green Was My Valley* or *Valley of Song* in Aberystwyth, though it did generate enough interest on its three-day run in June 1940 to be booked for a further two days the following month.[97]

Welsh audiences seldom had the opportunity to see themselves portrayed on screen, but when film companies in Britain or the United States did decide to produce pictures that used Wales as a setting, they attracted considerable interest. Films such as *Proud Valley* and *Valley of Song*, which were not great commercial successes in Britain, were actually among the most popular films screened in some Welsh cinemas. For the most part, however, audiences did not go to the cinema to see what was familiar, but what was different, glamorous, or exotic. With the exception of the Gainsborough melodramas of the 1940s, such films were almost always American, rather than British in origin.

Summary

Cinema audiences in Wales, like those in the rest of Britain, enjoyed programmes of entertainment that incorporated much more than the main advertised feature film. Short films, serials and newsreels had been a feature of cinema entertainment from its earliest days, and the continued presence of this element of variety in cinema programmes well into the second half of the twentieth century served as a reminder of its fairground origins. For the early audiences who gathered in showmen's booths or penny gaffs moving pictures may have been just the latest and most novel fairground attraction. The enormous commercial potential of the new medium, however, meant that showmen soon sought to broaden its appeal to as wide an audience as possible. The development of the feature film helped in this process, as did the provision of more comfortable and elegant cinema buildings. In the interwar period variety entertainment was increasingly provided by cinemas in their attempt to attract a new, more up-market audience. By the 1940s middle-class audiences were for the first time also offered a regular supply of critically acclaimed British films. In Wales, such attempts to broaden the cinema's appeal made less of an impression than in other parts of the country. Modern 'dream palaces', we know, were few and far between, while the provision of live variety entertainment was likewise restricted to only a small minority of halls. The improved quality of British films in the 1940s, similarly, appeared to make little impression on the preferences of most Welsh cinema-goers. The occasional appearance, from the late 1930s onwards, of films with a Welsh setting did hold a strong appeal (whether British or American made), but for most Welsh audiences it was the American made shorts, 'B' movies and feature films that held the greatest appeal.

Interior and exterior views of Porth's Central Cinema

The manager of Porth's Central Cinema (front row, left) with his staff

Traditional methods of showmanship persist well into the 1920s

THE RUTHIN CINEMA COMPANY LIMITED

Summary of Accounts for period ending 31st July, 1926

RECEIPTS

By reserved 1/3d seats net	697 6 3			
" Tax	133 8 5	900 14 8		
1/- Seats net	867 5 .			
" Tax	173 9 .	1040 14 .		
6d Seats		325 .		
" Transfers		11 2 6		
9d Seats	12 11 3			
" Tax	2 10 3	15 1 6		
3d Seats		42 3 .		
Private Box	10 8 .			
" Tax	1 13 6	11 19 3		
Rents		41 . .		
Hire of Hall (Thos Roberts)	10 . .			
Quidella refund re miscellaneous payments 'smouldering Films'	4 6 6			
Hire of Hall (Purcess Williams)	7 10 .	21 16 6		
		2259 11 10		
Value Tax Tickets in hand and payment due in respect of advertisement slides to 1st August, 1926	45 . .			
Proportion of Rents to 1st August	11 4 7	56 4 7		
ESTIMATED DR. BALANCE		12 6 6		
		£ 2278 4 11		

EXPENDITURE

To paid hire of Films	523 19 10
Carriage of Films	39 17 5
Posters, Printing, Advertising	151 3 8
Wages	378 3 9
Entertainments Tax	335 19 .
Rates, Taxes and Insurance	89 3 .
Lighting and Fuel	94 7 11
Stationery	5 8 2
Petty Cash and Postages (principally return Carriage on Films)	77 11 6
Miscellaneous	39 3 4
Expenses Booking Films	40 . .
Pianoforte Music & Tuning Piano	3 8 6
transfer to Capital Account	300
	2257 4 11
	21 0 0
	2278 4 11

Audited etc. Pros Robts

The balance sheet of the Ruthin Cinema Company shows the range of prices charged for different types of cinema seat – and the popularity of each

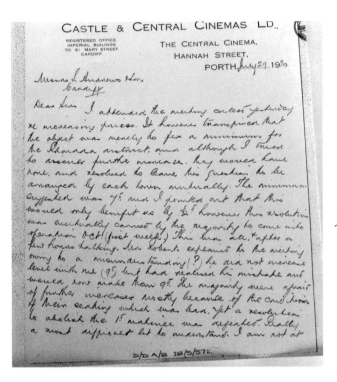

CASTLE & CENTRAL CINEMAS LD.,
REGISTERED OFFICE.
IMPERIAL BUILINGS
70. S! MARY STREET
CARDIFF

THE CENTRAL CINEMA,
HANNAH STREET,
PORTH, July 29 19—

Price fixing at Rhondda cinemas.

The manager of Porth's Central Cinema fails to persuade his counterparts to increase prices by any more than 0.5d for the cheapest seats

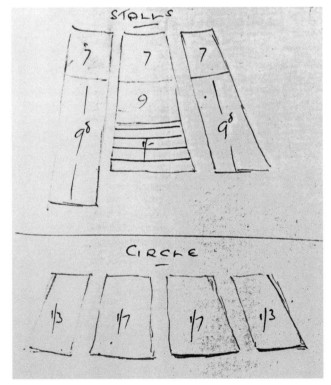

The revised pricing structure is illustrated in this sketch

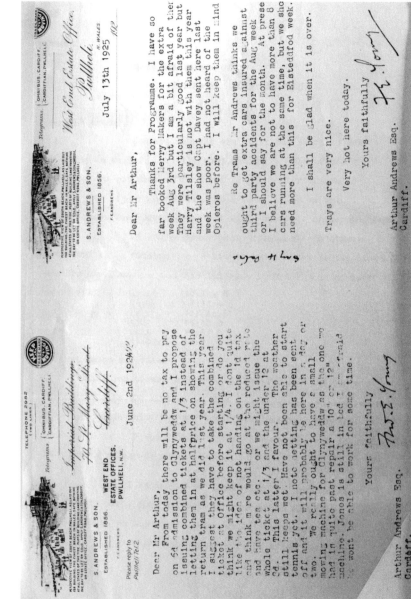

TELEPHONE 2982
(TWO LINES)

Telegrams { OMNIBUS, CARDIFF.
CARDIFFIAN, PWLLHELI.

S. ANDREWS & SON.
ESTABLISHED 1856.

WEST END
ESTATE OFFICES,
PWLLHELI, N.W.

Please reply to
Pwllheli Tel 2

June 2nd 1924

Dear Mr Arthur,

From today, there will be no tax to pay on 5d admission to Glynyweddw and I propose issuing combined tickets at 1/3 instead of letting them in at halfprice on showing the return tram as we did last year. This year I suggest they have to take the combined ticket at Office before starting or do you think we might keep it at 1/4. I dont quite like the idea of not handing on the 1d tax and think m re would go at the reduced rate and have tea etc. or we might issue the whole ticket at 1/3 and the under 12 at 6d. This latter I favour. The weather still keeps wet. Have not been able to start tennis yet. I note letting has been sent off and it will probably be here in a day or two. We really ought to have a small mowing machine for Glynyweddw as the one we had is quite past repair a 10" or 12" machine Jones is still in bed I am afraid he wont be able to work for some time.

Yours faithfully,

Fras.E. Young

Arthur Andrews Esq.
Cardiff.

Telegrams { OMNIBUS, CARDIFF.
CARDIFFIAN, PWLLHELI.

West End Estate Office,
Pwllheli.
N. WALES

S. ANDREWS & SON,
ESTABLISHED 1856.

July 13th 1925
192

Dear Mr Arthur,

Thanks for Programme. I have so far booked Merry Makers for the extra week Aug 3rd but I am a bit afraid of them They were particularly good last year but Harry Tilsley is not with them this year and the show Capt Davey sent here last week was poor. I had not heard of the Opleros before. I will keep them in mind

Re Trams Mr Andrews thinks we ought to get extra cars insured against third party accidents for the Aug week or I should say for the month. At prese I believe we are not to have more than 8 cars running at the same time, but we sho need more than this for Eisteddfod week.

I shall be glad when it is over.

Trays are very nice.

Very hot here today.

Yours faithfully

F.E. Young

Arthur Andrews Esq.
Cardiff.

The Central Cinema,
HANNAH STREET, PORTH.

Thursday Afternoon, December 14th, 1922
at 2.30

AMY EVANS
THE WORLD FAMOUS SOPRANO

"A singer with a voice of gold."   "Worth trudging miles barefoot to hear."

AND

FRASER GANGE

THE WORLD-RENOWNED SCOTTISH BARITONE.

"An artist to his finger-tips."   "A magnetic personality and voice of arresting quality."

—Westminster Gazette.

"*Their success was prodigious*"

WITH

MR. SYDNEY THOMAS
The Well-known Pianist.

Reserved and Numbered Seats, **5 9** and **3 6** : Unreserved Seats, **2 4** : Admission, **1 3**
all including Tax.

Plan and Tickets at Messrs. Jones & Jones' Music Stores, Hannah Street.

Doors open at 2 p.m.

Vail & Co., London, E.C.1.

Cinema managers were keen to attract a 'higher class of patron' by offering alternative
forms of entertainment. For this valleys cinema, however, the attempt to introduce variety 'did not pay off'

The New Film Society
COLWYN BAY

SECOND
Annual General Meeting

to be held at the

St. Paul's Church Room, Rhiw Road
COLWYN BAY

on

WEDNESDAY, 31st MAY, 1944

at 7.30 p.m.

AGENDA

1. To receive the Second Annual Report and audited Accounts

2. Election of Officers and Committee

3. Election of Honorary Auditor

4. Any other business

JOYCE HERBERT,
Hon. Secretary.

The membership of Colwyn Bay's film society had reached 820 by 1944.

FILMS SHOWN DURING THE SECOND SEASON, 1943-44

MAIN FILMS

Un Carnet de Bal	France, 1937	September 26th
Lenin in October	U.S.S.R., 1937	October 10th
Le Roi s'Amuse	France, 1938	October 31st
Film and Reality	Great Britain, 1942	November 21st
The Virtuous Isidore	France, 1931	December 12th
Burgtheater	Austria, 1937	January 9th
Citizen Kane	U.S.A., 1941	January 30th
Masquerade	U.S.S.R., 1941	February 20th
Stage Coach	U.S.A., 1939	March 12th
Hotel du Nord	France, 1939	April 2nd

SHORT FILMS
Documentary and Travel

Memories of Europe	U.S.A., 1942	September 26th
Inside Fascist Spain	U.S.A., 1942	October 31st
Malta Convoy	Great Britain, 1943	December 12th
Listen to Britain	Great Britain, 1942	December 12th
Quebec at War	Great Britain, 1942	January 9th
St. Moritz	Great Britain	March 12th
Athens	France	April 2nd
Danger Area	Great Britain, 1943	April 23rd
Cowboy	U.S.A., 1943	April 23rd
Autobiography of a Jeep	U.S.A., 1943	April 23rd
Pipeline	U.S.A., 1942	April 23rd
West Indies Calling	Great Britain, 1943	April 23rd
The Silent Village	Great Britain, 1943	April 23rd

Historical and Technical Interest

Calling Mr. Smith	Great Britain, 1943	February 20th
Brahms' Hungarian Dance	Germany, 1931	January 9th

Here is a selection of the films screened

III

Responses to Film-Going in Wales

The final section of this book addresses the responses generated by the cinema's mass appeal, and in doing so demonstrates the extent to which cinema had become a central component of Welsh popular culture. For the representatives of Liberal and Labour Wales, the remarkable appeal of cinema entertainment could be seen either as a threat or an opportunity. The fear was that mass consumption of this commercial (and mostly American) entertainment would erode the traditional values and beliefs that constituted Welsh culture and identity. The hope was that, properly used, cinema might serve to promote such values and beliefs, and strengthen existing cultural traditions within Wales. Responses to this form of entertainment, accordingly, took two distinct forms. Chapter 6 recounts how critics and cultural commentators in Wales highlighted the failings of existing commercial cinema entertainment, and sought to encourage a body of film-making that would reflect the cultural and political concerns of the Welsh themselves. This took a variety of forms, from the creation of film societies to calls for a Welsh Films Council. Ultimately, however, such efforts failed to have any influence on the type of entertainment screened in commercial cinemas. Chapter 7 focuses on the role played by political and cultural leaders in regulating and controlling the potentially harmful influence of cinema-going. Most of the regulations enforced by local authorities in Wales, concerning issues of health and safety or the attendance of children, were in line with developments elsewhere in Britain. The Sunday opening of cinemas, however, was widely regarded as a threat to an important (if only recently 'invented') national tradition, and was firmly resisted by representatives both of Liberal and Labour Wales.

6

CRITICS

Cinema-going in the 1930s was famously described by the historian A. J. P. Taylor as the 'essential social habit of the age'.[1] This book argues that this was as true of Wales as any other part of Britain. Yet while cinema-going had become a regular weekly activity for at least one third of the population, the majority of films shown were American-made. Cinema may have been the most popular form of mass public entertainment in Britain, but this entertainment was not usually British and it was almost never Welsh. How did those most concerned about the protection, and promotion, of British or Welsh culture respond to such a state of affairs?

This chapter examines the views expressed in different sections of British and Welsh society about the mass appeal of the cinema, and explores the efforts made by various groups to utilize the medium for their own cultural or political interests. The chapter devotes roughly equal amounts of space to the critical response to the cinema in Britain as a whole, and to Wales in particular. Part of the reason for this is that the national, London-based papers were widely read in Wales. The Welsh local or regional papers tended to be read in addition to, not instead of, the national press. It is also necessary to write at some length about the social/cultural context from which British film criticism emerged because relatively little attempt has been made to do this before. The contrasting styles of film journalists in London and Wales did not necessarily reflect national differences. Film columnists in the local or regional press, however, do provide a quite different insight into the way the cinema was regarded than that which we get from the national press. It is in the local papers that the cinema's position as a social institution, rather than just a place for screening films, comes across most clearly.

The chapter is divided into four sections. In the first it is argued that conflicting attitudes to the cinema held by different sections of the English middle class reflected deep-seated social and cultural divisions within that social group. The second section focuses more specifically on what was written about the medium by contemporary newspaper critics and reporters in Britain as a whole at this time. It seeks to identify and explore the distinction between 'critic' and 'reporter'. In the third section attention is turned to Wales where the political and cultural mores of a relatively recently established middle class were plainly evident in critical debates surrounding the cinema. It also demonstrates that there was a demand in Wales for films other than the regular output of Hollywood studios: a number of film societies and workmen's institutes screened non-commercial films in this period which often held particular cultural or political interest for local audiences. The final section examines the output of film reporters in Wales. Writing specifically for a local audience, they tended to take a rather different approach to London-based critics, focusing the attractions offered by individual cinemas, rather than the appeal of particular films.

Cinema and the middle classes in Britain

The emergence of film criticism in Britain was by no means synonymous with the development of the cinema. For roughly the first twenty-five years of its existence the cinema was not taken seriously by those who aspired to any kind of social or intellectual respectability. No national newspapers had a regular film critic, and there were no specialist journals devoted to serious analysis of films. An impression of the way in which educated middle-class opinion viewed the cinema is provided by C. A. Lejeune, whose film reviews for the *Observer* were to make her one of the most popular and respected critics of her generation:

> When I first went to the pictures, I remember how my friends and I used to hide behind the bill-boards outside the theatre, in case one of our relations came by and discovered us in the queue, or some other girl from school told tales about the way we spent our evenings. And even some time later, at college, I remember how we thought our Professor of English a very gay old dog, because he paid his sixpence regularly to see Nazimova and Pauline Frederick at the local picture house.[2]

Even as Lejeune made these comments, the commercial products of the British and American film industries were still viewed with disdain by many critics. The medium itself, however, had at least managed to win some new and influential converts. But which sections of the middle class had been won over, and what role did film critics have to play in their conversion?

In a famous and much quoted essay written during the Second World War, George Orwell contrasted two 'important sub-sections of the middle-class', which he regarded as 'symbolic opposites'. 'One was the military and imperialist middle class, generally nicknamed the Blimps, and the other the left-wing intelligentsia.' The Blimps, the Empire builders and administrators, had even before 1914 begun to lose some of their vitality. Their brand of blind patriotism and anti-intellectualism, however, was never far below the surface of both popular and official opinion in inter-war Britain. The intelligentsia, on the other hand, although not without influence, had largely been excluded from positions of official authority:

If you had the kind of brain that could understand the poems of T. S. Eliot or the theories of Karl Marx, the higher-ups would see to it that you were kept out of any important job. The intellectuals could find a function for themselves only in the literary reviews and the left wing political parties.

To literary reviews can easily be added film criticism, for the qualities that characterized the English intelligentsia, as Orwell saw it, were precisely those that underpinned the more serious film reviews. He asserted, for instance, that 'the English intelligentsia are Europeanized. They take their cookery from Paris and their opinions from Moscow.' Film critics, similarly, were most enthusiastic about the work of directors such as Eisenstein, Pudovkin, Pabst and Clair. The contempt which Orwell claimed the intellectuals had for 'every English institution, from horse racing to suet puddings' also applied to British films. Further, the journals that Orwell cites as the principal organs of the intellectual left, the *New Statesman* and the *News Chronicle*, were precisely those in which such critics wrote.[3]

By the 1930s, the intellectual wing of the English middle class dominated the writing of serious film criticism. Indeed, it could be said that they had a profound influence on the development of film in Britain more generally. How had this happened? The establishment of the Film Society in 1925 was certainly an important development. It was set up 'in order that works of interest in the study of cinematography, and not yet easily accessible, might be made available to its members'. The members themselves were drawn from a variety of fields, and included H. G. Wells, George Bernard Shaw, Julian Huxley, J. B. S. Haldane and John Maynard Keynes. As Jen Samson has observed: 'The new and controversial foreign films which the Film Society imported into Britain during the late 1920s and throughout the 1930s not only increased esteem for the medium among the intelligentsia, but also had an effect on the development of British film production.'[4] In the same year (1929) as Grierson's *Drifters* was first shown to the Film Society, he also set up a film unit at the Empire Marketing Board.

Within two years of the first Film Society meeting, the first journal devoted to serious film criticism had been launched. As Charles Barr has noted: '*Close-Up* belongs to the early years of the Film Society movement, and the discovery by a generation of intellectuals of the cinema as an art form.'[5] In 1932 *Cinema Quarterly* first went into print, a journal with close associations to the documentary movement. This period also saw the launch of *Sight and Sound* and *World Film News*, as well as the introduction of film criticism in such journals as the *Spectator, News Chronicle, New Statesman, The Listener* and on the BBC. A generation of British film critics emerged in the late 1920s and 30s who regularly contributed to these journals, among them Roger Manvell, Paul Rotha, R. S. Lambert, Dilys Powell, C. A. Lejeune, Richard Winnington, William Whitebait, Graham Greene and Alistair Cooke. While Graham Greene and Alistair Cooke are much more well known for their work in other fields, they can legitimately be viewed as part of a generation of film critics who sought to highlight the artistic and educational properties of this new medium.

These critics, though important in lending the cinema a new artistic and intellectual respectability, were not alone in attempting to take films up-market. Among the more patriotic elements of the middle class were also to be found advocates of the new medium. For this group, the cinema's potential as a medium of national expression, rather than its artistic development, was the primary concern. As a letter, published in *The Times* in 1932, argued:

> No close study of films and talkies is needed to convince one that the British point of view is neglected oversea[s]. There is little enough shown with 'home' as a setting; practically nothing of the Empire, that treasure-house of colour and drama . . . the remedy lies with the layman at home. If he encourages our own people to produce work which by sheer merit outsails that of the other man on every tack; if he insists on clean humour, on technical excellence, on plots which can be shown to children without hesitation and to the East without scruple he will get what he wants: that link will be forged. But if he goes on tolerating foreign extravagances which proclaim the white races to be nothing but degenerate half-wits, we shall pay the cost some day.[6]

The paper itself strongly endorsed these sentiments: 'The British Empire should know itself; and the world should know the British Empire.'[7] Such concerns had led to the establishment, in 1929, of the Commission on Educational and Cultural Films. The Commission's 1932 report, *The Film in National Life*, devoted a chapter to 'The Cinema and the Empire' in which it was argued:

> The backward races within the Empire can gain more and suffer more from the film than the sophisticated European, because to them the power of the visual medium is intensified. The conception of white civilisation which they are receiving from third-rate melodrama is an international menace, yet the film is an agent of social education which could be as powerful for good as for harm.

The authors of the report concluded that a National Film Institute needed to be established, 'an important branch' of which 'should deal with Imperial and Colonial film affairs'.[8]

The concerns expressed in this report and in editorials in *The Times* were by no means new. Patriotic initiatives to promote British film production pre-date the establishment of the more highbrow Film Society. The British National Film League was established in 1921, which aimed 'to encourage the production and exhibition of British-made films'. One of the ways it attempted to do this was by launching a campaign of British Film Weeks. The intention was to arrange as many bookings as possible for British films in a single week, which could then be shown in different areas on successive weeks. The first of the Film Weeks was scheduled for November 1923, and according to *Bioscope* among those present at the launch of the campaign were 'leading members of the diplomatic corps, Colonial and Dominion representatives . . . Members of Parliament, legal luminaries, civic dignitaries, the Army and Navy, and practically everyone who matters in the social scale.'[9] The campaign, which did not eventually get underway until February 1924, did little to stimulate British film production. However, the interest clearly taken by the traditionally patriotic sections of the middle class in raising the prestige of British films is worth noting. Their influence can also be detected in the 1927 Films Act, which sought to stimulate British film production (if not to encourage the development of a specific type of British film).[10]

The lack of interest shown in the artistic properties of the film infuriated highbrow critics. Indeed, the blind support shown to British pictures (regardless of their 'quality') by journalists and politicians led Paul Rotha to argue that the British film lay on a 'hollow foundation':

> It rests upon a structure of false prestige, supported by the flatulent flapdoodle of newspaper writers and by the indifferent goodwill of the British people . . . Well-merited castigation would have laid bare, and therefore more easily remedied, the root of the evil. Instead, there have been British Film Weeks and National Film Campaigns which have nourished the cancer in the film industry. As it is, the British film is spoon-fed by deceptive praise and quota regulations, with the unhappy result that it has not yet discovered its nationality.[11]

What concerned Rotha and others was that British studios in the 1920s had failed to develop their own distinctive style of film-making. The British Film Weeks, which intended to promote 'British films for British people', were an anathema to critics who did not necessarily regard a film made in Britain as a truly British film.[12] One of the films promoted as part of the Film Weeks campaign was Cecil Hepworth's *Comin' Thro' The Rye* (1923). Here was an example of a film which made every effort both to be distinctively British, and to appeal to a higher class of audience. As Andrew Higson has demonstrated, however, though widely praised in the national press, the film failed to match up to the artistic standards set by the emerging generation of cinema critics, and has seldom featured in discussions on British cinema since.[13]

Hepworth claimed in his autobiography that: 'It was always in the back of my mind from the very beginning that I was to make English pictures, with all the English countryside for background and with English atmosphere and English idiom throughout.' His adaptation of Helen Mathers's 1875 novel was clearly an attempt to do just this. The film can be seen as part of the process of mythologizing the English countryside, which reached new heights during the inter-war period.[14] Higson regards it as a 'heritage film' and argues that it represents an early (pre-Film Society) attempt to appeal to more up-market audiences, and to utilize film for artistic purposes. The thoroughly traditional notion of Englishness represented in this literary adaptation, however, was totally at odds with the modernist principles upon which film was later to establish itself as an art form. Higson, recognizing that historians of British cinema from Rachael Low to Roy Armes have tended to dismiss the film as 'retrogressive', draws attention to the mixed response it received at the time. Its emphasis on tradition, landscape and heritage, as opposed to more modern editing techniques and narrative structures was 'neither summarily dismissed nor unhesitatingly celebrated'. Further, the most positive reviews came from the *Bioscope* and *The Times*, suggesting, perhaps, that Hepworth's film had some success in appealing to the more patriotic sections of the middle class.

The lack of intellectual film criticism in 1923 makes it difficult to compare high- and middlebrow responses to *Comin' Thro' The Rye*. It can only be asserted that while the film did win a certain amount of acclaim from reporters at the time, it has been largely overlooked by critics ever since. Hepworth's film was clearly far removed from the product of Hollywood studios, and he might be viewed as attempting to take British films up-market by aiming at the more patriotic section of the middle class. By the early 1930s, however, the intelligentsia (limited as they were to 'the literary reviews and left wing political parties') had come to determine what constituted an 'artistic' film. The relative influence of these two sections of the middle class over British cinema is hinted at by the only Government sponsored film unit. When established in 1929 the unit was located within the *Empire* Marketing Board. It was soon dominated, however, by the most *intellectually* acclaimed of British film-makers – the documentarists, led by John Grierson. Within a couple of years the unit had been rehoused at the GPO.

Critics and reporters in the national press

The more patriotic element within the English middle class continued to exert influence over government film policy in this period, but it was from the intelligentsia that the emerging generation of film critics were drawn. To focus too closely on the writings of the above critics, however, obscures the fact that much else was being written about the cinema in the national press in the 1920s and 30s. The growing popularity of the cinema (as a form of entertainment rather than an art form) led many of the national daily papers to devote more attention to Hollywood films, and their stars, in order to attract and interest readers. A distinction came to be drawn in the 1930s, therefore, between 'critics' and 'reporters'.

'Critics' usually wrote in weekly or monthly publications and were most interested in the intellectual possibilities that the medium provided. Above all they wanted to see films that would make audiences *think*, but recognized that such films would not be made unless there was a demand for them. Critics, therefore, saw their role as being essentially an educational one: to teach their readers to appreciate, and demand, intelligent films. As Dilys Powell, reflecting on her early days as film critic for the *Sunday Times* admitted: 'I suppose in a kind of impertinent way I did want to educate my readers. I probably thought I must persuade people to go and see this film which I liked very much, which moved me.'[15] These critics were often as damning of what they saw as the indiscriminate consumption of 'film-addicts' as they were of individual films themselves. For the likes of Roger Manvell and Richard Winnington, unless the cinema-going public learned to be selective in their choice of films, major studios would have no incentive to provide audiences with anything other than 'mental dope'.[16]

Reporters, on the other hand, were less interested in shifting popular taste than in reflecting it. Those who reviewed films in the national daily press often had little or no specialist knowledge of film-making or of the cinema industry. As Guy Morgan, film 'reporter' for the *Daily Express* explained, they were simply journalists who happened to be writing about films. As such 'the "lay" critic's first responsibility is to his editor, for a feature in his paper that people, not necessarily filmgoers, will read on its own merits.' He went on to argue that

> There is no difference between the film critic of a popular newspaper and a reasonably observant film fan except that the former has more regular opportunities for seeing films, wider standards of comparison and greater practice in summing up films quickly according to the journalistic require-ments of his paper. For this reason 'film reporter' is a fairer designation than 'film critic'. His approach is of necessity more informative than critical.[17]

Graham Greene, film critic of the *Spectator*, had made the same distinction between critics and reporters two years earlier (in 1936). He placed himself firmly within the former category:

> One need not deny to either books or films of popular middle-class entertain-ment a useful social service, as long as it is recognised that social service has nothing to do with the art of the cinema or the art of fiction. What I object to is that it is the *critic's* business to assist films to fulfil a social function. The critic's business should be confined to the art.

The problem that Greene went on to identify was that, because only 'two or three films in the year can be treated with respect', the serious critic had a limited amount of material about which to write. The solution he proposed was for critics to be more 'satirical'. 'We need to be rude, rude even to our fellow reviewers ... Indeed, I am not sure whether our fellow critics are not more important subjects for our satire than the cinema itself, for they are doing as much as any Korda or Sam Goldwyn to maintain the popular middle-class Book Society *status quo.*'[18]

This distinction between critics and reporters was also alluded to by C. A. Lejeune in 1934. She felt that 'it is one of the cinema's misfortunes that film criticism . . . has been consistently bad both in this country and America, while film journalism . . . has been consistently efficient.' Although a respected film critic herself, Lejeune also considered herself a film fan, and felt that there was a need for the gulf between critics and reporters to be bridged: 'What we need, and what we have not yet got in this country, is a catholic criticism, which will recognise the distinctive qualities of the best continental pictures, but give just as much care and attention to the mass products of England and America.'[19]

The obstacles in the way of bridging this gap and developing a more 'catholic' criticism were formidable. The comments of Graham Greene and Guy Morgan illustrate not only that critics and reporters were aware of their differences, they saw themselves as performing quite separate roles. They wrote for very different readerships, coming from contrasting cultural backgrounds and whose views of what cinema should represent can be seen as polar opposites:

Critic	Reporter
Cinema as art	Cinema as entertainment
European/international	British/patriotic
Intellectual	Popular
Experimental use of film	Adaptations from literature/theatre
Modernist aesthetics	Traditional settings/genres

Not all those who wrote film reviews in this period fitted neatly into one of the above categories. The distinction was real enough, however, for Paul Rotha to draw attention, in 1934, to 'two different tendencies' within contemporary cinema:

> On the one side, there is the accepted standard of story-film, making use of orthodox ideas of acting and studio routine and still having much in common with the theatre; while on the other there is the increasing interest being taken in documentary cinema, which springs direct from the fundamental requirements of the medium and is principally concerned with an approach to modern existence. The two types are well contrasted in *The Private Life of Henry VIII* and *Kameradschaft.*[20]

A brief comparison of these two films is instructive. To take the latter first, G. W. Pabst's *Kameradschaft* (1932) in many respects epitomizes the sort of qualities most frequently praised by the highbrow film critics. Set on the Franco-German border, the film tells the story of a mining disaster in which trapped French workers are rescued by their German counterparts. The film demonstrates the artificial nature of national boundaries, and its implied message ('workers of the world unite') evidently appealed to those who could 'understand the theories of Karl Marx'. It was not so much the film's political message that attracted critical acclaim, however, but its distinctive cinematic style, which applied documentary-like realism to a feature film.[21] The sort of lavish praise the film received at the time was clearly expressed by Francis Birrell in *The New Statesman*:

> It is not easy to convey to the reader the singular beauty of the photography, which is placed in this realistic and murky setting. Yet the photography has a rhythm of its own, which becomes more apparent with familiarity. There is nothing pretentious about it. You never feel that either the settings or the actors have been elaborately posed before the camera in order to get an 'artistic' shot. The whole thing is a 'movie'.[22]

Similar sentiments were expressed in *The Spectator* and *Close-Up*, while Roger Manvell, re-assessing the picture for *Sight and Sound* in 1950, argued that the film survives 'as the work of an artist, and not as an effective example of contemporary propaganda'.[23] Highbrow critics were clearly impressed by the film's realism, while its innovative cinematic style and structure were clearly regarded as artistic (though not 'arty'). Its influence can be measured by the number of mining films that followed in its wake.[24] It is possible, however, to detect a rather different emphasis in the reviews of the national 'lay' press. *The Times*, for instance, though approving of the film's realism in terms of photography, settings and acting, argued that 'it is more important that this admirable technique is put at the service of an emotional conflict, a story which is really fascinating'.[25] Even this organ of respectable middle-class opinion apparently felt that entertainment was as important as art in the making of feature films.

Sue Harper has described *The Private Life of Henry VIII* as 'a significant cultural innovation' but for rather different reasons. She points out that 'Korda had developed a film theory which eschewed realism', and that he believed the film's (female) target audience to be unreceptive to 'historical exactitude'. Korda's intention was clearly to appeal to popular taste, not to aim above it. As such he distanced himself from 'characterless' international pictures, arguing that 'the more typically national a film is . . . the more general its appeal will be.'[26]

The Private Life of Henry VIII was a huge commercial success, not just in Britain, but also in Europe and the US. The critical response to the film in Britain, unsurprisingly, was mixed. It would be an oversimplification to draw too clear a distinction between, on the one hand, highbrow contempt for the film, and on the other, patriotic delight that a British film had at last proved a match for the most successful Hollywood productions. The acting of Charles Laughton, in particular, won acclaim from the more intellectual critics, while there were those of a more patriotic persuasion who felt the film presented the wrong image of Britain to overseas audiences. Lord Cottenham, writing in *The Daily Telegraph*, thought the picture showed Henry to be a 'dissolute buffoon' and argued that 'those who love the empire contemplate with anger and disgust the world-wide distribution of a vulgar travesty of history such as this'. Nonetheless, attitudes to this film were largely determined by one's position on the broader question of what exactly the cinema was meant to be. Those most concerned with the artistic properties of the medium had more cause to view the film in a critical light than those for whom cinema was primarily a form of entertainment.

Significantly, the views expressed by Lord Cottenham in *The Daily Telegraph* were not echoed by that paper's film reporters: 'Whether this is Merrie England is a matter on which dons may differ. It is certainly first rate cinema.' Similarly, *The Times* reviewer felt that 'Neither comment [on situations] nor arrangement [of characters], would be altogether bearable in a book, but they are very amusing in a film'. What matter if 'it is an emotional and ignorant picture of the past' asked *The Evening News*, when 'the childish imaginings in dusty schoolrooms have been suddenly and warmly brought to life'? To the film reporters of the national press, it would appear, *Henry VIII*'s artistic deficiencies were more than compensated for by its sheer entertainment value.[27]

There is evidence to suggest that the more intellectual critics took a far less tolerant attitude to the film's shortcomings. Alistair Cooke, in *Sight and Sound*, complained that '*Cavalcade* and *The Private Life of Henry VIII* have between them a lot to answer for. Either of them might have been spared so that we might also have been spared the pre-occupation with Epic which they have unwittingly provoked.'[28] Cooke, writing a year after *Henry VIII*'s release, was much more critical than many 'highbrow' reviewers had initially been. He attacked the popular response to the picture as much as the film itself. For Cooke, and many critics like him, films such as *Kameradschaft* were true 'movies' while 'epics' like *Henry VIII* were merely commercial enterprises with no artistic merit. That the latter were so popular with audiences was a matter for regret, but also a situation which critics felt it their 'duty' to try and change.

Critical responses to the cinema in Wales

Patriotism and intellectualism were both in evidence in Wales in this period, though the polarized distinction which Orwell drew between Blimps and highbrows is of less value when applied to the middle class in Wales. This was a social group that emerged and developed a distinctive identity in the latter part of the nineteenth century. In an incisive essay on culture and identity in late modern Wales, David Smith identified a Welsh 'clerisy' which 'traced out the elements of higher Welsh culture'.[29] The emergence of this distinctively Welsh middle class was a feature of the increasing sense of self-confidence so characteristic of Liberal Wales. It could count among its number the likes of T. E. Ellis and David Lloyd George: men with an acute awareness of their distinctive Welsh identity, but who took equal pride in Wales's central position within the British Empire. Thus Tom Ellis, in replying to a toast at the British Empire Club in 1892 to 'The Principality of Wales', asserted that '[t]he more Wales has the power of initiative and decision in her own affairs, the more closely will she be bound to the very texture of the imperial fabric.'[30]

Smith identifies a politically and economically confident middle class which was proudly patriotic. Yet he also argues that this was a class 'consumed with the guilt of an achievement that implicitly denied its origins'.[31] The new-found prosperity and political centrality of Liberal Wales was rooted firmly in the industrialization of (mainly) south Wales. The huge influx of migrants into the steelworks and coal mines of Glamorgan and Monmouthshire, which saw the combined population of those two counties rise from under 600,000 in 1871 to over 1.7 million half a century later,[32] provided the bedrock upon which Wales's contribution to the empire was built. Yet while almost two-thirds of the Welsh population lived in one of these two counties by the end of the First World War,[33] they had no place in the image of Wales which was being constructed by the main beneficiaries of this social and economic transformation. Rather, the Welsh 'clerisy' preferred to place a mythologized *gwerin* at the heart of its cherished national identity.

The *gwerin* can be broadly described as a classless folk: inhabitants of small, isolated communities in Welsh-speaking, rural Wales; yet highly cultured and 'enlightened' by a combination of self-education and Nonconformist religion. As Gwyn A. Williams noted: 'It was in the last decade before the War, when anything resembling a *gwerin* was fast disappearing from Welsh earth, that the *gwerin*'s self-appointed voices filled the Welsh air.'[34] Those self-appointed voices were those of the Liberal Welsh 'clerisy' whose hallmark was cultural nationalism. Thus, as Gareth Elwyn Jones puts it: 'There was some substance in the *gwerin* myth, but it ignored, or was antipathetic towards, that most revolutionary element in Welsh history, industrialisation.'[35]

Attempts to locate the national genius of modern industrial powers within a 'timeless' rural heritage is by no means unique to Wales. Similar tendencies have existed in, among other places, the US, Germany and England. In the very act of expressing their national identity and distinctiveness, therefore, the cultural 'establishment' within Wales were following a well established pattern. Something similar can be said of attitudes to the cinema commonly expressed by the Welsh middle class. The terms in which the commercial cinema was criticized within Wales, as we shall see, were broadly consistent with concerns being raised across Britain. Efforts to draw attention to the potential importance of the cinema as a national cultural institution in Wales were certainly in keeping with the values and assumptions of the more patriotic sections of the English middle class.

The emergence of the cinema in the early twentieth century was a significant feature in the process of modernization – indeed Americanization – of Welsh society. Unsurprisingly, there were serious objections raised about the cultural threat this new form of popular amusement posed. Yet, while much of the entertainment provided in the picture houses was subject to moral or intellectual condemnation, there was also an acknowledgement that the medium itself provided a valuable means by which traditional Welsh culture might be brought to a much wider audience. This was certainly a common theme in many of the serious articles concerned with the cinema in Welsh newspapers. Ifor Evans, a professor of English Literature at Southampton University, was one who made the point forcefully, recognizing that 'the cinema is not merely an idle amusement, but an international power of no mean importance in the world of today'. Yet he went on to ask:

What is being done in Wales? As a nation we are sometimes accused of not treating the arts, apart from music, with sufficient seriousness, and certainly as far as literature is concerned we are not known to the world at large. It is said that the ghost of a puritan conscience lurks amongst us that leads us to consider drama and the kindred arts as the wanton pastimes of the Evil One . . . [Yet] it is a fallacy to condemn any instrument because that instrument is at times abused. One might as well condemn music because one dislikes some piece of jazz played by some hack orchestra in a dance hall . . . In a superlative way the cinema is the medium through which a small nation can express itself to the world. Few foreigners will master our language, but through this silent language of the film we can tell the world much of our customs and our history.[36]

An editorial in the same edition of the *Western Mail* warmly endorsed such sentiments, adding that:

In the development of the cinema we must avoid making the mistake that was made in the development of the drama – the mistake, we mean, of allowing these old prejudices to blind us to its tremendous possibilities as an art, as a vehicle of expressing contemporary life, and also as a means of communicating to the world our rich heritage of folk-lore, history and romance.[37]

An article published in the same paper the following year went as far as to suggest that the northern coastal resort of Colwyn Bay might become a 'Hollywood for Wales'. It argued that the attractive marine and mountain scenery, the atmosphere (which was suitable for photography) and the climate (which 'would enable the production work to proceed without a halt all year round') made Colwyn Bay 'an ideal place for a British Hollywood'.[38]

There is clearly a certain amount of overlap between the sentiments being expressed here, and those of the patriotic wing of the English middle class.[39] Middle-class commentators in Wales did not exhibit the sort of anti-intellectualism that Orwell detected among the Blimps, but there certainly was a strong emphasis on the importance of projecting a positive national image to the rest of the world. Further, the suggested themes are those of romantic legends, beautiful landscape and ancient heritage. In Wales, as elsewhere, middle-class interest in the cinema was provoked at least as much by cultural nationalism as it was by any intellectual concern for film art.

For those who saw the representation of Wales on screen as an important objective, film criticism was not necessarily regarded as a means of achieving it. Whereas film critics in the national press hoped that by writing intelligently about film they could create a demand for the kind of pictures they deemed to be of artistic merit; within Wales, the total cinema going-public was simply too small to generate the sort of demand that might attract the interest of film companies in London or the US. Not until the Second World War, and then for rather different reasons, did British studios make a conscious effort to include Welsh characters and settings into their films.[40]

Those expressing the desire for an image of Wales to be projected onto cinema screens in the inter-war decades felt that the initiative needed to come from within Wales itself. The encouragement of indigenous film production, rather than a more enlightened criticism of what was being made elsewhere, preoccupied the more film-minded Welsh middle class. Early suggestions as to how this might be brought about were, at best, highly optimistic. Ifor Evans, for instance, having outlined a grand vision of what a Welsh film industry might be able to achieve, could only pose the question: 'Does there exist in Wales the man of wealth and initiative who will give Welsh art an opportunity?'[41] By the 1930s the debate had moved on. The publication of *The Film In National Life* in 1932 and the subsequent establishment of the British Film Institute (BFI), led those who hoped that the cinema would become a 'respectable' cultural force within Wales to call for a Welsh Film Council. In October 1936 a group of Welsh members of the BFI decided to form themselves into a body called the Film Institute Society of Wales. They gathered together representatives of religious organizations, local authorities, social services, public institutions and academic bodies at a meeting in Cardiff University to call for the formation of a Film Council of Wales. Also present was the general manager of the BFI, Oliver Bell, who expressed support for the idea of a central administrative organization which could cater for the particular cultural and educational needs of Wales.[42] The idea was warmly endorsed in an article by Harold Dowling in the *Western Mail* the following week:

> Very little thought is needed to show that if this council can become a really effective working instrument Wales cannot but reap enormous benefit from its

activities. The film, a method of education, culture and propaganda as yet in its infancy, will in the future become an increasingly potent influence in the life of the nation. Its possibilities as an instrument of enlightenment are only limited by the technique of its art, a technique which is approaching nearer to perfection every day.

The group of intellectual, religious and political authorities that were represented at this meeting were about as reflective of a bourgeois Welsh 'clerisy' as it was possible to be. It is interesting to note, therefore, that in discussing the make-up of a future Film Council of Wales, Dowling was quick to stress that, 'its activities must not be confined to Cardiff or even to South Wales . . . It is only common sense to suggest that such bodies as the National Museum, the National Library, the Free Church Council, the YMCA and the universities should be strongly represented on the executive body if the council is to be truly representative of the nation.'[43]

Just as the landscape and traditions associated with the rural *gwerin* were felt to provide the obvious background for screen depictions of Wales, so the institutions established by the middle class of Liberal Wales were seen as being 'truly representative of the nation'. There was evidently no place in such a national outlook for trade unions, miners' institutes, or any other institution that reflected the social and cultural experience of industrial south Wales. Yet how far did this view of Wales, and of the cinema's position within Welsh society (usually expressed in the pages of the *Western Mail*), actually reflect the views of the Welsh middle class? The question cannot be answered with certainty, but evidence of alternative viewpoints can be detected in a debate among readers generated by one such article, and published in the paper's letter columns.

In 1938 D. P. Williams wrote a long article in the *Western Mail* entitled 'It is Time Wales Told Her Story on the Screen'. The gist of his argument was familiar enough. He began by suggesting that 'Wales must by this time be almost, if not quite, the last country in Europe which has not tried to use the film as a means of self-expression'. Yet he felt that 'Our country is a paradise of the film director and cameraman', in terms of both subjects and settings. Indeed, he claimed that 'there is enough potential drama in Wales to keep the studios of London and Hollywood working for a lifetime'. However, Williams was not content to rely upon British or American film companies to produce screen images of Wales. He hoped that a body of Welsh film-makers would emerge who could create authentic, if low-budget, pictures of their own country. 'The important thing', he stressed, 'is not to ape foreign methods, but to make films that really express Wales.' Thus, while he congratulated the Cardiff Amateur Cine Society in 1937 for making an apparently successful film at a tiny cost,[44] 'the Welshman in me was pained to see this effort wasted on a thriller about a Chinese cabinet that might equally well have been made in Leeds or Inverness or Norwich'.[45]

The initial response to this article was supportive. Expressing contempt for the mainstream feature films with the greatest popular appeal, a correspondent with the pen-name 'Anti-Box Office' complained that

> The immense output of the commercial studios in the United States, Britain and France has made the term cinema synonymous with the machine-made products with which the public is almost exclusively familiar. Stripped of the 'production values' . . . 99 per cent of these stock articles are built on the tattered formula of 'boy meets girl'.

This criticism, like much of that coming from middle-class 'critics' elsewhere in Britain, identifies commercial interests and systems of mass-production as the reason for the cultural paucity of most film entertainment. Yet, pointing to the success of such countries as Finland and Sweden in producing 'films of imperishable' quality on low budgets, this correspondent saw no reason why the same could not be achieved within Wales. Indeed, he argued that 'the cinema has such a great potential value for Wales that it should be seriously studied and adapted by some cultural organisation which would safeguard it from the abuse to which it is so easily open'.[46]

The views of 'Anti-Box Office' correspond closely to those expressed in various articles published in the *Western Mail* in the inter-war period. An alternative position, however, was taken by another correspondent, this time named 'Realist', who was apparently much closer in outlook to highbrow intellectual opinion. Equally dismissive of mainstream commercial films, 'Realist' argued that the root of the problem was one of demand rather than supply:

> If the people who live in Wales had the slightest desire to see films which have any cultural, educational or national value, or even films which offer some measure of intellectual entertainment, they could have voiced that desire long ago . . . I do not suggest that the Welsh are less appreciative of good entertainment than the English, but I do maintain that if the Welsh really wanted more intelligent films they could easily get them. They need not make the films themselves.

The important objective, according to this argument, was that Welsh people should be encouraged to appreciate high-quality entertainment (whatever its country of origin), preferably through a state-aided circuit of specialist cinemas. The medium's potential to provide a means of national self-expression was a secondary consideration.

> What grounds has 'Anti-Box Office' for suggesting that Wales is in any way specially adapted for the task of raising cinematographic art from the depressing level to which it has sunk in Britain and America? . . . Welsh history and Welsh scenery and institutions doubtless offer scope for good films, but

so, for that matter, do the history, scenery, and institutions of England and most other countries.

'Realist' went on to defend the Cardiff Amateur Cine Society against the criticism it had received from D. P. Williams for failing to make films about Welsh life. He pointed out that only one member of the Society was actually Welsh, and that 'they make films for their own amusement and not with the idea of contributing to Welsh nationalist propaganda'.[47]

With two differing viewpoints so forcefully expressed, a debate was soon underway. 'Anti-Box Office' was quick to defend his/her position, and launched into a further attack on 'Realist's' suggestion that there should be a state-aided cinema in every town. 'Anti-Box Office' argued that the cinema suffered from 'enough capitalistic, political, religious and moral suppressions without putting the millstone of State aid round the neck of a young movement that must have absolute freedom if it is to live at all'.[48] The Rector of St Athan, Stanley Gibbon, joined the debate by expressing support for 'the end "Realist" has in view'. He was also opposed to the idea of state aid, however, and argued for the establishment of a network of voluntary film societies across south Wales which could screen cultural and intellectual films.[49] 'Realist', for his part, made a spirited defence of the argument for state support for the film industry.[50] Other contributors to the debate included Reginald Coath, the secretary of the Cardiff Amateur Cine Society, who, pointing out that his society had 'at least produced something tangible', called for constructive advice or assistance rather than damning criticism from those who claimed to care about film making in Wales.[51] Oliver Bell, by now Director of the BFI, also added his opinion that a documentary film of Wales would be a welcome addition to the body of work already in existence, and that such a film would find a ready market in film societies and schools throughout Britain.[52]

In a second article on the subject of Wales and film, D. P. Williams reiterated his original position while taking account of some of the views that had been expressed since then. He pointed to the twin threats posed to the cinema by those for whom it was no more than escapist entertainment and those who regarded it purely in terms of its 'highbrow' intellectual content. Yet he suggested that they bore little relevance to Wales: 'Sex-appeal and high-browism are not, happily, among the more noticeable failings of Welsh people.' Williams suggested that cinema's popular and intellectual appeal could be married within a national context. He wrote of an industry 'with traces of an art about it' and argued that 'story-documentaries . . . would be popular throughout Wales'.[53]

The question of national identity lay at the heart of the debate. 'Realist', and others, regarded Welsh cinema audiences as being no different to those elsewhere in Britain. Their concern was that such audiences should be encouraged and educated to appreciate better films, whatever their nationality. 'Realist's' suggestion of a state-aided circuit of cinemas would not, presumably, have been limited to Wales. Many of those who expressed their opinions in the Welsh press, on the other hand, clearly did consider the Welsh audience to be a distinct entity, and that by making films of national interest other differences could be overcome.

The majority of the articles relating to the cinema that were published in the *Western Mail* adopted broadly the same position as that of 'Anti-Box Office'. The view expressed by 'Realist', on the other hand, that film should be treated as a serious cultural form rather than an opportunity for national expression, also had its adherents within Wales. This outlook lay behind the establishment of film societies such as that at Colwyn Bay in 1942. Within two years this society, which met on Sunday evenings at the town's Arcadia Theatre, had 820 members and generated an annual surplus of £120. Its programmes usually provided a diverse range of pictures: 'There was clearly a strong demand for Continental films, especially French, but there were also requests for main films with English dialogue.' The society frequently screened films by French and Russian directors, and the programmes usually included at least one documentary, short or animated film. In addition a number of films of 'historical and technical interest' were shown, such as *The Great Train Robbery* (1903) and *The Invisible Thief* (1909).[54]

If the debate between 'Realist' and 'Anti-Box Office' reflected a gulf between two sincerely held points of view, it was not necessarily an unbridgeable one. Even those lacking much sense of cultural nationalism, and who regarded film as having great artistic and intellectual potential, usually had their own local or regional cultural preferences which set them apart from the highbrow London-based critics. A national, as well as an intellectual, outlook was certainly evident within the Cardiff Film Society, established shortly after the end of the Second World War. As well as screening films of intellectual interest, it also sought to take the lead 'in establishing a Welsh group of film societies which, with financial support from the British Film Institute, would be able to help any body of interested people in Welsh towns and villages to establish a local film society'.[55] Here was a body concerned with film on both an artistic and a national level. It saw its role, perhaps, in similar terms to the way in which the Film Society operated between 1925 and 1939, but with a Welsh, rather than British focus.

One of the founding members of this society, and for three years its chairman, was Idris Evans. There was certainly a good deal of overlap between his attitude to the cinema, and that of London-based critics, yet he maintained a concern for the Welsh national interest.

It is probably no exaggeration to say that during the past seven years in Wales 90 per cent of pupils have left school without ever having had a single lesson in film appreciation and film criticism. It is hardly remarkable in the circumstances that our young people's taste in films is unrefined and that all many of them require of the commercial cinema is hackneyed stuff with little or no intellectual content. To put it bluntly: Welsh education authorities missed the film boat years ago and even in the intervening time have been rather pathetically paddling after it.

Evans, who had acted as Film Officer for Wales in the Ministry of Information during the Second World War, had long championed the cause of a Film Council for Wales. He had been among those present at the meeting in Cardiff University in 1936 when calls for such a council were first voiced. In an article in the *Western Mail* several years later he outlined in some detail what he felt such a council could do. He saw its potential largely in educational terms, hoping that it would foster a Welsh film library, and forge closer links with schools and universities – both so that film was more widely used as an educational aid and that film-making techniques could be properly taught. He also suggested that such a council should 'collaborate with Welsh religious bodies in equipping church and chapel halls for the use of films to teach religious knowledge and social betterment'. As well as encouraging a greater appreciation of the artistic and educational potential of the cinema, Evans also called for a more concerted effort to put Wales on the screen. He envisaged 'a film production unit of Welsh experts to make films about Wales, her history, culture, traditions and industries. Both Welsh and English copies of these films will be made.' Evans, rather like George Orwell and Humphrey Jennings in England, combined intellect with patriotism. He wanted the Welsh to appreciate better films, but he also wanted Wales to be depicted on screen. Further, it was not a narrow view of Welshness which he sought to promote, but bilingual accounts which took in her industrial background as well as older rural traditions.[56]

Evans's patriotic leanings, which set him apart from the more cosmopolitan intellectual film critics, would almost certainly have been shared by many others from a Welsh middle-class background. Yet the demand for non-commercial films that bore relevance to the cultural outlook of Welsh audiences was not restricted to the middle classes. Similar sentiments were at times expressed in the working-class communities of the south Wales coal field where, on the surface at least, it appeared that some of the attitudes expressed by highbrow London critics had an appeal.

Bert Coombes, a self-educated miner whose writing is often quoted by historians of the south Wales coalfield, was as critical as anyone of mainstream Hollywood entertainment – especially if it found its way into the miners' institutes:

My complaint about Glynneath is that the regular nightly film shows have driven all other interests away. Unless you want to see a picture it is better to keep away after early evening, for you will get neither room nor peace. I do not believe it was the ideal to compete with other cinemas when the welfare Halls were built . . . What the halls were for was to supply a permanent place where other types of culture should be nurtured, and I believe all that was intended was that they should be self-supporting.[57]

He was apparently not alone in holding such a view. When the Ystradgynlais Miners' Hall began operating in competition with local commercial cinemas it provoked a boycott by some of its own members who, like Coombes, felt that the whole purpose and ethos of the halls was being corrupted by 'cine-maisation'.[58] Thomas Jones was another who decried the fact that in the institutes of the 1930s 'cinema and billiards [were] going strong and education going weak'.[59]

The showing of films was less a concern for the more culturally minded miners than the type of entertainment being screened and the commercial use to which it was put. The occasional screening of the 'right sort' of film was considered to be entirely appropriate for the miners' halls. The range of cultural opportunities available at Resolven Welfare Hall, for instance, met with Coombes's approval. Here, 'The large upstairs concert room is reserved for cultural occasions when visiting or local dramatic societies perform, or good class operas or musical comedies are given. Educational and documentary films are shown there.'[60] To Coombes, it would appear, only 'educational and documentary films' qualified as being 'cultural' and therefore worthwhile. Such films were no more popular among regular cinema-goers in the south Wales valleys than in any other part of Britain. The mining communities of south Wales did, however, provide a working-class audience for certain films that could be termed 'alternative'.

It would almost be fair to say that south Wales miners were more likely to appear in a Griersonian documentary than to pay to go and see one.[61] However, when films appeared on subjects in which the miners had a genuine interest, such as Spain, they were readily booked by the institutes. The Tredegar Workman's Hall, for example, screened both *They Shall Not Pass* and *Spanish Earth*, while the hall at Maerdy was able to show the Progressive Film Institute's (PFI's) *Defence of Madrid* which was released on 16mm stock.[62] This demand for films dealing with the Spanish Civil War underlines Bert Hogenkamp's claim that films at the miners' cinemas fell not just into the categories of entertainment or education, but also of politics. Ivor Montagu, head of the PFI in the 1930s, once claimed that the miners' cinemas 'were among our best customers'. What is more, a number of these halls were occasionally able to secure permission to screen films denied a certificate by the BBFC on the grounds of their politically 'controversial' content. Thus audiences in Cwmbach, Nantymoel and Maerdy had the opportunity to see Pudovkin's *Mother* in the early 1930s.[63]

In 1934 a Rhondda Film Society was established 'with the object of privately exhibiting films not ordinarily available to the public ... The programmes will include films of international repute and of educational, scientific and aesthetic interest.' An apparently 'crowded audience of members' was told that *Battleship Potemkin* and *The Cabinet of Dr. Caligari* were among the films the society intended to screen.[64] It is unclear for how long, or how successfully, this society continued to function, but its existence demonstrates that there was a demand in this part of south Wales for films of artistic as well as political significance. This point is supported by the fact that the Tredegar institute, after many years of discussion, also established a Film Society in 1944, to show 'Italian, French, Russian and non-commercial American films'.[65]

Film reporters in the Welsh press

The success of film societies in different parts of Wales points to the fact that there was an audience for non-commercial films. For the vast majority of the cinema-going population in Wales, however, the existence of film societies and the writings of the more highbrow critics were quite irrelevant. Film reviews in the Welsh press were almost entirely the work of reporters rather than critics. This is not to say that there was no demand within Wales for a more intellectual approach to film criticism, or for 'artistic' films. Such sentiments were voiced from time to time in letters pages and editorials (as discussed above), but not within the format of a weekly film column. If Welsh residents wished to learn of the latest developments in film technique in Europe or America, it was to the London-based press that they had to turn. Welsh newspapers, with a local or regional distribution, made little attempt to appeal to such minority interests.

What do these film reviews, which were aimed at the majority of cinema-goers within their regions, actually tell us? First, a distinction must be drawn between weekly titles, which generally had a small, local circulation; and the much larger dailies, which could be described as regional papers. Journalists writing for weekly titles such as the *Caernarfon and Denbighshire Herald*, the *Cambrian News* or the *Cardigan and Tivyside Advertiser* were not in a position to attend advance press screenings of the latest films. Unable to view films ahead of their readers, film reviewers in the local Welsh press were limited in what they could actually write. For the most part their notices provided little more than a brief factual description of the basic plot, and a list of the leading players. This information was usually gleaned from the standard reviews provided by the trade press. When local papers in Wales did want to draw attention to a film's critical acclaim, they often relied on quotations from reviews in the national press.[66] The local weekly newspapers in Wales had neither the resources nor the inclination to provide a thorough analysis of the week's films. Audiences in most parts of Wales would have learned all they needed to know about the best films months before they arrived at their local cinema. What they demanded of the local weekly paper was not so much criticism as information. The format in which this information was presented, however, tells us rather more than the content of the film reviews themselves.

This book has argued that cinemas were important local centres of popular entertainment in their own right; they were visited by audiences on a regular basis as a matter of routine; and the individual film shown was not only factor determining whether or not people went to the cinema. This comes across clearly in the way that film reviews were presented in Welsh local newspapers. They were not organized on a film-by-film basis, but rather on a cinema-by-cinema one. Each cinema was given a similar amount of exposure, and so preference could seldom be given to one individual film over another. Further, the reviews concerned themselves with whole programmes of entertainment, not just the main features. Information, however brief, was therefore provided about the second feature and any short films or live entertainment. It seems unlikely that many people would have decided which cinema to attend on the basis of the reviews in the local press. Both the format and content of these reviews seemed to be geared towards those who wanted to check what was on at their local cinema, and not those who may have wished to discover which was likely to be the most interesting or appealing film.

The film reviews provided by the daily provincial newspapers within Wales were rather more detailed than those of the local press. Titles such as the *Western Mail* and the *South Wales Evening Post* made more effort to advise their readers of the particular merits and weaknesses of individual films. The tone of the reviews was very much in the style of the reporter rather than the critic. This was entirely consistent with developments in the Welsh press since the 1880s. The adoption of the principles of New Journalism in the late nineteenth century by daily titles, especially in south Wales, meant that these papers were becoming much more popular in terms of their presentation and appeal. In the case of the *Western Mail*, for instance, Joanne Cayford has shown that far from being able to impose its political views on a south Wales readership, the paper, along with its rival the *South Wales Daily News*, 'became increasingly consumer orientated. They catered for what they perceived to be popular taste, encouraging reader participation and reader purchase.'[67] In the 1890s this was most evident in the introduction of a *Ladies' Own* supplement and a huge expansion in the coverage of sport. The increasing commercialization and popular appeal of the daily Welsh press provides the context in which the film reviews of the 1930s can be best understood. Yet the adoption of the principles of New Journalism by sections of the Welsh press did not simply mean that they aped the presentation techniques of the more popular national titles. As Aled Jones has argued, 'such Cardiff-based papers as the *Western Mail*, succeeded in constructing a new and crucially undifferentiated audience that was conceived of as being essentially *Welsh* in character.'[68] This was evident in the writing of the film reporter for the *South Wales Echo*, Walter Grossey, or 'The Prompter' as he was known to his readers. The *Echo*, it should be noted, had employed Langford Reed as a regular film reporter since 1920 and was far ahead of most Welsh papers in its coverage of cinema news. To give a sense of the style in which Grossey wrote, as well as an analysis of his views, he is quoted at some length here.

'The Prompter's' entertainment notes appeared regularly in the *Echo* from 1927 until the 1940s. The majority of his column inches were taken up by cinema news, but he did not limit himself to film reviews; he also reported on theatre performances and any other entertainment that was deemed newsworthy. A play in the New Theatre or a film in the Capitol were treated on their own terms as equally valid cultural pursuits. Indeed, there were occasions when he found it necessary to defend himself against allegations that 'I invariably depreciate the stage to the advantage of the films'.[69]

When dealing with films, 'The Prompter' would discuss cinema programmes, not just the main feature. He believed that cinema audiences (his readers) expected to be entertained for a whole evening, and quoted to them the complaints of cinema managers who at times failed to match these expectations:

> 'One of these pictures alone ought to give them their money's worth ... Instead of that happy feeling of a shilling well spent I have known lots of my regular customers leave the theatre with the remark, "Of course, the big picture was fine, but the second was simply terrible." '[70]

Under the heading of 'All about next week's shows', 'The Prompter's' cinema notes dealt with the supporting programmes offered by Cardiff's cinemas, as well as the main features. He was enthusiastic, for example, about the introduction of cine-variety at the Capitol in the 1930s, advising his readers to look out for acts like 'Herschel Hentere, the famous pianist; Terry's 24 Tots, a big music-hall act; and the popular Gershom Parkington Quintet, whom I last heard in a West End drawing room.'[71] Not all live entertainment met with his approval, however, and he was known to express amazement 'at rounds of applause given acts after 25 minutes of what in the old days of variety would have been regarded as wearisome drivel'.

Attention to the role of the manager was recurring theme in this weekly column. Expanding on what he considered his role as a film critic to be, Grossey did not define his position against that of the film producer or advertising executive, but against that of the local manager.

> Well, I try to be critical and kind at the same time, but bless your heart, a Chicago gunman would get less abuse for a 'killing' than the provincial critic who fires one real shot at the stage or screen. 'Ah', they [the managers] say, 'what do you know about this game of providing a satisfying programme, week after week, of back stage difficulties, temperamental audiences, and so

on?' To which I reply, 'what matters how much I know of sound-systems, tabs, back cloths, accoustics, the art of booking shows, and so on. That's your job. I merely report on the audience reactions to all these things; whether they say "It is" or "It isn't", whether I think their opinion is genuine and deserved; whether it is liable to reflect opinion of Cardiff folk generally.'

Significantly, Grossey refers to himself as a 'provincial critic'. Whereas critics in the national press sought to provide an appraisal of a film's worth to set against the hype generated by the publicity departments of major film studios, the role of the provincial critic was to provide an opinion which was clouded neither by the boasts of cinema managers, nor by the outpourings of the national press.

> Because a selective 'audience' in an intimate West End theatre raves over this or that play, giving enormous press publicity, it neither follows that the play is great, nor that provincial audiences are unintelligent because their sense of the artistic does not lead them to gushing flattery.[72]

This reluctance to follow the critical opinions expressed in London, was reflected in his attitude to British films. He was not at all concerned, for instance, that the majority of cinema programmes consisted of American films, or even that US companies had begun to take control of leading provincial cinemas, such as Cardiff's Capitol. To the contrary, he commended the fact that '[e]very penny necessary for the maintenance and general equipment [of the Capitol] is spent locally.' Further, 'Paramount and other big corporations are making British pictures, employing British artists in British studios.' His attitude to the films themselves was influenced by their level of popular appeal, not their nationality:

> Anyhow, the public does not care a rap whose film they pay to see, provided its good entertainment. All the 'bad' American films are getting 'the bird' when they deserve it, and so are the British productions that fail to reach the standard . . . Hang it all. The most successful stage musical comedies of recent years have been American. When we have glutted the market with something equal, if not better, then lets raise the cry, 'All British'.[73]

It was not necessarily the lack of artistic integrity in British films that concerned this film reporter, nor their failed attempts to imitate the methods of Hollywood studios. Rather, he pointed to broader cultural reasons why they failed to appeal to south Wales audiences:

> Let us be fair. Give the Americans their due. If the nasal accent grates upon British ears like a circular saw, how much do our Yankee friends suffer to hear a mixture of the Oxford-cum-Cockney language spoken on English films? If they give the artist and the film 'the bird' would you blame them? I would not.

The audience at the Pavilion Cinema did 'bird' a British film one night this week . . . The amount of suburban chatter among the women must have got on the cinema patron's nerves, because when the traditional English 'silly ass' appeared he proved to be too great a burden. Having spent their money to be entertained, the folk in the pit began to guffaw and laugh in anything but a complimentary fashion, and I sympathised with them.[74]

When Grossey did offer words of praise for a British film, as in the case of *The Private Life of Henry VIII*, he did so by saying that 'I am going to offer an impression from one Provincial to another – in fact, to all of you who some-times find that the over-boosted film can easily be a bauble.'[75] In attempting to pitch his film reviews at the level of popular taste, this film reporter clearly found it necessary to distance his views from those of the national press. Walter Grossey may not have been typical of all those who wrote about films in the Welsh press. However, his approach does illustrate how Welsh-based newspapers could tailor the information and opinions within their film columns to the specific concerns of a local or regional readership.

Summary

The critics looked at in this chapter were not just those paid to watch and review films on a weekly basis in the national press, but also commentators who voiced concerns about the cultural influence of the cinema for British, and Welsh, society. In Britain, these cultural critics could mostly be divided into two groups: intellectual critics who wished to celebrate and promote the artistic qualities of film; and more patriotic commentators who wanted more films to project a positive image of Britain to the rest of the world. Both groups achieved at least partial success in promoting their interests. Intellectual critics helped provide cinema with a degree of cultural respectability in the inter-war years, and influenced the writing of film his-tory for several decades afterwards. Concerns about the national interest, on the other hand, led to government protection for the film industry (which succeeded in reviving British film production but did little to create a market for these films overseas).[76] The views of both these groups can be found in film reviews of the period, but neither group could claim to represent the voice of the typical British film-goer. Intellectual critics, in fact, were con-temptuous of film-goers who sat through a whole evening of cinema entertainment on at least a weekly basis, and complained that such indis-criminate viewing on the part of general public was the main reason why so few original and interesting films were ever made. For film reviews which sought to reflect, rather than shape, public taste we must look to film 'reporters', who treated films as entertainment rather than art.

In Wales, differing responses to the cinema (as an art form, mass-entertainment or a national institution) were also expressed. The popular appeal of the cinema for the majority of audiences was best captured by those 'reporters' writing in the provincial daily papers. They sought to address the interests of local or regional audiences, and in doing so wrote about whole programmes of entertainment at local cinemas, not just the main films. When it came to reviewing films themselves, however, film reporters like Walter Grossey had no interest in promoting the national interest or in raising the level of public taste. He drew attention to the pictures he felt would be most popular among local audiences, which for the most part were products of Hollywood studios.

Mainstream Hollywood entertainment did much to satisfy the demands of 'American Wales', yet those of a more intellectual persuasion also took an interest in the artistic potential which cinema had to offer. Indeed, the demand for 'alternative' films showed up both the diversity and continuity inherent within society and culture in Wales. Calls within the Welsh press for the cinema to be effectively utilized as a medium of national expression had their origins in the cultural nationalism of Liberal Wales. The audience that existed for non-commercial films in the valleys of south Wales, on the other hand, grew out of a working-class culture that had emerged in industrialized areas. These two groups had quite different cultural aspirations, as embodied in the *gwerin* and *working-class* myths. One was essentially rural, Welsh speaking and Liberal voting (closely associated with the pulpit); the other increasingly (though not exclusively) industrial in landscape, English in language and Labour in politics (often linked to the coal pits). While the differences between these cultures are clear enough, there were similarities also. Within both traditions Nonconformist religion, education, self-improvement and social respectability were highly valued. Even codes of dress, as David Smith has observed, remained very much the same: 'The Welsh working class accepted that they were only to wear their working clothes at work or in private; on the street, in public, at ceremonial moments they would wear the clothes of the bourgeois.'[77] The common concern for social and moral respectability within these cultures led elements within both to reject mainstream Hollywood entertainment. As we shall see, such opposition was most frequently expressed in debates about the regulation of cinema entertainment, and in particular on the question of Sunday cinema opening.

7

CENSORSHIP AND CONTROL

One of the clearest indicators of the social significance accorded to the cinema in Britain by the beginning of our period was the extent to which both the functioning and the influence of this form of entertainment was regulated. Perhaps the most widely known method of attempting this was film censorship, which in Britain began with the establishment of the British Board of Film Censors (BBFC) in 1912.[1] However, the censorship of films was just one feature of a much wider process by which cinema has been socially controlled and regulated. Regulations relating to the design of buildings, make-up of audiences and hours of opening were as important as the actual censorship of films in shaping the cultural experience that cinema to provided. These rules were drawn up and enforced on a local rather than a national level. If anything they served to strengthen the established position of the cinema in the local community, and they were usually given the full backing of film exhibitors.

The controls placed upon the cinema industry (regarding the content and advertising of films, and health and safety issues within the halls themselves) were essentially no different in Wales to any other part of Britain. This chapter will examine how local authorities in Wales sought to regulate the environment in which films were viewed. Such endeavours did not set Wales apart, but serve to illustrate how local authorities across Britain went about their task of cinema censorship. The important point is that control of the cinema as an institution, rather than just censorship of films, was taken seriously by local authorities.

The issue of Sunday opening of cinemas, however, was an area where clear differences did exist between Wales and most other parts of Britain. In almost the whole of Wales cinemas were prevented from opening on Sundays until the 1950s. In many parts of England, on the other hand, Sunday opening of cinemas had occurred throughout the period covered by this book. An examination of the debates over Sunday opening of cinemas in Wales from the early 1920s to the early 1950s points to deeper changes occurring in Welsh society at this time. Cinemas had remained shut on Sundays in Wales because calls for Sabbath observance had been supported by representatives from both the societies of Liberal and Labour Wales. This alliance of opinion meant that opposition to Sunday opening was increasingly presented as a national issue, rather than a moral or religious one. The eventual extension of Sunday opening into Wales (which came after the public themselves – the frequenters of the fleapits – had been allowed to vote) reflected the declining importance of religious observance in Welsh society as a whole.

The process of cinema censorship

Cinema censorship in Britain was not conducted by a single, all-powerful body, but emerged out of a fairly complex series of social/political interactions. Early attempts to regulate the cinema had been based on the 1780 Disorderly Houses Act, but in 1909 a new Cinematograph Act was introduced which legislated specifically for picture houses. The Act was drafted with the intention of ensuring safety within the halls, but was soon being used to enforce the censorship of films themselves. Under the Act local authorities were given the final responsibility for drafting and enforcing regulations, but their measures could only be expected to succeed when they were widely supported. Therefore, the interests of various local pressure groups: the cinema-going public, the film trade, the police, the national Government and the BBFC, all needed to be taken into account. Where the interests of one or more of these groups were ignored, enforcement of the regulations became extremely difficult. The controversial decision of Liverpool JPs in 1930 not to admit children to films with an 'A' certificate (even when accompanied by an adult) was enforced for less than two years.[2] The attempt by councillors in Beckenham to introduce their own system of film censorship was even shorter lived, lasting for barely six months.[3]

Cinema censorship was a process rather than a single act, and one which could be regarded as constructive as well as constraining. In this respect Michel Foucault's conception of power can be usefully applied to the regulation of the cinema:

> If power were never anything but repressive, if it never did anything but to say no, do you really think one would be brought to obey it? What makes power hold good, what makes it accepted, is simply the fact that it doesn't only weigh on us as a force that says no, but that it traverses and produces things, it induces pleasure, forms knowledge, produces discourse. It needs to be considered as a productive network which runs through the whole social body, much more than as a negative instance whose function is repression.[4]

Following Foucault, Annette Kuhn has argued that the development of cinema censorship should be regarded as an essential part of the process by which the cinema emerged as a 'public sphere'. Any form of censorship or regulation which impinges on individual liberties, she argues, is much more likely to be accepted if it is regarded as performing a wider, public role. Within little more than a decade of its invention, the cinema came to be regarded as a public institution on a number of levels. The cinema buildings themselves were public spaces, audiences were broad based enough to constitute a cinema-going public, and thus the cinema could be regarded as a potential threat to public safety or public morality. To Kuhn, censorship was not only a product of the cinema's increasingly public status, it was a productive force in shaping the cinema as a public sphere. Censorship, therefore, was much more than simply a negative or repressive force – something *done to* films. Rather, it was part of a much wider process by which both films themselves and the cinema more generally were shaped and developed.[5]

Far from being imposed on the cinema industry once the medium achieved a certain level of popularity, the process of censorship was productive in that it helped to shape the public experience of cinema-going in the decades of its greatest appeal. There is certainly no reason to suppose that controls were imposed upon a reluctant, or even a passive, film trade whose freedom to conduct its own affairs was subsequently diminished. On the contrary, the 1909 Cinematograph Act was passed with the full backing of the trade. Initially welcomed as a 'picture showman's charter', it was hoped that the Act would invest the industry with a greater measure of social respectability. Even when it became clear that the powers granted to local authorities under the Act were more wide ranging than they had initially realized, the trade responded by setting up its own film censorship body: the BBFC (see below). There were few groups with a greater interest in the establishment of the cinema as a respectable social and cultural institution than exhibitors themselves. Representatives of the film industry were, therefore, very much a part of the overall process by which the cinema was regulated on both a local and national level.

Controls over the cinema were evidently not imposed on managers or audiences by a single, powerful institution. Regulations were only properly developed once the cinema had been established as a public institution, and they only proved effective in cases where it could be agreed that they were for public benefit. The process of censorship, therefore, was one which involved a number of institutions, organizations and pressure groups, each protective of their own interests. Struggles inevitably arose when these interests clashed. The story of cinema censorship, is the story of how these struggles were fought and resolved.

Regulation of the cinema as a public space

The earliest attempts to regulate the cinema were centred not on the films themselves, but the physical environment in which they were presented. Only when film shows began to regularly take place in buildings used primarily as cinemas (as opposed to music halls, penny gaffs or showmen's booths) did specific legislation relating to the cinema become necessary. This legislation, ostensibly at least, was designed to protect public safety: not to regulate the entertainment on offer. Just because the Cinematograph Act was later used to sanction film censorship, and a host of other controls and regulations, did not mean that the initial concerns over public safety had become any less important. Indeed, even after the passing of the 1909 Act, previously existing legislation (such as the Disorderly Houses Act and Public Health Act) continued to be used to regulate the cinema.

The public concerns expressed in this period about the physical conditions inside cinemas during performances can be divided into three categories: safety, health and morality.

Public safety

Safety concerns centred largely on the threat of fire breaking out during a performance. By 1909 the fire hazard had, according to Annette Kuhn, 'become almost mythical', even though there had been no major cinema fires caused by inflammable stock in Britain by this date.[6] Safety concerns were at the forefront of parliamentary debates surrounding the Cinematograph Act, and the Act itself dealt predominantly with fire regulations. Thus, it became necessary for the projection room to be sealed, for films to be stored in fireproof cases, and for the auditoriums to have sufficient provision of exits and fire extinguishers. It was relatively straightforward for local authorities to ensure that these provisions were in place before granting a cinema license.

Less easily dealt with was the problem of over-crowding. Gwyn Thomas has recalled, with characteristic humour, some of the practices employed by unscrupulous cinema managers who sought to get as many paying customers into their halls as possible (see chapter 4). To the licensing authorities, however, the matter was rather more serious. In March 1920 the concern was expressed at a meeting of the Swansea Watch Committee 'that in a number of kinemas the rule of keeping the gangways clear was not observed'.[7] A month earlier the Rhondda Urban District Council had discussed the same issue, having heard from the Porth Trades and Labour Council that the problem was becoming critical:

> Councillor Morgan Rees alleged that at certain halls chairs were placed in the aisles so as to 'get every penny piece'. He described the conditions as 'really deplorable', and said the overcrowding was so acute that in the case of an outbreak of fire many people might be trampled to death even if they escaped the fire . . . It was decided that the attention of the police should be called to the matter.[8]

The Superintendent of Glamorgan did conduct an inspection of Rhondda cinemas, but found no evidence of overcrowding.[9] This was not entirely surprising, given that local cinema managers would have known an inspection was imminent. Clearly, the enforcement of regulations intended to prevent overcrowding was fraught with difficulties. At the beginning of our period problems were caused by the clash of interests between exhibitors anxious to pack as many paying customers as possible into their cinemas, and licensing authorities concerned about public safety. Concerns about overcrowding, however, diminished as the 1920s wore on and were virtually unheard of by the 1930s. This cannot simply be attributed to a more effective enforcement of regulations on the part of the police. A more likely explanation is that with cinema firmly established as public institution, managers were increasingly concerned with protecting the long-term interests of their business, rather than making a quick profit while the opportunity existed.

Public health

Nowhere were the exhibitors' aspirations to present a positive public image more evident than when it came to questions of hygiene and cleanliness. The reputation that many cinemas had acquired as 'fleapits' or 'bug houses' was not easily shaken off. P. Morton Shand, describing the cinema as 'a sort of public lounge', claimed that '[s]choolboys, whose holidays are drawing to a close, know that prevalent epidemics can be caught there.'[10] Anecdotes relating to the unhygienic conditions within particular halls can be found in most towns and cities. One of the most well known is Leslie Halliwell's recollection of the Atlas cinema in Bolton in the 1930s: 'The local joke was that they loaned you a hammer with your ticket.'[11]

If the fleapits are often remembered with an element of affection, however, their reputation was one which managers were anxious to shed. The trade press was full of advertisements in this period for disinfectants and deodorants which would enable managers 'to put forward the claim that his house is absolutely germ proof, and that patrons can visit it without the slightest fear of infection'.[12] As well as maintaining high standards of hygiene and cleanliness, those halls most concerned with presenting a positive public image made sure that they were *seen* to be doing so. Aberystwyth's Coliseum cinema, therefore, placed notices in the local press, not just to advertise forthcoming attractions, but also to stress that 'This hall is disinfected with Jeyes fluid'.[13]

Clearly, business concerns were uppermost in the minds of cinema managers, who wanted to create an environment that would attract as many patrons as possible. The role of the licensing authorities, however, was also something that needed to be taken into account. In February 1920, for instance, *Kine Weekly* warned that with another outbreak of influenza, even if less severe than previous epidemics, there is every possibility of more severe legislation, for the authorities have been attacked so heavily for previous laxity that they will no doubt the next time go to the other extreme. The fanatic opponents of the kinema will also take advantage of an epidemic to air their views and force the hands of the authorities, where possible, to the most stringent measures.[14]

The worst fears of the trade may not have been realized in 1920, though health and safety issues were increasingly a concern for local and national authorities. In October of that year the Home Office sent out a communication to surveyors complaining of the unsatisfactory sanitary conditions in some cinemas. Though the government could not force licensing authorities to improve the situation, this was a problem to which a number of local officials were already turning their attention. Addressing a meeting of the Welsh School of Social Service at Cardiff University, Lleufer Thomas, stipendiary magistrate for Pontypridd,[15] referred to some cinemas as 'barracks', with no adequate system of ventilation. He went on: 'The cinema had come to stay, and they should insist, from the point of view of public health, on the buildings being flooded with sunshine by means of sliding roofs.'[16] Sliding roofs were, alas, never to become a feature of cinema architecture in south Wales.[17] Concern about public health, however, continued to feature in debates about the cinema in this period. While cases of cinemas having licences refused because of their failure to meet minimum sanitary requirements were rare (if they existed at all), it was quite common for licensing authorities to cite public health concerns as a reason for introducing new regulations. Again, Lleufer Thomas was to play a prominent role in this respect. His primary concern, unsurprisingly perhaps, being the physical health and development of children.

Thomas had asked Dr J. D. Jenkins, Medical Officer of Health to the Rhondda Urban District Council, to report to the magistrates at the Licensing Sessions in Pontypridd what he considered to be the likely effect of cinema attendance on those aged under fourteen. The evidence was actually provided by the Assistant Medical Officer, Dr Murphy, and it was damning. He raised four areas of concern. The first was that visits to the cinema in the evening prevented children getting their necessary ten hours sleep. Secondly, the flickering screen was apt to cause eye strain, especially after a long day.[18] Thirdly, there was an 'increased risk of infection from germs at night, and in places which were overcrowded personal contact was much closer and resistance of disease was lowered'. Finally, children were especially 'liable to colds and bronchial trouble when they came out of the kinemas . . . into the night air'. According to Dr Murphy: 'There was no doubt that children who went to kinemas at night suffered mentally and physically, and at school the following day showed general lassitude.'[19] On hearing this testimony the local magistrates were left in little doubt that the best course of action would be to stop children from entering, or remaining in, cinemas after 8.30 p.m.

The exhibitors were loath to be seen not to share these general concerns, but they did oppose the measures suggested. The manager of Porth's Central Cinema (G. W. Robinson) said of the magistrates' intention to prevent the admission of children to evening performances: 'personally I quite agree with them, unless the restrictions should be extended to children accompanied by adults.' The health risk posed by visiting the cinema was presumably the same for children whether accompanied by their parents or not, but this was clearly not Robinson's primary concern. He realized that the proposal 'would be a serious hit at the business', and feared takings could be down by as much as a quarter. Rather than confronting the justices head on, however, Robinson sought to convince them that he was sensitive to their concerns, and that formal regulations were unnecessary:

> As a licensee I am not the least keen on fighting the authority who grant these. I agree with the views of the stipendiary and was bound to admit this in the box on Tuesday last. He says he would like the public to be educated on the point, I wish he would allow us to do so voluntarily, by means of slides and advertising gradually, not to make it an immediate condition upon acceptance of a license.[20]

The refusal of the magistrates to accept a voluntary agreement brought Rhondda exhibitors round to the point of view initially expressed by Will Stone on behalf of the CEA. Stone had tactfully refused to express his personal opinion as to whether evening cinema performances had any harmful effects on children, but stated that he was prepared to legally challenge the justices' decision. The solicitor to the CEA, Mr Norman Hart, was therefore invited to south Wales to defend the exhibitors interests. He argued that under the Cinematograph Act of 1909 only conditions that were deemed reasonable could be imposed on the granting of a cinema licence, and that the proposed measure was *ultra vires* and, therefore, illegal. Lleufer Thomas, explaining the justices' decision, accepted that the Cinematograph Act did not give them the authority to impose such a condition, but pointed out that the Public Health Act did. To this, the CEA solicitor had no effective response, and the exhibitors were forced to accept the magistrates' decision.[21]

The authorities in the Rhondda were not alone in their attitude to public health. The following year the county medical officer for Carmarthenshire expressed concerns about the lack of sunlight ('that great disinfecting agent'), paucity of ventilation and stagnation of air within cinemas. Describing the buildings as potential 'hotbeds of disease', he went so far as to question the value of building isolation hospitals when children were allowed to attend crowded cinemas. Like the Pontypridd justices he felt that children under fourteen should be kept out of cinemas in the evenings, and he even suggested that those under five years of age should be prohibited entirely.[22]

It was not only the health of children that was at issue where cinema regulations were concerned. The question of sanitary conditions inside picture houses also entered the debate on Sunday opening.[23] In response to the much used argument that the closing of cinemas left people with nothing to do other than roam the streets, opponents of Sunday opening contrasted the virtues of a breath of fresh air with the risk of contamination (both physical and mental) posed by the cinema. 'Young couples', opined Lord Colum Crichton-Stuart in the *Western Mail*, 'are undoubtedly better off walking in the open than sitting holding each other's hands in a dark, stuffy cinema seeing the "close-ups" of the Hollywood stars, who demonstrate the latest ritual of love expression.'[24]

Cleanliness and godliness were, apparently, near neighbours, and moral concerns about conditions inside cinemas were never far from those relating to public health.

Public morals

The first section of a 1917 report by the Cinema Commission of Inquiry, which dealt with 'Moral and Social Aspects of the Cinema', considered the dangers posed by the cinema 'as a place of entertainment' before it raised the issue of the 'character of the films'.

> A distinction must be made between moral evils *incidental* to the picture house and those *consequential* on the kind of film shown. The charge has been brought against the picture house that the darkness encourages indecency, especially where there are boxes, though this is the case in very few houses; and that the promenade or the standing room at the back of the building, where such exists, affords opportunities for improper conduct.[25]

The report acknowledged that such charges could easily be exaggerated, but insisted that they were not without foundation. At worst, it was claimed that conditions inside cinemas afforded opportunities for 'solititation' and 'the molestation of children',[26] though one London exhibitor argued that '[w]hen investigation is made it is usually found that the alleged misconduct is nothing more than the privileged manifestation of affection between the sexes.' Whatever the seriousness of the allegations, it seems that concerns about indecent conduct within cinemas were enough to convince a number of chief constables to insist on increasing the amount of lighting inside cinemas during performances.[27] Licensing authorities in Wales, too, shared such concerns.

When Rhondda magistrates undertook to prohibit the attendance of children at cinema shows in 1920, they also introduced a clause into licences stating that the auditorium was to be adequately lit during performances.

This would appear to be a clear example of moral considerations influencing cinema regulation. It did not become an important *censorship* issue because exhibitors themselves made no attempt to challenge the ruling. When the manager of the Central cinema was informed that 'the justices hope to visit as many of the halls in the area as possible in order to see the type of poster etc. displayed in the lobbys [*sic*], and also the lighting of the interiors during the performance', he maintained that 'they are welcome here any time'.[28] Mr Norman Hart, when expressing the opposition of Rhondda exhibitors to regulation dealing with children at the cinema, was careful to point out that they 'had no objection to the condition as to the lighting of the premises'.[29] There seemed to be a consensus among those involved in the cinema trade in the early part of this period that measures needed to be taken to limit the opportunities for indecent behaviour in cinemas.

As well as increased interior lighting, this also meant that cinema attendants were to have a more prominent role in overseeing the behaviour of cinema audiences. The actions of torch-wielding cinema staff were in many ways more intrusive a form of control over the cinema-going experience than any policy devised by local or central government. An example of what this meant for audiences in the Rhondda is provided by Gwyn Thomas: 'I remember that in one cinema there were a pair of funereal-looking ushers who roamed the aisles hissing, "Put 'at light out. What're you up to? Shurrup", on the general principle that someone somewhere must be doing something which was covered by some part of the statement.'[30] Problems connected with safety, health and morality inside picture houses often required specific action to be taken on the part either of local authorities or central government, particularly in the early part of this period. These issues also informed wider debates about the cinema's social role, and the regulations by which it was to be controlled. Such regulations, clearly, were concerned with more than just the censorship of films. However, attempts to control the entertainment provided by cinemas were a common feature of the period.

The films and their audiences

The legal basis for film censorship in Britain can be traced back to the Cinematograph Act of 1909. The Act was introduced to regulate public safety within cinemas, but local authorities quickly sought to use their licence-granting powers to control the content of films. In a landmark ruling, the High Court confirmed that local councils had 'a free power to impose such terms, conditions and restrictions as they thought fit' when granting licenses.[31] Faced with the prospect of each local council acting as a film censor, the film trade responded by gaining the approval of the Home Secretary, Reginald McKenna, to establish the BBFC. The BBFC was an industry-funded body which in 1913 began the task of issuing certificates to those films it considered suitable for public exhibition. Initially it was regarded with scepticism by local councils, but the Board went to great lengths to establish its credentials as a responsible and impartial authority.[32] Presidents and Secretaries of the BBFC were pillars of the British 'establishment' (usually retired military officers, senior civil servants or Conservative politicians), and the Board took great care to ensure that scenes likely to offend moral or religious sensibilities were kept well away from cinema screens.

Under the presidency of T. P. O'Connor, the BBFC wasted little time in compiling a catalogue of taboo subjects.[33] By 1917 a set of rules had been established, known as 'O'Connor's 43', which tightly regulated the portrayal of, among other things, royalty, religious subjects, criminal behaviour and any kind of immorality – ranging from bad language to prostitution. Additions and amendments were made throughout the period, but the fundamental principle remained: that subjects likely to arouse controversy should be kept off the cinema screen.[34] Despite the best efforts of the BBFC to cut, ban or generally discourage the filming of sensitive topics, however, films continued to create controversy throughout our period. This was partly because the content of individual films was not the only factor that created censorship controversies. The BBFC report of 1930 outlined the problem concisely:

> One such film by itself may not be prohibitive, but the board cannot help feeling that a continuous succession of them is subversive, tending to invest a life of irregularity with a spurious glamour. There is evidence of quite definite disapproval of this type of film among the regular cinema-going public.[35]

The censors, clearly, found themselves in a difficult position. They were able to prevent the public exhibition of particularly objectionable scenes or images in individual films; but they had no control over the alleged long-term effect of certain *types* of film that audiences so regularly went to see. The habitual routine of cinema-going, it would seem, posed as many problems for those involved in the censorship process as the actual films themselves. Certain films, felt to have slipped through the censors net, did occasionally arouse the ire of moralists, educationalists, critics and local authorities. Behind all this, however, lay deeper concerns about the influence of Hollywood films on British, and Welsh, society.

Areas of concern

In a useful discussion of English criticism and American culture, Richard Maltby argues that censors and critics perform parallel functions. He points to a distinction between 'art' and 'entertainment', whereby it is only the former which is allowed to be 'socially disruptive', and argues that such 'cultural frontiers are policed by the institutions of censorship and criticism. Regimes of censorship ensure that entertainment conforms adequately to its socially prescribed role; regimes of criticism define entertainment as trivial, and maintain the distinction.'[36] This observation helps to explain a complaint raised by BBFC President Edward Shortt in 1933: 'I have never been able to understand why it is that with a certain section of highbrowed people nothing is really high art unless it is beastly.'[37]

Shortt's job, and that of the board as a whole, was to ensure that such 'beastly things' were kept off the cinema screen. They were able to do this precisely because the vast majority of films were not considered to be 'high art' – an opinion that 'highbrowed' critics played an important part in fostering and maintaining.

The extent to which a body of critical opinion could be incorporated into the overall censorship process was evident in Wales, even though there was no journalistic outlet for highbrow film criticism. Film *reporters* in Wales, as was argued in the previous chapter, were mostly favourably inclined toward Hollywood's output and treated it at face value – as a highly popular form of entertainment. In Wales, criticism of Hollywood films came not from film reviewers, but from groups more closely associated with the censorship process, such as religious leaders, educationalists and local councillors. As well as lamenting the negligible cultural value of Hollywood films, these critics were also anxious to highlight their potential social impact. One speaker at a meeting of the Swansea Citizen's Union in 1920, for example, complained that 'one of the causes of young girls going astray, was their inordinate love of excitement and pleasure – visiting picture halls and theatres at every opportunity' . . . 'Many of the pictures shown in our town are of a very low standard, and create a love in these girls of aping a society of foolish standards of living and life. These artificial standards are fatal to the interests of the community.'[38] A Cardiff delegate at a conference of Christian workers in 1932 made the point more forcefully. Claiming that Hollywood films were 'a direct affront to the Christian Church' he warned that '[w]e must take great care to see that the foundations of society in this country are not interfered with by these foreign eruptions of bestiality.'[39] A Lampeter vicar, similarly, harboured fears that the pictures were causing the Welsh people to 'lapse into paganism'. His concerns are worth quoting more fully since they incorporate many of the anxieties being expressed about what young Welsh audiences were watching in cinemas at this time:

> [p]ictures in which battle, murder and sudden death are glorified, where what is known as 'sex appeal' is very much in evidence, and where marital infidelity is exhibited as a matter of course. Children who are brought up on this sort of filth cannot help developing a moral twist, for the spirit of emulation is strong in the young.[40]

Fears about juveniles emulating the criminal behaviour seen at the pictures are almost as old as the medium itself. In the period when cinema's popularity among youngsters was unmatched by any other form of entertainment, however, such concerns were voiced with particular frequency and urgency.[41] One of the most vitriolic and sustained denouncements of much of Hollywood's output came from R. G. Burnett and E. D. Martell. Their account (that concluded that too many films were 'concocted by depraved minds for depraved palates'), argued that the cinema was, among other things, 'the greatest crime-producing agency of this generation'.[42]

Burnett and Martell were certainly two of the more zealous of Hollywood's accusers, but their opinions were shared by many in Wales. Dr George Green, for instance, lecturer in education at the University of Wales in Aberystwyth, often addressed meetings in different parts of Wales where he would talk on subjects such as 'the truth about the film'.[43] For the Cardiff Head Teachers' Association the 'truth' was of no small concern. In a letter to the local authority they pointed to the harm done to children by the 'unavoidably vitiated atmosphere' of the halls and the loss of sleep caused by evening visits. 'Even more serious still', they insisted, was 'the pernicious effect that many of the films have on the vivid imagination of children, perverting their moral sense, and, doubtless, often inciting them to actions of an undesirable, if not criminal, nature.'[44] At a head teachers' conference in London, moreover, concern was expressed that it was not only violent films which could induce impressionable young people to commit crime, but also those with a distinct sexual element:

> Many films had this sex appeal, and its effect on children was serious. It had been discovered that a child who was too early stimulated to sex might develop undesirable qualities and become anti-social. It brought about irritability, laziness, strained love relations, and any kind of crime from pilfering to violent assault.[45]

Objection to films on the basis of their overt 'sex appeal' was, in fact, much the most frequently voiced complaint against cinema entertainment in this period. It was widely recognized, however, that the problem ran deeper than the images on the screen themselves. Just as concerns were expressed about audiences who sided with criminals in films, even though they were brought to justice in the end, censorship authorities displayed a certain amount of anxiety about not just the depiction of sexual relations on screen, but how such scenes could be interpreted. The bishop of Edinburgh, speaking at a conference in Cardiff in 1920, felt that 'kinema films, whilst not directly indecent, were suggestive, and, after all, it was a suggestion which was operative in this matter of immorality'.[46]

Edward Shortt elaborated on the same point over a decade later.

Complaining of 'the tendency on every conceivable occasion to drag in scenes of undressing, bathroom scenes, and in the exhibition of feminine underclothing, which are quite unnecessary from the point of view of telling the story', the president of the BBFC concluded that

> They are solely introduced for the purpose of giving the film what is termed in the trade a 'spicy flavour'. The cumulative effect of a repetition of such scenes as can be described as 'suggestive' is very harmful and properly evokes adverse criticism, although isolated instances may do no harm and call for no comment.[47]

The difficulties facing local licensing authorities who sought to clamp down on the exhibition of immoral or excessively violent pictures were neatly captured by a Swansea councillor, who was reported to have complained that 'a film at which he made strong protest was liked very much by other members of the committee when they went to view it. Action appeared to be difficult because they could not agree on what was indecent.'[48] At the same meeting, the city's chief constable apparently said 'he wished he had time for a local censorship, but did not think the Committee would agree with many of his decisions'. However strong the consensus of opinion that debased and immoral films posed a serious threat to the social fabric, there was little local councillors were able to do as far as individual films were concerned. (There were occasional cases of films being cut or banned by local authorities in Wales, such as when the Cardiff Chief Constable demanded cuts to an educational film, *The Mystery of Life*. Censorship of major Hollywood pictures, however, was not the most practical means of controlling the cinema's influence.)[49] This is not to say that they did nothing, rather, that in order to counter the dangers associated with Hollywood's perceived cultural hegemony, attention was focused on areas other than the screen itself.

Methods of control

While he regretted not being in a position to administer a local censorship of films, Swansea's most senior police officer did, at least, point to the fact that 'posters were now censored'.[50] As well as being a task that local authorities actually had the resources to conduct, this form of regulation was widely felt to serve an important social function. Critics such as Burnett and Martell argued that the cinema's influence was considerably enhanced by the way in which it was publicized, and that in this respect poster advertising was central:

> The posters are often worse than the films themselves . . . [here the] sex-cum-crime mania flaunts itself. The much larger posters, usually printed in several

gaudy colours, are exhibited either outside the cinemas themselves, or on huge roadside hoardings ... More often they are blatantly lurid and intended to suggest that 'this film is hot stuff'.

As well as demanding a stricter censorship of posters, complaints were also levelled at the titles of films which, they felt, were 'deliberately concocted to deceive'.[51] Concerns centred on the way films were perceived, not just the content of the pictures themselves. The regulation of advertising, therefore, was treated as seriously as film censorship.

As early as 1920 Rhondda exhibitors were having their premises inspected by local justices who wanted 'to see the type of poster etc. displayed in the lobbies'.[52] At least one member of Swansea's Watch Committee was also alert to the problem, urging her colleagues that

> Something might also be done with regard to hoardings, which were having a detrimental effect upon children. She happened to be living opposite a hoarding and they would be surprised to see the numbers of small children who stood before it and criticised the pictures they were shown on it.[53]

That this councillor should have been especially concerned about the effect of posters on children was entirely consistent with what was being written about the influence of cinema more generally in this period. With the interpretation placed upon films being as great a concern as pictures themselves it is unsurprising that impressionable young minds were considered most prone to corruption at the hands of the Hollywood studios.

Complaints that the cinema acted as a corrupting influence over the young were evident in Welsh newspapers during this period. In a *Western Mail* article of 1933, Ray Hopkins warned that 'in the average cinema the child to-day is shown for the most part a travesty of life, seen through the distorting lens of Hollywood'.[54] A decade and a half later the same paper ran a leader article stating that 'too often children are admitted to cinemas to see films which are obviously beyond the capacity of their impressionable minds to assimilate in a healthy manner'.[55] These concerns were reflected in the attempts of local authorities to impose stricter controls on when children were allowed to attend cinemas, and what sorts of films they were allowed to see.

Moves by councillors in Pontypridd, Swansea and elsewhere to prevent children from visiting cinemas in the evening have already been discussed. As well as the public health justification for doing this, however, it was also argued that the viewing of pictures in the evening was more likely to cause nightmares and/or loss of sleep. This was a point made by Dr George Green who, recognizing that the cinema could be a force for good as well as evil, reasoned that: 'On the whole, it seemed advisable that children's performances should be given in the afternoon rather than in the evening, as that had a less disturbing effect on sleep.'[56] Likewise, a delegate at a head teachers' conference in 1924 complained that 'children went to the films and were then afraid of the dark, and spent their nights in dreams of horror'.[57]

Regulation of posters and the prohibition of children from cinemas after a certain hour were measures designed, in part at least, to limit the influence that films had on younger audiences. The policy of banning minors from cinemas showing 'A' certified films, even when accompanied by parents or guardians, was a much more direct form of control, and this, too, had its supporters in Wales.[58] A delegate from Cardiff proposed, at the conference of the National Federation of Christian Workers in 1932, that an appeal be made to the Home Office to introduce legislation preventing even accompanied children from watching 'A' classified films. As he saw it: 'The trouble lies in the fact that you never know what seed has been planted in the minds of those young people by films marked "A". The result may not now be apparent, but God knows it will be revealed later on in life.'[59] Neither the Home Office nor the BBFC approved of the idea, but this did not stop local authorities from pursuing precisely such a policy. It was adopted most famously by Liverpool JPs in October 1930, who felt that parents were 'not always the best judges of what a child should see'.[60] Burnett and Martell described this decision as 'an outstanding victory for decency',[61] and a number of other local authorities followed Liverpool's example. Demands that children be kept away from pictures deemed suitable for adult audiences, however, were made before the 1930s. In 1920 Lleufer Thomas, a key figure in the decision to ban children from evening cinema performances in the Rhondda, spoke of the need for more exhibitions of films for children only.[62] By 1929, at least one member of Swansea's Watch Committee felt 'there was no doubt that films were being shown that children should not see'.[63] Within a year Swansea councillors had decided to ban all children under the age of sixteen from cinemas where 'A' films were being shown: some nine months before the Liverpool JPs did so.[64]

The measures introduced by local authorities to keep children away from cinemas at certain times, or during particular sorts of performances, were by no means set in stone. Under pressure from both exhibitors and audiences most of these decisions were eventually reversed. By taking such action, however, local licensing authorities demonstrated that they were serious about their role in the censorship process. They may have been unable to do much to control the content of individual films, but they did what they could to limit the cinema's potential as a harmful influence.

Another way in which local councils sought to control the cinema's influence was by carefully monitoring the types of films shown at particularly sensitive times. Four Pontypridd cinemas found that the renewal of their licences had been placed in jeopardy in 1931 because they had 'shown films at Christmas other than those permitted by the magistrates'.[65] More significantly, perhaps, in 1926 a Swansea cinema was forced to change its programme on Armistice Day because of the public outcry surrounding the film *The Unknown Soldier*. The tradition of the unknown soldier was by no means unique to Britain, but it nonetheless embodied powerful national sentiments. The notion that an *American* film company should be able to profit by releasing a film on the subject, and at such a sensitive time, was clearly too much for some of the more patriotic members of the public. Neither the BBFC President, T. P. O'Connor, nor the Home Secretary, who was forced to defend the film in the House of Commons, could find anything objectionable in the film's content. The author of one letter to the *South Wales Daily Post*, however, insisted that 'the offence to British sentiment cannot be over-emphasised':

> It is revolting to think that an American film company should hoax the British public into patronising a film of this type, by causing a title so endeared to all British hearts . . . The Unknown Soldier is revered throughout the Empire. I feel sure that the Welsh people, as members of this vast Empire, will feel the insult to British sentiment and pride.[66]

The manager of the Castle Cinema, unperturbed by such sentiments, assured the proprietor that 'the whole matter will probably be forgotten by Monday'. He nonetheless considered it necessary to withdraw the picture on Armistice Day itself – though not for the rest of the week when it played to packed houses.[67] The tone of the criticism directed at this film, along with its popularity with audiences, suggest that the controversy was an expression of much deeper concerns about the spread of American culture throughout British society. Such anxieties were never far from the surface in debates about the cinema in this period. They were pushed to the fore in this instance because Hollywood had been seen to have penetrated one of Britain's most important national traditions.

The idea that commercial cinema entertainment might impinge on a Welsh national tradition – the 'Welsh Sunday' – led to much the most impassioned debates about the role of cinema in Welsh society in our period.

Sunday opening of cinemas in Wales

Many of the concerns raised about the cinema generally, were expressed with added intensity whenever it was suggested that picture halls should be opened on Sundays. In debates over Sunday opening accusations that the cinema was a threat to public morals, or an agent of Americanization, were particularly forcefully made. An examination of the factors which lay behind the controversy over Sunday opening, therefore, may help to explain the rationale behind attempts to control or regulate the cinema in Wales.

In Wales, the issue of Sunday opening was much more sensitive than in most other parts of Britain. Evidence of the actual extent to which Wales (and

Scotland) were out of step with England in terms of Sunday cinema attendance is provided by the statistical survey of cinema attendance conducted by Browning and Sorrell in the early 1950s. In 1951, they calculated that in the north of England one in ten cinema visits occurred on a Sunday, in the south the proportion was more like one in eight. However

> The experience in Scotland and Wales is in marked contrast to England. In Scotland only about one in twelve cinemas were open on Sunday in 1951 (compared with two out of three in the country as a whole) and under 1 per cent of all admissions were on Sunday; in Wales the corresponding proportions were one in ten and 2 per cent. This is perhaps some indication of the strength of nonconformist traditions in these countries.[68]

Opponents of Sunday opening in Wales often took exception to the nature of cinema entertainment, on the grounds that it was wholly inappropriate for exhibition on the sabbath. Cinemas were, in fact, allowed to open on Sundays in Wales for most of our period, but only for 'sacred concerts' at which no films were shown nor profits made. When the Cardiff Watch Committee met to discuss the possibility of opening cinemas on Sundays in order to raise funds to relieve distress, it was implicitly accepted that a stricter standard of censorship than that already existing would need to be enforced on Sundays.[69] The lord mayor expressed the view that cinemas 'were opened for concerts now, and if they could get some kind of censorship of the pictures that would be shown he saw no reason why the people should not be in cinemas rather than walking around on the streets'.[70] Similarly, Mrs Rhoda Parker 'did not see any objection as long as pictures of the right sort were shown and if the cinemas were opened after church hours'.[71] Even for those in favour of Sunday opening, it seems, the moral standards to which films had to conform from Monday to Saturday were insufficient to warrant the granting of Sunday licences. When films were found which were suitable for exhibition on the sabbath, however, it was known for attitudes to become more relaxed. Both the Watch Committee and the local chief constable were willing, for instance, to allow Swansea YMCA to screen religious films on Sunday evenings in 1931.[72] There was little objection within Wales to the idea of incorporating the cinema, as a social institution, into the existing tradition of the Welsh Sunday. What caused concern was the introduction of entertainments that ran counter to traditional notions of sabbath observance. As a secular, commercial, and for the most part foreign medium of entertainment, the cinema provided much scope for concern.

The question of Sunday opening came to prominence every ten years or so throughout the period under examination here. In 1921 a request by Lord/Earl Haig that cinemas should be opened on a single Sunday (April 3) to raise money for his Officers' Association fund, led to the issue of Sunday cinemas being discussed by local licensing authorities across Wales. Though there was a general acceptance that something should be done to assist the cause, the suggestion that cinemas be opened on a Sunday, albeit as a one-off gesture, was felt to be the thin end of the wedge, and most Welsh licensing authorities rejected the idea. The same year saw a number of requests for cinemas to be (temporarily) opened on Sundays to support various local charitable causes – such as the purchase of a war memorial in Pontypridd and the relief of distress caused by unemployment in Cardiff.[73]

Much of the most prolonged debate on the issue of Sunday opening (in Britain as a whole, not just Wales) came in the early 1930s. Until this time it had been widely assumed that any local licensing authority could grant cinema licences on Sundays – on the proviso that all profits went to charity. However, an unexpected legal decision in 1930, based on the Sunday Observance Act of 1780, ruled such actions illegal. This led in turn to demands for new legislation to replace what was seen as an outdated Act. A Sunday Opening Bill came before parliament in 1931, therefore, proposing that local authorities should be allowed to grant licences for the showing of films on Sundays provided a public demand for this could be demonstrated. There was some dispute as to what exactly constituted 'public demand', but in effect the Bill simply attempted to re-establish, on a secure legal footing, the situation that had existed before 1930. Scotland and Northern Ireland were excluded from the Bill on the grounds that the 1780 Act had not applied in these territories in the first place. There was a committed group of Welsh MPs who also argued that Wales should be excluded from the legislation. Before the Bill could pass into law, however, the country was plunged into economic and political crisis and the legislation was postponed.

The whole matter was debated once again in 1932 and this time a Bill was passed (in which Wales was included) that permitted local authorities to grant Sunday cinema licences. The only authorities automatically entitled to do this, however, were those where Sunday film shows had regularly taken place before 1930. Those authorities, including all Welsh ones, which had previously refused to grant Sunday licences needed to submit a draft order to the secretary of state before permission for them to do so could be granted. Furthermore, in all boroughs and urban districts a draft order could not be submitted until a poll of local residents had been taken and a majority approval of Sunday opening demonstrated. Despite these stringent conditions the great majority of Welsh MPs still voted against the Bill – for reasons which will be discussed below.[74]

With the onset of the Second World War the question of Sunday opening was again raised. The 1932 Act was amended, making it easier for local authorities to issue Sunday cinema licences, and there were demands that, in certain parts of Wales at least, restrictions on the Sunday opening of cinemas should be relaxed. It was (unsuccessfully) argued, for instance, that troops stationed in Welsh towns should have the opportunity to visit picture houses on Sunday evenings.

For the most part, Sabbatarians had been able to rebuff attempts to introduce Sunday opening into Wales, most of which had been generated by developments elsewhere in Britain. In 1950, however, after a fiercely fought referendum campaign, the people of Swansea voted in favour of the Sunday opening of cinemas. Thereafter it was only a matter of time before other parts of Wales followed suit.[75] In retrospect it seems that opponents of Sunday opening were engaged in a battle they were always doomed to lose. Eventually, forces of commercialization and secularization rendered the foundations of Welsh Sabbatarianism obsolete. Interestingly, the arguments marshalled against Sunday cinema in Wales gradually shifted in emphasis over the period covered here, with the issue increasingly treated as a national, rather than a religious one. The main areas of debate can be broadly divided into four areas.

The argument most frequently advanced by supporters of Sunday opening was that by allowing cinemas to open, people would have something to do on Sunday evenings other than roaming the streets. The prospect of young people spending their Sunday evenings in the local picture hall, so the argument ran, was a good deal less harmful than having them out on the streets. One Wrexham councillor made the point directly when debating the issue in 1942. He appealed to his colleagues that 'they must admit that Wrexham on a Sunday night was a disgrace. The streets were thronged. It was worse than any other night. A number of young men from the district were being packed home by the police.'[76] Similarly, when the renewal of a seven-day dramatic licence for a Bargoed cinema was discussed, one councillor argued that 'young people are better off in cinemas than running about the roads and rambling over the mountains. It is better for the morals of the people.'[77] Sabbatarians, on the other hand, flatly rejected the notion that the opening of cinemas on Sunday could achieve any advance in public morality. They tended to regard the cinema as a dubious moral influence as it was, and to extend licences to permit Sunday opening was, for them, ungodly as well as unnecessary. The Revd F. W. Cole of Penarth made the point succinctly: 'I maintain that it is far better for them [young people] to take a walk along the cliffs, with the fresh wind of God on their faces, than in a cinema, where the winds blow from Hollywood.'[78]

A second argument employed by proponents of Sunday cinemas was that it would serve a valuable social purpose by raising money for local charitable causes. It was solely as an aid to such causes that Sunday opening had first been seriously proposed in parts of Wales in the early 1920s. These proposals were turned down by most local councils, however, on the grounds that they represented the 'thin end of the wedge'. Defenders of the 'traditional' Welsh Sunday were, no doubt rightly, suspicious of the claims that all profits would go to charity. They realized that once the principle of Sunday opening had been established the desire to help local charities would soon diminish, and cinemas would be run on the same basis for seven days a week. Lord Colum

Crichton-Stuart, for one, was sceptical of reassurances that the Bill before parliament in 1931 would prevent exhibitors from pocketing the profits from Sunday opening:

> Many cinema proprietors are against the Bill, but, of course, there is money in it. There are the receipts from advertisements and the publicity they will get for the week's fresh films. But is anyone so simple as to doubt that in the course of a short time there will also be a substantial share in the receipts, if not the whole, to bank on Monday morning?[79]

When the Sunday Opening Bill came before parliament once more in 1932, Major Goronwy Owen led the Welsh opposition to the proposals, by arguing that 'The trouble and danger of this Bill is that it gives the sanction of law for the first time to inroads upon the Christian Sunday, and it would open the way to a further secularisation and commercialisation of the one day of rest.'[80]

Against this, a third (libertarian) argument that people had as much right to visit the cinema on a Sunday evening as they had to go to church cut little ice with Sabbatarians, and indeed it was a point seldom advanced. Demands for increased personal liberty could easily be interpreted by the more religiously minded as simply putting more temptation in peoples' way. Further, by raising the issue of personal choice, supporters of Sunday opening left themselves open to the counter-argument that cinema workers would be required, against their will, to work on Sundays.

The fourth area of debate surrounding the issue was the question of nationality. Just as protesters at a demonstration in Cardiff against the 1881 Sunday Closing Act had demanded 'British rights for British working men',[81] there were those half a century later who similarly felt that the rights enjoyed by many people in parts of England should also be extended to Wales. On learning, in 1921, that Sunday opening was permitted by the London County Council, one Cardiff councillor complained that he failed 'to see why London should be favoured or disfavoured – according to the point of view – more than Cardiff'.[82] Such a view, when stated at all, remained a minority view within most Welsh councils. The alternative position was expressed by, among others, Lord Crichton-Stuart. Arguing that capital cities, by their very cosmopolitan nature, tended to be more lax about Sunday observance than outlying areas, he went on to suggest that 'London is unique in attempting to force its failings, not only upon its own provinces, but upon another country – Wales – as well'.[83]

The twin assumptions implicit in this argument – first, that Wales was a distinct national entity in itself; and secondly, that it was opposed, *as a nation*, to Sunday opening – became increasingly important as the debate wore on. Key to the success that Welsh Sabbatarians were able to achieve in delaying the spread of Sunday opening into Wales, however, was not the strength of their arguments, but the amount of influence they could exert in Welsh society. Who, then, were the supporters of the Sabbatarian cause?

According to Stephen Ridgwell, 'the churches and chapels' played 'an absolutely central role in moulding and organising this hostile opinion'.[84] Despite declining church attendance, religious authorities and Nonconformist denominations in particular, continued to wield considerable influence throughout this period. This was only partly the result of individual ministers berating congregations from their pulpits. More important was the role played by bodies such as the Free Church Council and the Lord's Day Observance Society both in holding demonstrations and, crucially, sending deputations to lobby licensing authorities. In both 1921 and 1940 such deputations played an important role in convincing Cardiff councillors not to permit Sunday opening.

It is unlikely that the arguments advanced by various religious bodies would have proved very effective, however, had local politicians not been sympathetic to their position in the first place. Much is made of the fact that the 1920s witnessed something of a watershed in Welsh politics, with the nineteenth-century Liberal hegemony being replaced by that of a Labour Party more in tune with the needs of an industrial working class. Nonconformist religion had been intimately bound up with the identity of Liberal Wales, as reflected by its political achievements from the Welsh Sunday Closing Act of 1881 to disestablishment of the Church in 1919. If the debates over Sunday cinemas tell us anything, it is that the decline of the Liberal Party and of chapel attendance, did not bring to an end the influence of Nonconformity in Welsh political society.

Ridgwell describes the controversy over Sunday cinemas in Wales as 'the "tip of an iceberg", the visible extremity of something far deeper':

> Since the turn of the century the 'traditionalists' had been struggling to hold on to their idea of a distinctly Welsh culture against the threatening advance of an urbanised, commercialised and anglicised counter-culture ... The cinema, and especially the Sunday cinema, came to crystallise this clash of cultures.[85]

He observes that the six Welsh MPs who voted in favour of the Sunday Opening Bill in 1932 all represented south Wales constituencies, and that the remaining Liberal strongholds in north and west Wales remained staunchly opposed. It is important to recognize, however, that support for any opposing 'counter-culture' to the traditions of Liberal Wales was seldom found in the Labour Party at this time. The transformation of Welsh politics in this period was more evolutionary than revolutionary with continuity just as discernible as change. Ridgwell is aware of these continuities but still 'can't help feeling that had the Labour Party in Wales, particularly in south Wales, pressed the case for Sunday cinemas, their arrival would have been a good deal hastened'.[86] No doubt, but the crucial point is that the Labour Party in Wales had no reason to press the case for Sunday opening. Indeed, the secular and commercial forces that informed the logic of Sunday opening were as much anathema to Welsh Labour men as they had been to their Liberal predecessors. As Peter Stead has remarked, the Labour Party in south Wales was led after 1918, 'by men whose careers had consisted not of sectional activities but of service to the community as a whole'. It is significant, therefore, that 'most of them were active in Nonconformist chapels'.[87] A closer look at the south Wales MPs who voted for the 1932 Sunday Opening Bill is revealing in this respect. All six represented south Wales constituencies, but it is surely significant that three of them were Conservatives.[88] Reginald Clarry, who had won a by-election in Newport in 1922 on the back of his opposition to the Liberal Government's extension of the 1881 Sunday Closing Act to Monmouthshire, was one such supporter of the Bill. Clarry had 'gained the support of local licensed victuallers'[89] in his 1922 election campaign, and the concern that he, and other Conservatives, had for the interests of local traders (whether publicans or cinema managers) accounted for just as much of the support for the Sunday Opening Bill in Wales as did any sympathy on the Labour benches for the rights of working-class men and women. The sort of arguments that were most likely to persuade Labour supporters were almost invariably employed by opponents of Sunday opening. It was repeatedly stressed, for instance, that cinema workers needed a day of rest on the sabbath, yet the fact that it was illegal for any cinema employee to work for seven consecutive days was largely overlooked.

In contrast to the breadth of support on which Sabbatarians could rely, supporters of Sunday opening had few representatives in positions of authority. Even cinema exhibitors in Wales were reluctant to be seen pushing the case for Sunday opening too forcefully. When the Sunday Opening Bill was being debated in 1931 the south Wales branch of the CEA argued that Wales should not be exempted from the legislation, but in doing so stressed that 'If there is no general demand in an area for Sunday opening, the kinemas will remain shut'.[90] The view of the trade was that Sunday opening should only come about if the public demanded it, but they did very little to influence public opinion themselves.

The length of time it took for Sunday opening to be established in Wales suggests that the 'traditional' values espoused by Liberal Wales continued to hold considerable moral authority until the second half of the twentieth century. As the debates wore on, however, opponents of Sunday opening appealed less to deep seated religious sentiments than to national ones.

National consciousness had been as much a feature of Liberal Wales as had Nonconformist zeal. The establishment of institutions such as the University of Wales, the National Library and the National Museum had been important achievements, and a powerful sense of national sentiment had also underpinned arguments in favour of the Welsh Sunday Closing Act of 1881, disestablishment of the Church and, of course, Home Rule. The society and culture that emerged out of the industrialized areas of (mainly south) Wales, however, had no place in the outlook of this generation of Welsh nationalists. Abhorrence at the industrialization of south Wales was particularly marked among the more radical Welsh nationalists, who had sought a political outlet of their own after the post-1918 decline of the Liberal Party. Saunders Lewis's poem, 'The Deluge 1939', effectively captures their sense of disenchantment. The opening stanza reads as follows:

> The tramway climbs from Merthyr to Dowlais,
> Slime of a snail on a heap of slag;
> Here once was Wales, and now
> Derelict cinemas and rain on the barren tips;
> The pawnbrokers have closed their doors, the pegging clerks
> Are the gentry of this waste;
> All flesh had corrupted his way upon the earth.[91]

If cinemas were regarded as unwelcome and alien institutions by the defenders of 'traditional' Welsh culture, Sunday opening was an even more direct affront to their sense of national identity. In opposing the Sunday opening Bill of 1932 Major Goronwy Owen MP (Lib. Caernarvon) claimed to 'know the views of the great number of the Welsh nation with regard to the Bill and with what repugnance and abhorrence they viewed any legislation which tended to detract from the holiness of Sunday.' Making direct reference to the 1881 Sunday Closing Act, he argued that 'The position of Sunday in Wales was quite different from England'.[92] The 1881 Act was important in this respect because it had been the 'first distinctively Welsh Act of Parliament' that applied 'a distinct legislative principle for Wales, as distinct from England'.[93] This was a precedent that those of a nationalist persuasion were enthusiastic to see extended.

The national element to debates over Sunday opening in the early 1930s was highlighted by the fact that all but four Welsh MPs voted against the Bill in 1931 (a figure that increased to six the following year.) This also explains why Goronwy Owen and his supporters were less concerned to see the Bill defeated as to ensure that Wales was excluded from it altogether. The apparent contradiction in their arguments – that, on the one hand, there was no demand in Wales for Sunday opening, and on the other, that local option should not be granted to Welsh constituencies – were seized on by defenders of the legislation. When another Welsh MP, Mr. Llewelyn-Jones (Lib. Flintshire), put the case for Welsh exclusion in Standing Committee, the Home Office Under Secretary, Oliver Stanley, replied that: 'The hon. Member must have very little confidence in the desire of Welshmen to preserve their Sunday if he really believes that this provision is going to be a temptation to them.'[94] For many Welsh Liberals, however, local option was opposed precisely because the issue was felt to be a national, rather than a local one.

Concerns about the protection of Welsh identity were also evident when

Sunday opening was debated during the Second World War. The Pontypridd councillor who announced in 1940 that he opposed Sunday cinemas on the grounds that 'it is a step in the direction of eliminating all that is best in the life of the Welsh nation',[95] was expressing what had become the standard argument against Sunday opening. The Revd Dr Rees Griffiths, similarly, appealed to Cardiff councillors that 'Wales is what it is because it has had this institution for centuries'.[96]

The increasing frequency with which the national card was being played in Sunday opening debates, however, was more indicative of the decline in popular religious sentiment than any increasing nationalist fervour. Shortly after Cardiff councillors had voted against Sunday cinemas in 1940, the Revd William Yorwerth published an article in which he argued that

> The tragic and undeniable fact is this, that the decline in Sabbath observance is not so much due to indifference of the masses as to the increasing apathy of those in normal membership with the churches, to whom Sabbath observance has no personal and vital meaning . . . The revolt of modern youth from organised religion is due not to a growing materialism but to the failure of the churches to square up to new conditions.[97]

The arguments being advanced by those opposed to Sunday opening bore less relevance to those of a younger generation who had grown up in a very different society. Appeals to the national heritage of Liberal Wales, with its emphasis on Sabbath observance, may have influenced those in positions of authority in the inter-war years, but by the 1950s a new generation of political leaders was emerging, to whom such considerations were quite unimportant. The authors of a survey titled *Social Change in South-West Wales*, note that '[d]uring the discussions about Sunday cinemas in Swansea in 1950 a substantial number of Labour councillors were in favour of them opening'. They argued that such councillors were part of a 'newer generation of active trade union Socialists . . . [who] are gradually ousting the more old-fashioned Socialists whose activities and opinions alike show their chapel background'.[98]

The length of time it took for Sunday opening to become established in Wales is testament that the values of Victorian Wales survived into the mid-twentieth century. The eventual arrival of Sunday cinemas, however, was a clear signal that such values would have little role to play in the shaping of post-war Wales. The traditional Welsh Sunday was being, as it were, 'uninvented', and the issues that most concerned post-war Welsh nationalists were much more secular and overtly political.

Summary

There was little by way of active censorship of films in Wales, partly because local authorities simply did not have the resources to carry it out, but also because they did not need to. The standards upheld by the BBFC in this period were usually quite acceptable to authorities in Wales as well as the rest of Britain. Cinema managers did not need to be overly concerned with the films they showed in order to avoid licensing difficulties, but they did need to take account of how the pictures were locally marketed and received. The environment in which films were seen, the make-up of the audience who saw them and the times at which they were screened were matters to which licensing authorities paid close attention. The intention was to ensure that the institution of the cinema conformed to standards of respectability that were acceptable to leaders of Welsh society. These standards evolved as Welsh society itself changed and new leaders emerged. In the period covered by this study, the vast majority of Welsh cinemas were either independently managed or part of a small, locally run chain. Control over the way that films were exhibited and received, therefore, lay almost entirely in local hands. For the most part, cinema managers and local councillors in Wales acted much like their counterparts in the rest of Britain. Their autonomy, however, did enable them to express local, and in the case of Sunday opening, national differences.

CONCLUSIONS

Film-going was the most popular form of publicly consumed entertainment in Wales between the 1920s and the 1950s. Welsh households spent more on cinema tickets than theatre and sporting events combined, though expenditure on film-going remained only a small part of that typically allocated for recreation, and just a tiny fraction of overall household spending. The cultural influence of the cinema cannot, of course, be measured simply by the amount of money people allocated to film going. One of the reasons cinema was so popular was that it was cheap and represented quite remarkable value for money. Statistics on consumer expenditure do remind us, however, that cinema was just one of a range of recreational pursuits available to people. Its appeal was certainly impressive in comparison to attendance at football matches or theatre performances, but less so when set against the consumption of tobacco products, alcohol or even books and magazines.

There was nothing particularly remarkable or distinctive about the appeal of film-going in Wales compared to other parts of Britain. Frequency of cinema attendance in Wales was no higher than the British average and somewhat lower than in northern England and Scotland. Where Wales differed from other British regions was not in the popularity of films, but in its provision of cinemas.

The large cinema circuits that increasingly came to dominate film exhibition in Britain in the 1930s made very little investment in Wales. For many of the larger towns and cities in Britain the 1930s was 'the age of the dream palace', but in Wales older patterns of film exhibition, based around small, locally owned cinemas remained the norm. The persistence of this more traditional pattern of film exhibition did nothing to dampen the appeal of film-going in Wales, but it did mean that the environment in which films were consumed was locally controlled. As well as local centres of entertainment, cinemas were also local employers. They did not always offer particularly generous wages, particularly to female staff such as cleaners and usherettes, but they were nonetheless a valuable source of employment (and income) during periods when little other work was available.

Measured by aggregate levels of attendance cinema was far more popular than other forms of publicly consumed entertainment, but as local institutions, individual cinemas faced real competition from other forms of popular culture. We have seen that rival attractions, such as travelling fairs, excursions or touring operas could lure away even the most regular film-goers. Cinema managers could not take their customers for granted and developed their own advertising and publicity campaigns to keep the audiences coming in. On some occasions cinema managers had cause to be thankful for the influence of other forms of popular culture: cinema attendance in Cardiff and Swansea was known to rise significantly on weekends when these towns played host to major rugby internationals.

What set the cinema apart from most of the other forms of entertainment against which it competed was the contrast between the social and the cultural experiences it offered. Socially, the cinema's appeal remained rooted in local traditions: familiarity, convenience and accessibility were the cornerstones of the popularity of local cinemas. Culturally, however, the films audiences most enjoyed were usually foreign and about as far removed from local tradition as it was possible to get. Whether melodrama, western or romantic, films offered audiences the opportunity to escape temporarily into another world which seemed glamorous or exotic or both. The provision of escapist entertainment, for little cost, in a socially familiar and friendly environment, was a potent combination. High-minded critics often referred to cinema entertainment as a form of drug or dope, and the most regular film-goers as 'addicts' dependent on their weekly or twice-weekly fix of entertainment. Yet the addiction metaphor should not be pushed too far. Film audiences were not victims of a clinical addiction, but rather enthusiastic consumers with a healthy appetite for filmed entertainment. The appeal of 'the pictures' lay not so much in the inherent properties of the cinematic medium itself, but in the startling contrast between the world depicted on the silver screen and that in which audiences actually lived. A combination of increasing consumer affluence and the widespread availability of television (which brought visual entertainments into the most local and familiar environment of all – the home) sent cinema attendance into steep decline in the second half of the twentieth century.

Between the 1920s and the early 1950s, when film-going was at its peak, different cinemas appealed to different groups, in part by providing different programmes of entertainment. The largest and most prestigious cinemas in the big towns were often converted theatres that had been comprehensively refurbished in the 1920s or 30s. These cinemas were popular with all social groups, but with slightly higher admission charges than other halls, particularly for balcony seats, they consciously sought to attract a 'better class' of patron. One way in which they did this was by continuing to provide live stage performances, as well as films, in an attempt to retain the patronage of their former variety audiences. The most prestigious of the newly built cinemas in the 1930s also introduced variety acts into their programmes, and some even employed musicians to keep customers entertained in their cinema cafés. Such cinemas were the 'first-run' halls, so-called because they were the first to screen the latest releases in their locality. These 'dream palaces' did help to make cinema-going more respectable for middle-class audiences, but just as importantly a visit to such a cinema was an affordable luxury for the working classes too.

While cinemas such as Cardiff's Capitol or Swansea's Plaza were much loved institutions, the type of film-going experience they offered was atypical. More common by far were visits to small, 'second-run' cinemas that showed films which had either been passed over or long since screened by the major circuits or leading independent cinemas. These halls could not compete with the large city-centre cinemas in terms of the films they screened, nor did they embellish their programmes with live variety or musical entertainment. Yet by offering a reliable staple of Hollywood entertainment that was both cheap and conveniently accessible, they provided the bedrock on which the cinema-going habit was built. In some of the larger Welsh towns a number of local cinemas were constructed in the inter-war period, but in smaller communities in most parts of Wales the local cinema was more typically a converted hall, skating rink or part of a miners' institute.

Within a few short years at the beginning of the twentieth century cinema grew from a fairground novelty into one of the most popular cultural institutions in Welsh society. How did representatives of other cultural traditions respond? For those whose identities were shaped by the values of the pulpit or the coal pit, the cinema's appeal posed both an opportunity and a threat. Neither ministers of religion nor union officials saw much merit in the content of most commercially produced films, regarding them as suspicious on either moral or political grounds, or both. Yet there was also a feeling, regularly expressed in the Welsh press, that cinema was a medium with the potential to make Welsh culture more relevant and accessible to a new and expanding audience. Concerns about national identity, so important a feature of the Wales of the pulpits, were evident in calls for a Welsh Films Council and the frequent demands that more be done to promote film-making in Wales itself. Despite the best efforts of a few committed individuals, however, little was achieved in this regard. The screen depictions of the Welsh that most audiences saw in this period were provided by Twentieth Century Fox or MGM (producers of *How Green Was My Valley* and *The Citadel*), not local independent film-makers like Ifan ab Owen Edwards. Similarly, attempts within the society of the coal pit to use cinema to promote a progressive political agenda made little headway. A number of miners' cinemas did screen films dealing with subjects such as the Spanish Civil War and revolutionary Russia, evidence that the medium was being used to serve the political and cultural interests of Labour Wales. The screening of 'political' films, however, was the exception rather than the rule, and miners' cinemas, like those elsewhere, had to rely on popular Hollywood entertainment to attract regular custom. The societies of both the pulpit and the coal pit hoped to use cinema to promote their own social and cultural identity, but such attempts were no match for the entertainment provided by commercial film studios.

The influence that religious or political leaders were able to exert over cinema-going in Wales related less to the content of films themselves than to the context in which they were received. The design and positioning of advertising posters, the lighting and seating arrangements within cinemas, and the attendance of children at evening performances were matters that local authorities took seriously. In these respects councillors in Wales acted in much the same spirit as their counterparts in the rest of Britain. Debates over the Sunday opening of cinemas, however, provide the clearest evidence of attempts to protect 'traditional' Welsh society (both pulpit and coal pit) from a more commercial and consumer oriented 'American Wales'. The idea of allowing cinemas to open on a Sunday aroused passionate opposition in Wales and was resisted until the 1950s – decades after it had become commonplace in England. Opponents saw themselves as defenders of the traditional 'Welsh Sunday', which they regarded as an important feature of national identity under threat from commercial interests. By voting to allow the Sunday opening of cinemas, the people of Cardiff and Swansea began a process by which this particular Welsh tradition became 'uninvented'. Much the same pattern would be followed decades later in debates, and local referenda, on the Sunday opening of pubs in Wales – with the same result.

This book set out to explore the reception of cinema entertainment in Wales during the period of its greatest appeal. It has done so by examining the institutions through which the pictures were brought to audiences; the appeal of the entertainments for audiences themselves; and the response to this new cultural form from different sections of Welsh society. The central argument is that although the international film industry was dominated by American firms, whose films were certainly popular with Welsh audiences, the social experience of cinema-going remained an intensely local one. Socially, cinemas established themselves as popular local institutions at the heart of Welsh communities, while culturally, they offered a form of entertainment that lay outside the traditions of Liberal or Labour Wales. The so-called 'fleapits' were probably the most visible symbol of the Welsh as consumers in the mid-twentieth century, just as the pulpits and coal pits symbolized the Welsh as worshippers or workers. As such these local cinemas might be taken as the most visible evidence of a consumerist 'American Wales'.

American Wales did not, however, exist in a vacuum. It was no more independent of the culture and traditions of Liberal and Labour Wales than these two societies were of each other. This history of film-going provides a vivid illustration of how American popular culture could be enthusiastically embraced by Welsh audiences, yet still consumed in a manner reflective of local cultural traditions. The mass appeal of Hollywood films provides compelling evidence of the existence of an 'American Wales' in the mid-twentieth century; the nature of the film-going experience reminds us that 'American Wales' was at least as firmly rooted in the culture of Wales as it was of America.

NOTES

Introduction

1 David Berry, *Wales and Cinema: The First Hundred Years* (Cardiff, 1994).
2 Gerben Bakker, 'Entertainment industrialized: the emergence of the international film industry, 1890–1940', *Enterprise and Society*, 4, 4 (2003), 579–85.
3 For example, Janet Staiger, *Interpreting Films: Studies in the Historical Reception of American Cinema* (Princeton, NJ, 1992); Annette Kuhn and Jackie Stacey (eds), *Screen Histories: A Screen Reader* (Oxford, 1998); Melvyn Stokes and Richard Maltby (eds), *Identifying Hollywood's Audiences: Cultural Identity at the Movies* (London, 1999); Nicholas Hiley, '"Let's go to the pictures": the British cinema audience in the 1920s and 1930s', *Journal of Popular British Cinema*, 2 (1999), 39–53; Annette Kuhn, *An Everyday Magic: Cinema and Cultural Memory* (London, 2002).
4 For example, David Bordwell, Janet Staiger and Kristen Thompson, *The Classical Hollywood Cinema: Film Style and Mode of Production to 1960* (London, 1985); Richard Maltby, *Hollywood Cinema* (Oxford, 2003 edn); Tino Balio (ed.), *The American Film Industry* (Madison, 1976); Tino Balio, *Grand Design: Hollywood as a Modern Business Enterprise, 1930–1939* (Berkeley and Los Angeles, 1993); Thomas Schatz, *The Genius of the System: Hollywood Film-making in the Studio Era* (New York, 1988).
5 Richard Maltby, 'Introduction', in Stokes and Maltby (eds), *Identifying Hollywood's Audiences*, p. 4.
6 Kenneth O. Morgan, *Rebirth of a Nation: Wales, 1880–1980* (Oxford, 1981), p. 36.
7 R. Merfyn Jones and Ioan Rhys Jones, 'Labour and the Nation', in Duncan Tanner, Chris Williams and Deian Hopkin (eds), *The Labour Party in Wales, 1900–2000* (Cardiff, 2000), pp. 241–63.
8 R. Merfyn Jones, 'Beyond identity? The reconstruction of the Welsh', *Journal of British Studies*, 31, 4 (1992), 330–57.
9 Gwyn A. Williams, *When Was Wales? A History of the Welsh* (Harmondsworth, 1985), p. 241.
10 Alfred E. Zimmern, *My Impressions of Wales* (London, 1921), p. 29.
11 See, for example, David Smith, 'Wales through the looking-glass', in David Smith (ed.), *A People and a Proletariat* (London, 1980), pp. 215–39.
12 Walter Haydn Davies, *Ups and Downs* (Swansea, 1975), pp. 46–7.
13 Ibid., pp. 46–7.
14 Emlyn Williams, *George* (London, 1961), pp. 130–3.
15 Leslie Thomas, *In My Wildest Dreams* (London, 1984), pp. 43–4.
16 For example, J. B. Priestley, *English Journey* (London, 1934); George Orwell, *Keep the Aspidistra Flying* (London, 1936).
17 Albert Jenkins captained Llanelli, and Wales, in the 1920s. Lord Elwyn-Jones, *In My Time* (London, 1983), pp. 19–20.

[18] Gareth Williams, *1905 And All That: Essays on Rugby Football, Sport and Welsh Society* (Llandysul, 1991), p. 127.

[19] Wilde to Castle and Central Cinemas, 10 July 1931. Glamorgan Record Office [GRO hereafter], D/D A/B, 18/11/1.

[20] Ministry of Labour and National Service, 'Weekly expenditure of working-class households in the United Kingdom in 1937–1938' (unpublished report, July 1949), The National Archives [TNA hereafter], Lab 17/7.

[21] Harry Libby, *The Mixture: Mumbles and Harry Libby* (Swansea, 1962), p. 46.

[22] See, Stephen Ridgwell, 'South Wales and the cinema in the 1930s: the functioning and reception of a mass cultural form' (M.Phil. thesis, Swansea, 1993).

[23] Robert Morgan, *My Lamp Still Burns* (Llandysul, 1981), p. 46.

[24] Roy Denning, in Stewart Williams (ed.), *The Cardiff Book* (Barry, 1973), p. 54.

[25] Robinson to Andrews, 20 May 1920. GRO, D/D A/B, 18/5/40.

[26] Robinson to Andrews, 22 June 1920. GRO, D/D A/B, 18/5/48.

Introduction to Part I

[1] Tony Garnett, quoted in Peter Stead, 'Wales in the movies', in Tony Curtis (ed.), *Wales: The Imagined Nation, Essays in Cultural and National Identity* (Bridgend, 1986), p. 161.

1. Consumers

[1] Barry Supple, *The History of the British Coal Industry Vol. 4, 1913–1946: The Political Economy of Decline* (Oxford, 1987); John Davies, *A History of Wales* (London, 1993), pp. 549–59; Gwyn A. Williams, *When Was Wales? A History of the Welsh* (Harmondsworth, 1985), pp. 252–72; Kenneth O. Morgan, *Rebirth of a Nation: Wales, 1880–1980* (Oxford, 1981), pp. 210–40; Gareth Elwyn Jones, *Modern Wales: A Concise History* (2nd edn, Cambridge, 1994), pp. 185–8; Philip Jenkins, *A History of Modern Wales, 1536–1990* (London and New York, 1992), pp. 366–72.

[2] Chris Williams, *Capitalism, Community and Conflict: The South Wales Coalfield, 1898–1947* (Cardiff, 1998); John Williams, *Was Wales Industrialised? Essays in Modern Welsh History* (Llandysul, 1995); Ina Zweiniger-Bargielowska, 'Miners' militancy: a study of four south Wales collieries during the middle of the twentieth century', *Welsh History Review*, 16, 3 (1992), 356–83; Hywel Francis and David Smith, *The Fed: A History of the South Wales Miners in the Twentieth Century* (London, 1980).

[3] David Smith, *Aneurin Bevan and the World of South Wales* (Cardiff, 1993); Chris Williams, *Democratic Rhondda: Politics and Society 1885–1951* (Cardiff, 1996); David Smith, *Wales! Wales?* (Hemel Hempstead, 1984).

[4] Competing theories of consumption are discussed in Ben Fine and Ellen Leopold, *The World of Consumption* (London, 1993).

[5] Matthew Hilton, *Consumerism in 20th-Century Britain* (Cambridge, 2003), p. 19.

[6] Hilton, *Consumerism*; Martin Daunton and Matthew Hilton, *The Politics of Consumption: Material Culture and Citizenship in Europe and America* (Oxford, 2001); Susan Strasser, Charles McGovern and Matthias Judt (eds), *Getting and Spending: European and American Consumer Societies in the Twentieth Century* (Cambridge and New York, 1998).

[7] The emergence of a consumer society has been attributed to various historical periods. See N. McKendrick, J. Brewer and J. H. Plumb, *The Birth of a Consumer Society: The Commercialisation of Eighteenth Century England* (London, 1982); Paul Johnson, 'Conspicuous consumption and working-class culture in late Victorian and Edwardian Britain', *Transactions of the Royal Historical Society*, Series 5, 38 (1988), 27–42; Jean-Christophe Agnew, 'Coming up for air: consumer culture in historical perspective', in John Brewer and Roy Porter (eds), *Consumption and the World of Goods* (London, 1993), pp. 19–39.

[8] John Benson, *The Rise of Consumer Society in Britain, 1880–1980* (London and New York, 1994), p. 4.

[9] Thorstein Veblen, *The Theory of the Leisure Class* (1899; New York, 1965), p. 85; also quoted in Johnson, 'Conspicuous consumption', p. 30.

[10] Hortense Powdermaker, *Hollywood the Dream Factory*, (London, 1951).

[11] A wealth of statistical material on consumer expenditure in Britain in the 1920s and 30s is available, but it is not broken down on a regional basis. Published statistics on consumer expenditure in Wales offer very little detail on the inter-war period. See Richard Stone and D. A. Rowe, *The Measurement of Consumers' Expenditure and Behaviour in the United Kingdom, 1920–1938*, 2 vols (Cambridge, 1954); John Williams, *Digest of Welsh Historical Statistics*, 2 vols (Welsh Office, 1985).

[12] Ministry of Labour and National Service, 'Weekly expenditure of working-class households in the United Kingdom in 1937–1938' (unpublished report, July 1949), The National Archives [TNA hereafter], Lab 17/7.

[13] Ministry of Labour and National Service, *Report of an Enquiry into Household Expenditure in 1953–54* (London, 1957).

[14] Brinley Thomas, 'Post-war expansion', in Brinley Thomas (ed.), *The Welsh Economy: Studies in Expansion* (Cardiff, 1962), pp. 30–50.

[15] Nicholas Hiley, ' "Let's go to the pictures": the British cinema audience in the 1920s and 1930s', *Journal of Popular British Cinema*, 2 (1999), 39–53.

[16] H. E. Browning and A. A. Sorrell, 'Cinemas and cinema-going in Great Britain', *Journal of the Royal Statistical Society*, 117, II (1954), 133–65; P. Perilli, 'Statistical survey of the British film industry', in J. Curran and V. Porter (eds), *British Cinema History* (London, 1983), p. 372.

[17] The figure of 28 cinema admissions per head in Britain in 1950 was unmatched by any other country at that time. The next highest figure was that of the United States, with 23, but no other country got above 19. Browning and Sorrell, 'Cinemas and cinema-going', p. 136.

[18] Between the late 1930s and the early 1950s, while the average price of a cinema ticket fell in real terms by 15 per cent, the average level of weekly household expenditure rose in real terms by 31 per cent.

[19] Entertainment duty was not charged at a flat rate on all cinema admissions, rather, there was a sliding scale with the cheapest tickets taxed less than the most expensive ones. See Geoffrey Macnab, *J. Arthur Rank and the British Film Industry* (London, 1993), pp. 188–98; A. P. Herbert, *No Fine on Fun: The Comical History of the Entertainment Duty* (London, 1957).

[20] The records can be found in the Andrews Collection held at the Glamorgan Record Office [GRO hereafter], D/D A/B Box 41.

[21] Film-goers tended to have very clear ideas about the relative merits of each of the cinemas in their locality. See Jeffrey Richards and Dorothy Sheridan (eds), *Mass-Observation at the Movies* (London and New York, 1987); Leslie Halliwell, *Seats in all Parts: Half a Lifetime at the Movies* (London, 1985); Annette Kuhn, *An Everyday Magic: Cinema and Cultural Memory* (London, 2002).

22 Political and Economic Planning [PEP hereafter], *The British Film Industry* (London, 1952), p. 181.

23 The cash books from Porth's Central cinema illustrate the point nicely. In the 1920s and 30s attendances invariably surged at specific times of the year (Christmas, Easter week and the August bank holiday) suggesting that there was a large group of people who would go to the cinema on certain occasions, but not as a matter of routine. By the 1940s, such seasonal variations were hardly evident at all, and average attendance levels were close to those previously seen during holiday periods. GRO, D/D A/B, box 41.

24 Kathleen Box, *The Cinema and the Public: An Inquiry into Cinema Going Habits and Expenditure Made in 1946* (London, 1946), p. 3.

25 See, L. Moss and K. Box, 'The cinema audience', an appendix to J. P. Mayer, *British Cinemas and their Audiences: Sociological Studies* (London, 1948), p. 253.

26 PEP, *The British Film Industry*, p. 182.

27 A more detailed regional and social breakdown of cinema audiences in England can be found in Ross McKibbin, *Classes and Cultures: England 1918–1951* (Oxford, 1998), pp. 419–56.

28 For a theory of film choice developed on the basis of British audiences in the 1930s see John Sedgwick, *Popular Filmgoing in 1930s Britain: A Choice of Pleasures* (Exeter, 2000).

29 Nicholas Hiley, 'The British cinema auditorium', in Karel Dibbets and Bert Hogenkamp (eds), *Film and the First World War* (Amsterdam, 1995), pp. 160–70.

30 S. Harper and V. Porter, 'Cinema audience tastes in 1950s Britain', *Journal of British Popular Cinema*, 2 (1999), 66–82.

31 Jeffrey Richards, *The Age of the Dream Palace: Cinema and Society in Britain, 1930–1939* (London, 1984); Stephen Ridgwell, 'South Wales and the cinema in the 1930s: the functioning and reception of a mass cultural form' (unpublished M.Phil. thesis, Swansea, 1993).

32 Peter Miles and Malcolm Smith, *Cinema, Literature and Society: Elite and Mass Culture in Inter-War Britain* (London, 1987), p. 164.

33 David Docherty, David Morrison and Michael Tracey, *The Last Picture Show? Britain's Changing Film Audiences* (London, 1987); Philip Corrigan, 'Film entertainment as ideology and pleasure: a preliminary approach to a history of audiences', in Porter and Curran (eds), *British Cinema History*, pp. 24–35.

2. Cinemas

1 Nicholas Hiley, '"Let's go to the pictures": the British cinema audience in the 1920s and 1930s', *Journal of Popular British Cinema*, 2 (1999), 39–53.

2 Skating was one of the popular fads of the early twentieth century and disused rinks were regularly converted into cinemas. In Tredegar, for example, one of the cinemas used throughout this period was called the Rink and Pavillion.

3 See also Nicholas Hiley, 'The British cinema auditorium', in Karel Dibbets and Bert Hogenkamp (eds), *Film and the First World War* (Amsterdam, 1995), pp. 160–70.

4 An amusing discussion of the role of usherettes in controlling cinema audiences can be found in Ernest Dyer, 'Cinema pests', *Sight and Sound*, 6, 24 (1937–8), 192–3.

5 Hiley, '"Let's go to the pictures"', p. 45.

6 Jeffrey Richards, *The Age of the Dream Palace: Cinema and Society in Britain, 1930–1939* (London, 1984).

[7] Peter Miles and Malcolm Smith, *Cinema, Literature and Society: Elite and Mass Culture in Inter-War Britain* (London, 1987); Ross McKibbin, *Classes and Cultures: England 1918–1951* (Oxford, 1998), pp. 419–56.

[8] See, for instance, the discussion between Robert Allen and Charles Musser in *Studies in Visual Communication*, 10 (1984), 24–52.

[9] J. K. S. Poole, quoted in Janet McBain, *Pictures Past: Recollections of Scottish Cinemas and Cinema-Going* (Edinburgh, 1985), p. 14.

[10] The earliest example seems to have been the Balham Empire, which became a cinema in 1907. See Rachael Low, *The History of the British Film, 1906–1914* (London, 1948), pp. 15–16.

[11] 'Penny gaffs' were usually converted shops or houses in which films were screened in the evenings.

[12] Nicholas Hiley points out that 'most of the new venues were built by local speculators eager to cash in on the cinema boom and were no more than small halls with very limited catchment areas'. See Hiley, 'The British cinema auditorium', p. 160.

[13] Dennis Sharp, *The Picture Palace and Other Buildings for the Movies* (London, 1969), p. 59.

[14] Low, *History of the British Film, 1906–1914*, pp. 16, 17.

[15] Sharp, *Picture Palace*, p. 66. The erroneous forecast was made by one John Palmer.

[16] David Atwell, *Cathedrals of the Movies: A History of British Cinemas and their Audiences* (London, 1980); Sharp, *The Picture Palace*; Allen Eyles, *ABC: The First Name in Entertainment* (Burgess Hill, 1993); Allen Eyles, *Gaumont British Cinemas* (Burgess Hill, 1996); Rosemary Clegg, *Odeon* (Birmingham, 1985).

[17] Robert Atkinson, 'The design of the picture theatre', in *Journal of the Royal Institute of British Architects*, XXXVIII, third series (June, 1921), 441–55.

[18] Low, *History of the British Film, 1906–1914*.

[19] The largest cinema to be built in Britain at this time was Green's Playhouse in Glasgow, seating 4,400.

[20] J. Eberson, quoted in Atwell, *Cathedrals of the Movies*, pp. 76–7.

[21] Atwell, *Cathedrals of the Movies*, pp. 46–7.

[22] McKibbin, *Classes and Cultures*, p. 423.

[23] The attitudes expressed by British film critics in this period are dealt with in chapter 6.

[24] P. Morton Shand, *Modern Theatres and Cinemas* (London, 1930), p. 19.

[25] Shand, *Modern Theatres*, pp. 9, 20.

[26] Shand, *Modern Theatres*, p. 16.

[27] Shand, *Modern Theatres*, p. 9.

[28] See Robert Murphy, 'Oscar Deutsch', in David Jeremy (ed.), *Dictionary of Business Biography* (London, 1984), pp. 89–93.

[29] Atwell, *Cathedrals of the Movies*, p. 159.

[30] Oscar Deutsch, in a Foreword to a Special Cinema Supplement of *Architectural Design and Construction*, VII, 5 (March, 1937), 183.

[31] Robert Cromie, 'What I really think of present day cinemas', *Architectural Design and Construction*, VIII, 3 (March, 1938), 89.

[32] J. R. Leathart, 'Cinema facade: the task of the modern cinema architect', in *Sight and Sound*, 4, 13 (1935), 12.

[33] Sharp, *Picture Palace*, p. 176.

[34] Audrey Field, *Picture Palace: A Social History of the Cinema* (London, 1974), p. 79.

[35] Atwell, *Cathedrals of the Movies*, p. 75.

[36] Quoted in Field, *Picture Palace*, p. 108.

[37] He mentions the Carlton and Castle cinemas, see Atwell, *Cathedrals of the Movies*, p. 29.

[38] See chapter 3.

[39] Simon Rowson, 'A statistical survey of the cinema industry in Great Britain in 1934', *Journal of the Royal Statistical Society*, vol. XCIX (1936), 67–119; H. E. Browning and A. A. Sorrell, 'Cinemas and cinema-going in Great Britain', *Journal of the Royal Statistical Society*, 117, II (1954), 133–65.

[40] In 1934 Wales accounted for 7.5 per cent of all cinemas in Britain, yet it accounted for only 3.3 per cent cinemas constructed in the previous two years.

[41] Scotland, in fact, boasted some of the largest and most impressive cinemas in the whole of Britain and the average size of cinemas there was well above the national average. Rowson, 'A statistical survey of the cinema industry', 76; Browning and Sorrell, 'Cinemas and cinema-going in Great Britain', 138–40.

[42] Average cinema size was just 677 seats in north Wales. The regions with the next smallest cinemas were the south-west and eastern counties of England. Rowson, 'A statistical survey of the cinema industry', 76.

[43] The percentage of the population living in towns over 100,000 in these areas in 1950 were as follows: Scotland, 38; north-west, 44; Midlands, 43; London and south-east, 55; Wales, 24. Browning and Sorrell, 'Cinemas and cinema-going in Great Britain', 138–40

[44] David Smith, *Aneurin Bevan and the World of South Wales* (Cardiff, 1993), p. 92.

[45] The period covered is April 1950 to March 1951.

[46] Philip Jenkins, *A History of Modern Wales, 1536–1990* (London, 1992), p. 366.

[47] Peter Stead, 'Wales and film', in Trevor Herbert and Gaerth Elwyn Jones (eds), *Wales Between the Wars* (Cardiff, 1995), pp. 161–85: 161.

[48] This had been true also of the earliest purpose-built cinemas in the years before 1914. See Low, *History of the British Film, 1906–1914*, p. 17.

[49] The appeal of the cinema for different social groups, and the social function it performed is dealt with more fully in chapter 4.

[50] M. J. Daunton, *Coal Metropolis: Cardiff, 1870–1914* (Leicester, 1977).

[51] The prediction was made in a special edition of the *Daily Mail*, 31 December 1900, quoted in Ian Christie, *The Last Machine: Early Cinema an the Birth of the Modern World* (London, 1994), p. 9.

[52] These figures, and all subsequent population totals, are taken from census reports.

[53] These figures, and a great deal more information on Cardiff's cinemas, have been gleaned from Brian Hornsey, *Ninety Years of Cinema in Cardiff* (Stamford, 1997); also the *Kinematograph Year Books*.

[54] See Jeffrey Richards, 'The cinema and cinema-going in Birmingham in the 1930s', in John K. Walton and James Walvin (eds), *Leisure in Britain, 1780–1939* (Manchester, 1983), p. 35.

[55] Of those that were built in the 1930s one opened in the last week of 1939 and can thus cannot have benefited inter-war audiences.

[56] The information regarding seating capacity comes from the *Kinematograph Year Book*, (1939), 668–9; see also Hornsey, *Ninety Years of Cinema in Cardiff*.

[57] *South Wales Echo*, 11 November, 1935, 8.

[58] Incidentally, it also happens to be the only Odeon opened in Wales in the 1930s that is still running under this name.

[59] *South Wales Echo*, 8 September 1936, 10.

[60] This information comes from a combination of press reports in the *Western Mail* and *South Wales Echo*, and also from Hornsey, *Ninety Years of Cinema in Cardiff*.

[61] The social makeup of the cinema audience is discussed in more detail in chapter 4.

[62] *South Wales Echo*, 20 October 1928, 2.

[63] The nature of the entertainment offered by different cinemas is considered more fully in chapter 5.

[64] *South Wales Echo*, 17 April 1937, 8.

[65] See chapter 3.

[66] The Tivoli was only built after Llandaff's existing cinema had been destroyed by fire.

[67] See Brian Hornsey, *Ninety Years of Cinema in Swansea: An Essay Celebrating the Cinemas* (Stamford, 1994); also *South Wales Evening Post*, 8 November 1976, 8, and 22 December 1976, p. 4.

[68] *South Wales Evening Post*, 5 December 1938, 6.

[69] These averages are based on the seating capacities given in the *Kinematograph Year Book* (1939).

[70] *Western Mail*, 14 February 1931, 5.

[71] Brian Hornsey, *Ninety Years of Cinema in Newport* (Stamford, 1994).

[72] *Kinematograph Year Books* (1914–).

[73] Figures taken from Hywel Francis and David Smith, *The Fed: A History of the South Wales Mines in the Twentieth Century* (London, 1980), p. 508.

[74] Peter Scott, 'The state, internal migration, and the growth of new industrial communities in inter-war Britain', *English Historical Review*, CXV, 461 (April, 2000), 329–53.

[75] Gwyn A. Williams, *When Was Wales? A History of the Welsh* (Harmondsworth, 1985), p. 246.

[76] The phrase comes from the *Western Mail*, 1 January 1901, and has been cited by various historians since. See, for example, Chris Williams, *Democratic Rhondda: Politics and Society 1885–1951* (Cardiff, 1996), pp. 12–28.

[77] Other forms of working-class culture in south Wales, notably rugby football and choral singing, were dealt a severe blow by the inter-war depression. See Gareth Williams, 'From grand slam to great slump: economy, society and rugby football in Wales during the depression', *Welsh History Review*, 9 (June 1983), pp. 338–57; Gareth Williams, *Valleys of Song: Music and Society in Wales, 1840–1914* (Cardiff, 1998).

[78] Jack Jones, 'Social effects of the coming of broadcasting', MS in National Library of Wales [NLW hereafter], no. 46 (1938), p. 19.

[79] *Merthyr Express*, 16 February 1929, 10.

[80] *Aberdare Leader*, 8 April 1939, 5.

[81] Hilda Jennings, *Brynmawr: A Study of a Distressed Area* (London, 1934).

[82] *Merthyr Express*, 16 February 1929, 10.

[83] Stephen Ridgwell, 'Pictures and proletarians: south Wales miners' cinemas in the 1930s', *Llafur: Journal of Welsh Labour History*, 7, 2 (1997), 69–80.

[84] See Dennis Thomas, 'Economic decline', in Herbert and Jones (eds), *Wales Between the Wars*, pp. 13–51.

[85] These figures are taken from the census returns of 1951, the corresponding figures were unfortunately not published in the inter-war years.

[86] See Brian Hornsey, *Ninety Years of Cinema in Wrexham* (Stamford, 1990); also Brian Hornsey *Cinemas of North Wales* (Stamford, 1996), pp. 91–7.

[87] *Wrexham Leader*, 19 March 1937, 7; see also commemorative section, celebrating the cinema's twenty-first anniversary in the *Wrexham Leader*, 7 March 1958, 8–10.

[88] *Caernarfon and Denbigh Herald*, 3 August 1934, 2.

[89] Hornsey, *Cinemas of North Wales*, pp. 8–14, 23–5.
[90] *Liverpool Post and Mercury*, 30 June 1931, 1.
[91] Hornsey, *Cinemas of North Wales*, pp. 33–5; 49–61; 78–88.
[92] The towns included in the sample are: from north Wales, Bangor, Caernarfon, Llandudno, Colwyn Bay, Rhyl and Wrexham; from south Wales, Newport, Cardiff, Port Talbot, Swansea and Llanelli.
[93] Dafydd Roberts, 'The slate quarrying communities of Caernarfonshire and Merioneth, 1911–1939' (Ph.D. thesis, Aberystwyth, 1982), p. 477.
[94] Hornsey, *Cinemas of North Wales*.
[95] *Carmarthen Journal*, 3 April 1936, p. 1.

3. Companies and employees

[1] Rachael Low, *The History of the British Film: Vols I–VII* (London, 1948–85); Margaret Dickinson and Sarah Street, *Cinema and State: The Film Industry and the British Government 1927–1984* (London, 1985); Sarah Street, *British National Cinema* (London and New York, 1997).
[2] This raised the problem of film historians judging the British industry by a quite different set of standards from those under which it actually operated. See Peter Stead, 'Hollywood's message for the world: the British response in the nineteen thirties', *Historical Journal of Film, Radio and Television*, 1, 1 (1981), 19–32; I. Jarvie, *Hollywood's Overseas Campaign: The North Atlantic Movie Trade, 1920–1950* (Cambridge, 1992).
[3] J. Sedgwick, *Popular Filmgoing in 1930s Britain: A Choice of Pleasures* (Exeter, 2000); J. Richards (ed.), *The Unknown 1930s: An Alternative History of the British Cinema, 1929–1939* (London and New York, 1998).
[4] For example, Gerben Bakker, 'Stars and stories: how films became branded products', *Enterprise and Society*, 2, 3 (2001), 461–502; Gerben Bakker, 'Building knowledge about the consumer: the emergence of market research in the motion picture industry', *Business History*, 45, 1 (2003), 101–27; Gerben Bakker, 'Selling French films on foreign markets: the international strategy of a medium-sized film company', *Enterprise and Society*, 5, 1 (2004), 45–76; John Sedgwick and Michael Pokorny, 'The risk environment of film-making: Warner Bros in the inter-war years', *Explorations in Economic History*, 35 (1998), 196–220; John Sedgwick, 'Product differentiation at the movies: Hollywood, 1946–1965', *The Journal of Economic History*, 62, 3 (2002), 676–705.
[5] See Tino Balio, *United Artists: The Company Built by the Stars* (Madison, 1976); Tino Balio (ed.) *The American Film Industry* (Madison, 1976); Tino Balio, *Grand Design: Hollywood as a Modern Business Enterprise, 1930–1939* (Berkeley and Los Angeles, 1993); David Bordwell, Janet Staiger and Kristen Thompson, *The Classical Hollywood Cinema: Film Style and Mode of Production to 1960* (London, 1985); Kristen Thompson, *Exporting Entertainment* (London, 1985); Thomas Schatz, *The Genius of the System: Hollywood Film-making in the Studio Era* (New York, 1988).
[6] See Rachael Low, *The History of the British Film, 1918–1929*; Allen Eyles, *ABC: The First Name in Entertainment* (Burgess Hill, 1993); Allen Eyles, *Gaumont British Cinemas* (Burgess Hill, 1996); Rosemary Clegg, *Odeon* (Birmingham, 1985).
[7] Quotation taken from Political and Economic Planning [PEP hereafter], *British Film Industry*, p. 151.

[8] In 1949 United Artists calculated that releasing pictures through independent cinemas would generate less than half the revenue of a circuit release. United Artists Archive [UAA hereafter], Series 6B, Arthur Kelly Papers, box 7, file 8.

[9] Ernest Betts, *The Film Business: A History of British Cinema, 1896–1972* (London, 1973), p. 79.

[10] H. E. Browning and A. A. Sorrell, 'Cinemas and cinema-going in Great Britain', *Journal of the Royal Statistical Society*, series A, part II, 117 (1954), 142, 146.

[11] Singleton cinemas are those not part of a chain; small circuits are those of between 2 and 10 halls; medium circuits are those with 11 to 50 halls; large circuits are those of over 50 halls.

[12] Robert Murphy, 'Oscar Deutsch', in David Jeremy (ed.), *Dictionary of Business Biography* (London, 1984), pp. 89–93.

[13] See Clegg, *Odeon*.

[14] Odeon cinemas, which usually seated between 1,400 and 1,800 people, were generally smaller than the two- or three-thousand seat Gaumonts and ABCs. This, perhaps, explains why Odeon built more cinemas in Wales than the other two major circuits.

[15] Odeons had also been planned for the south Wales towns of Swansea and Port Talbot. Building work was abandoned, however, with the outbreak of war.

[16] Eyles, *Gaumont British Cinemas*.

[17] Eyles, *ABC*.

[18] Neither Abertillery Theatres Ltd nor Ebbw Vale Theatres Ltd operated cinemas outside of their respective towns.

[19] A discussion of contemporary debates concerning transportation between north and south Wales can be found in Pyrs Gruffudd, 'Remaking Wales: nation-building and the geographical imagination, 1925–1950', *Political Geography*, 14, 3 (1995), 219–39.

[20] Although based in Hereford, all six of the cinemas operated by Plaza Cinemas were in mid Wales.

[21] According to the information in the *Kine Year Books*, the average size of Welsh circuits increased from 3.9 cinemas in 1922, to 5.2 in 1936.

[22] Reports of the court case appear in the *Western Mail*, 20–6 March 1925.

[23] For an introduction to the extensive business history literature on family firms see Mary B. Rose, 'The family firm in British business, 1780–1914', in M. W. Kirby and M. B. Rose (eds), *Business Enterprise in Modern Britain* (London, 1994), pp. 61–87; A. Colli, P. F. Perez and M. B. Rose, 'National determinants of family firm development? Family firms in Britain, Spain and Italy in the nineteenth and twentieth centuries', *Enterprise and Society*, 4, 1 (2003), 28–64.

[24] Browning and Sorrell, 'Cinema and cinema-going', 138–40, 154–9.

[25] *South Wales Echo*, 15 May 1971, 6.

[26] The actual programmes of entertainment provided by Welsh cinemas are examined in greater detail in chapter 5.

[27] Stephen Ridgwell, 'South Wales and the cinema in the 1930s', *Welsh History Review*, 17 (1995), 600.

[28] United Artists would typically spend between $10,000 and $15,000 advertising each of their films in Britain. See UAA, Series 4F, Walter Gould Papers, box 4, 'England 1937–1941: advertising appropriations'.

[29] The half-page rate for advertisements in the *Western Mail* and the *South Wales Echo* in 1934 was £75, and the rate for a single column inch was £1. The equivalent figures for the Swansea-based *South Wales Evening Post* were £32. 10s, and 8s 6d. UAA, Series 1F, Black Books, box 7, file 3, 'British Isles: advertising and publicity'.

30 *South Wales Echo*, 18 May 1971, 5.
31 *South Wales Echo*, 15 May 1971, 6.
32 Stephen Ridgwell, 'Pictures and proletarians: south Wales miners cinemas in the 1930s', *Llafur*, 7, 2 (1997), 69–80.
33 Hywel Francis and David Smith, *The Fed: A History of the South Wales Mines in the Twentieth Century* (London, 1980), p. 447.
34 Bert Hogenkamp, *Deadly Parallels: Film and the Left in Britain, 1929–39* (London, 1986), p. 143.
35 Bert Hogenkamp, 'Miners' cinemas in south Wales in the 1920s and 1930s', *Llafur: Journal of Welsh Labour History* 4, 2 (1985), 66, 71–2.
36 *South Wales Echo*, 17 May 1971, 5.
37 *South Wales Echo*, 14 May 1971, 5.
38 The actual increase in the numbers employed in cinemas is probably higher than these figures suggest since many theatres and music halls were either forced to close or convert into cinemas in this period.
39 According to the census there were 375 musicians employed in Welsh theatres, music halls and cinemas in 1921. It is likely that there were considerably more by the time the talkies arrived.
40 Michael Chanan, *Labour Power in the British Film Industry* (London, 1976), p. 14.
41 In many parts of Wales where electricity simply was not available for much of the inter-war period, older methods were preserved. Problems with electrical equipment, in areas where it could be used, meant that the skills of the 'handle turner' were often required in the 1920s.
42 Dick Lewis, who worked at Tonypandy's Empire, quoted in *South Wales Echo*, 17 May 1971, p. 5.
43 See Rachael Low, *The History of the British Film 1929–1939: Film Making in 1930s Britain* (London, 1985), p. 17.
44 *South Wales Echo*, 15 May 1971, 6.
45 *South Wales Echo*, 15 May 1971, 6.
46 The pianist, Adolphus Davies, worked in Cardiff's Globe cinema, see the *South Wales Echo*, 19 May 1971, 13.
47 *South Wales Echo*, 19 May 1971, 13.
48 Holidays with pay were enjoyed by relatively few workers in this period, see Stephen G. Jones, 'Trade union policy between the wars: the case of holidays with pay in Britain', *International Review of Social History*, 31 (1986), 40–67.
49 *South Wales Echo*, 17 May 1971, 5.
50 Glamorgan Record Office [GRO hereafter], Andrews Collection, D/D A/B 19/12/23i, letter from the Aeolian Co Ltd to A. Andrews, 14 September 1922.
51 He did initially promise his musicians that they could stay on to play incidental music. Unfortunately, however, the sound equipment installed in all of Will Stone's cinemas failed on the first night, forcing them to close. See the *South Wales Echo*, 17 May 1971, 5.
52 See *South Wales Echo*, 23 February 1976, 9.
53 *South Wales Evening Post*, 16 February 1931.
54 See the *Radio Times*, 22 November 1935.
55 Tom O'Brien, quoted in *The Daily Herald*, 2 July 1934, 3.
56 The author has encountered no examples of any female commissionaires.
57 This is the reminiscence of Connie Derrick, quoted in the *South Wales Echo*, 23 February 1996.
58 So remembers Reg Bennett, quoted in the *South Wales Echo*, 17 May 1971, 5.

59   The recollection is that of John Martin, quoted in the *South Wales Echo*, 23 February 1976, 9.

60   *The Daily Herald*, 2 July 1934, 3.

61   Robinson to Andrews, 2 October 1920, GRO, D/D A/B 18/5/74.

62   John Clarke and Chas Critcher, *The Devil Makes Work: Leisure in Capitalist Britain* (Basingstoke, 1985), p. 77.

63   The MP in question was Major Henry Procter, quoted in Stephen G. Jones, *The British Labour Movement and Film, 1918–1939* (London and New York, 1987), p. 66.

64   See Martin Pugh, 'Domesticity and the Decline of Feminism, 1930–1950', in Harold Smith (ed.), *British Feminism in the Twentieth Century* (Amherst, 1990), pp. 144–63.

65   Jane Lewis, *Women in Britain Since 1945: Women, Family, Work and the State in the Post-War Years* (Oxford, 1992), p. 18.

66   Economic activity rates for women in Wales were 23 per cent in 1921 and 21.5 per cent in 1931. The corresponding figures for England and Wales as a whole were 32.3 per cent and 34.2 per cent respectively.

67   Gwyn A. Williams, 'Women workers in Wales, 1968–82', *Welsh History Review*, 11, 4 (1983), 531.

68   Penny Summerfield, *Women Workers in the Second World War: Production and Patriarchy in Conflict*, (London, 1984); Harold L. Smith, 'The effect of the war on the status of women', in Harold L. Smith (ed.), *War and Social Change: British Society in the Second World War* (Manchester, 1986), pp. 209–29.

69   The figures are taken from the 1931 Census, *Industry Tables*, pp. 446–58.

70   Reg Bennett, quoted in the *South Wales Echo*, 17 May 1971, 5.

71   NATE had represented the backstage workers in the music halls: the performers were led by the Variety Artistes' Association, and the musicians by the Musicians' Union. See Chanan, *Labour Power*, p. 13.

72   Chanan, *Labour Power*, pp. 13–22.

73   Hogenkamp, 'Miners' cinemas', p. 69.

74   This was almost certainly because Swansea's Elysium cinema was built in 1913 as the main hall of the Dock, Wharf and Riverside General Workers Union. Those who worked at the Elysium would, therefore, have been members of the Dockers' Union, and it seems likely that some of them must have retained their membership after moving to other cinemas. See Brian Hornsey, 'The Elysium cinema, Swansea', *Mercia Bioscope*, no. 53 (1994); also City of Swansea Archives, File FAC. 180.

75   *Kinematograph Weekly*, 2 December 1920, 101.

76   Gambold to Andrews, 2 March 1920, GRO, D/D A/B 18/14/9.

77   Gambold to Andrews, 24 January 1920, GRO, D/D A/B 18/14/5.

78   The approach of the Dockers Union seems to have been effective. Their initial demands were not met, but a counter offer was accepted. Gambold informed Andrews that the new agreement 'will affect us to the extent of about £5 or £6 increase'. GRO D/D A/B 18/14/10–13ii.

79   *Kinematograph Weekly*, 16 December 1920, 101.

80   Gambold had no objection to musicians receiving extra payments, but contended 'that the MU should obtain payment from the BBC'. GRO, D/D A/B 18/15/132–3.

81   Chanan, *Labour Power*, pp. 13–22.

82   *Kinematograph Weekly*, 16 September 1920, 120.

83   Chanan, *Labour Power*, p. 51.

84   *Kinematograph Weekly*, 19 November 1936, 37.

85   Copies of the letters sent by NATKE to Arthur Andrews of Castle and Central cinemas in November 1936 are held at: GRO, D/D A/B 20/5/2–4.

86 *Western Mail*, 19 July 1937, 5; 24 July 1937, 10; 20 August 1937, 8.
87 *Western Mail*, 19 April 1938, 14; 21 April 1938, 14.
88 *Western Mail*, 30 July 1937, 6; 13 August 1937, 7.
89 Ridgwell, 'South Wales and the cinema', p. 599.

4. Cinema's appeal

1 Ernest Lindgren, *The Cinema* (London, c.1944), p. 11.
2 David Docherty, David Morrison and Michael Tracey, *The Last Picture Show? Britain's Changing Film Audiences* (London, 1987), p. 15.
3 Nicholas Hiley, ' "Let's go to the pictures": the British cinema audience in the 1920s and 1930s', *Journal of Popular British Cinema*, 2 (1999), 39–53; Ross McKibbin, *Classes and Cultures: England, 1918–1951* (Oxford, 1998), pp. 419–56.
4 Melvyn Stokes and Richard Maltby (eds), *Identifying Hollywood's Audiences: Cultural Identity and the Movies* (London, 1999); Gerben Bakker, 'Building knowledge about the consumer: the emergence of market research in the motion picture industry', *Business History*, 45, 1 (January 2003), 101–27.
5 John Sedgwick, 'Product differentiation at the movies: Hollywood, 1946–1965', *Journal of Economic History*, 62, 3 (Sept. 2002), 676–705; John Sedgwick and Michael Pokorny, 'The risk environment of film making: Warner Bros in the inter-war years', *Explorations in Economic History*, 35 (1998), 196–220.
6 Richard Maltby, 'Sticks, hicks and flaps: classical Hollywood's generic conception of its audiences', in Stokes and Maltby, *Identifying Hollywood's Audiences*, pp. 23–41.
7 Louis Moss and Katherine Box, 'The cinema audience: An inquiry made by the Wartime Social Survey for the Ministry of Information', an appendix to J. P. Mayer, *British Cinemas and their Audiences: Sociological Studies* (London, 1948), pp. 250–75.
8 Kathleen Box, *The Cinema and the Public: An Enquiry into Cinema Going Habits and Expenditure Made in 1946* (London, 1946), p. 3.
9 A survey carried out in 1934 clearly showed that East Anglia, the west of England and north Wales had fewer cinemas than more industrialized areas, and that they were smaller in size. Simon Rowson, 'A statistical survey of the cinema industry in Great Britain in 1934', *Journal of the Royal Statistical Society*, XCIX (1936), 67–119.
10 See Table 10, in chapter 1.
11 For example, D. C. Jones, *The Social Survey of Merseyside* (Liverpool, 1934); H. Llewellyn Smith et al. (eds), *New Survey of London Life and Labour* (London, 1934); B. Seebohm Rowntree, *Poverty and Progress* (London, 1941); the Carnegie Trust studies of youth unemployment in Glasgow, Liverpool and Cardiff (1941).
12 In a study of slate quarrying communities in north-west Wales it has been argued that it was from 'the early twenties on' that cinema-going became firmly established in the area, and that 'magic lantern shows had been fairly common in the years before 1914'. Dafydd Roberts, 'The slate quarrying communities of Caernarfonshire and Merioneth, 1911–1913' (Ph.D. thesis, Aberystwyth, 1982), p. 477.
13 Of those in the lower economic group 32 per cent never went to the cinema compared with 27 per cent in the higher group. More strikingly, 33 per cent of those not educated above elementary level claimed never to go to the cinema compared with just 18 per cent of university graduates. See Moss and Box, 'The cinema audience', pp. 257–8.

[14] The 1943 survey categorized the income groups as follows: lower, under £5 per week; middle, £5–10; higher, over £10. In the 1946 survey the categories were: lower, under £4 per week, middle, £4–£5 10s; higher, above £5 10s. Box, 'The cinema and the public', p. 3.

[15] Philip Corrigan, 'Film entertainment as ideology and pleasure: a preliminary approach to a history of audiences', in Vincent Porter and James Curran (eds), *British Cinema History* (London, 1983), p. 34.

[16] Roger Manvell, *A Seat at the Cinema* (London, 1951), p. 22.

[17] Stephen Ridgwell, 'South Wales and the cinema in the 1930s', *Welsh History Review*, 17 (1995), 594.

[18] See, for example, Sue Aspinall, 'Women, realism and reality in British films 1943–53', in Porter and Curran (eds) *British Cinema History* (London, 1983), pp. 272–93; Sue Harper, *Picturing the Past: The Rise and Fall of the British Costume Film* (London, 1994); Pam Cook, *Fashioning the Nation: Costume and Identity in British Cinema* (London, 1996).

[19] Richard Maltby, 'Introduction', in Stokes and Maltby (eds), *Identifying Hollywood's Audiences*, p. 8.

[20] H. L. Smith (ed.), *The New Survey of London Life and Labour*, vol. 9, *Life and Leisure* (London, 1935), p. 46.

[21] Ridgwell, 'South Wales and the cinema in the 1930s', 594.

[22] S. Glynn and A. Booth, *Modern Britain: An Economic and Social History* (London, 1995), p. 29.

[23] Moss and Box, 'The cinema audience', p. 254.

[24] Box, *The Cinema and the Public*, p. 3.

[25] See, for example, Richard Ford, *Children in the Cinema* (London, 1939); J. P. Mayer, *British Cinemas and their Audiences: Sociological Studies* (London, 1948).

[26] Docherty, Morrison and Tracey, *The Last Picture Show?*, pp. 18–19.

[27] Mary Stewart, *The Leisure Activities of Schoolchildren* (London, c.1947).

[28] Conversely, it may have been precisely because boys formed the bulk of cinema club membership that these films were the ones most regularly shown.

[29] Stewart, *Leisure Activities of Schoolchildren*, p. 9.

[30] Box, *The Cinema and the Public*, p. 5.

[31] Economic activity rates for women in Wales were 23 per cent in 1921 and 21.5 per cent in 1931. The corresponding figures for England and Wales as a whole were 32.3 and 34.2 per cent respectively.

[32] J. B. Priestley, *English Journey* (London, 1934), p. 401.

[33] Mildred Evans (b. 1920), quoted in Jeffrey Grenfell-Hill (ed.), *Growing up in Wales: Collected Memories of Childhood in Wales, 1895–1939* (Llandysul, 1996), pp. 169–70.

[34] Ivor Montagu, *Film World: A Guide to the Cinema* (Harmondsworth, 1964), p. 221.

[35] Nicholas Hiley, 'The British cinema auditorium', in Karel Dibbets and Bert Hogenkamp (eds), *Film and the First World War* (Amsterdam, 1995), p. 160.

[36] Hiley, '"Let's go to the pictures"'.

[37] P. Morton Shand, *Modern Theatres and Cinemas: The Architecture of Pleasure* (London, 1930), p. 9.

[38] Iris Barry, *Let's Go to the Pictures* (London, 1926), p. 3.

[39] A. J. Lush, *The Young Adult in South Wales* (Cardiff, 1941), p. 80.

[40] Herbert James (b. 1909), quoted in Grenfell-Hill (ed.), *Growing up in Wales*, pp. 97–8.

[41] Ridgwell, 'South Wales and the cinema in the 1930s', 595.

[42] Sidney L. Bernstein, 'Walk up! Walk up! – Please', in Charles Davy (ed.), *Footnotes to the Film* (London, 1937), p. 230.

43 Roger Manvell, *A Survey of the Cinema and its Public* (London, c.1947), p. 3.
44 Mrs Eirona Richards, interviewed by Beth Thomas, Museum of Welsh Life [MWL hereafter] tape 7583.
45 The cheapest seats in the Central were 4d compared with 9d in the Capitol in the late 1930s, these prices are taken from the *Kinematograph Year Book* (1939).
46 Mrs Cora Edwards, letter to the author, 11 February 1997.
47 Mrs Judy Godfrey Brown, letter to the author, 13 February 1997.
48 Quoted in Stephen Ridgwell, 'South Wales and the cinema in the 1930s', 597.
49 Mrs Judy Godfrey Brown, letter to the author, 13 February 1997.
50 Professor Graham Owens, letter to the author, 22 February 1997.
51 Ridgwell, 'South Wales and the cinema in the 1930s', 594.
52 Mrs Beryl Ellis, her recollections are held at MWL, file no. 3682/4.
53 Gwyn Thomas, quoted in *South Wales Echo*, 18 May 1971.
54 Mrs Cora Edwards, letter to the author, 11 February 1997.
55 R. L. Lee, *The Town That Died* (London, 1975), p. 103.
56 *South Wales Echo*, 18 May 1971.
57 Mrs Brenda Roberts, letter to the author, 12 February, 1997. According to Brian Hornsey, the Palladium was an 800 seat cinema opened in 1935. He claims that in the later 1940s prices ranged from 9d up to 3s, which suggests that the difference between the 1s and 1s 3d seats was probably only very marginal. See Brian Hornsey, *Cinemas of North Wales* (Stamford, 1996), p. 73.
58 John Prior (b. 1914), quoted in Grenfell-Hill, *Growing up in Wales*, p. 133. The surviving cash books for this particular cinema show that when this man was of school age the cheapest tickets cost 2d, while the most expensive balcony seats were 1s 3d.
59 Priestley, *English Journey*, p. 402.
60 Shand, *Modern Theatres and Cinemas*, p. 10.
61 G. Robinson to A. Andrews, 23 November 1920, Glamorgan Record Office (GRO), D/D A/B 18/5/86.
62 Mrs Cora Edwards, letter to the author, 11 February 1997.
63 Leslie Thomas, *In My Wildest Dreams* (London, 1984), p. 44.
64 Mildred Evans (b. 1920), quoted in Grenfell-Hill, *Growing up in Wales*, p. 169.
65 A concise account of the development of these, and other machines pre-dating the cinematograph, can be found in David Parkinson, *History of Film* (London and New York, 1995), pp. 7–22.
66 Michael Chanan, 'The emergence of an industry', in Vincent Porter and James Curran (eds), *British Cinema History* (London, 1983), p. 45.
67 Iris Barry, *Let's Go to the Pictures* (London, 1926), p. 31.
68 Jeffrey Richards, *The Age of the Dream Palace: Cinema and Society in Britain 1930–1939* (London, 1984); Hortense Powdermaker, *Hollywood the Dream Factory* (London, 1951).
69 Roger Manvell, *A Seat at the Cinema* (London, 1951), p. 60. This sort of criticism, it should be noted, was not confined to cinema audiences. Of equal concern were so-called 'tap-listeners' to the wireless.
70 Gertrude Keir, 'Psychology and the film', in *The Penguin Film Review*, 9, (1949), p. 68.
71 J. P. Mayer, *Sociology of Film: Studies and Documents* (London, c.1946), p. 53.
72 See chapter 6.
73 Docherty, Morrison and Tracey, *The Last Picture Show?*, p. 22.
74 Jack Jones, 'Social effects of the coming of broadcasting', NLW manuscript, No. 146 (1938), p. 13.

[75] Manvell, *A Seat at the Cinema*, p. 13. The statement was actually not strictly true. In 1951 there were forty-two 'news cinemas' in Britain, usually situated near stations or meeting places, which showed a continuous programme of newsreel footage. They proved popular until the widespread arrival of television. Political and Economic Planning [PEP hereafter], *The British Film Industry* (London, 1952), p. 199.

[76] Ian Christie, *The Last Machine: Early Cinema and the Birth of the Modern World* (London, 1994).

[77] See Michael Chanan, *The Dream That Kicks: The Prehistory and Early Years of Cinema in Britain* (London and New York, 1996 edn), p. 8.

[78] V. I. Pudovkin, quoted in Roger Manvell, *Film* (Harmondsworth, 1946 edn), p. 45.

[79] See Jen Samson, 'The film society, 1925–1939', in Charles Barr (ed.) *All Our Yesterdays: 90 Years of British Cinema* (London, 1986), pp. 306–13.

[80] For example, Terry Ramsaye, *A Million and One Nights: A History of the Motion Picture* (London, 1926).

[81] See chapter 6.

[82] Manvell, *A Seat at the Cinema*, p. 22.

[83] PEP, *British Film Industry*, p. 188.

[84] It is interesting that a number of films from the 1950s and 60s featured scenes in which television was portrayed in a less than flattering light. See Charles Barr, 'Broadcasting and cinema 2: screens within screens', in Barr (ed.) *All Our Yesterdays*, pp. 206–24.

[85] Sedgwick, 'Product differentiation at the movies'.

[86] Gerben Bakker, 'Stars and stories: how films became branded products', *Enterprise and Society*, 2, 3 (Sept 2001), pp. 461–502.

[87] Richard Dyer, *Heavenly Bodies: Film Stars and Society* (Basingstoke, 1986), p. 17; see also Richard Dyer, *Stars* (London, 1998 edn).

[88] Jackie Stacey, *Star Gazing: Hollywood Cinema and Female Spectatorship* (London, 1994).

[89] Elvis did, of course, star in a number of successful films though it could be argued that the movies needed Elvis more than he needed them.

[90] Docherty, Morrison and Tracey, *The Last Picture Show?*, p. 26. Bill Haley played to a packed Capitol Theatre in Cardiff in the mid-1950s.

5. Cinema entertainment

[1] Gerben Bakker, 'The decline and fall of the European film industry: sunk costs, market size and market structure, 1890–1927', LSE working paper, no. 70/03 (February 2003).

[2] See Margaret Dickenson and Sarah Street, *Cinema and State: The Film Industry and the British Government, 1927–1984* (London, 1985); Ian Jarvie, *Hollywood's Overseas Campaign: The North Atlantic Movie Trade, 1920–1950* (Cambridge, 1992).

[3] The belief that films helped to spread American ideas, and products, around the world gave the US industry considerable influence with the State Department. For the views of the manager of the Paramount corporation see Thomas H. Guback, 'Hollywood's international market', in Tino Balio (ed.), *The American Film Industry* (Madison, 1976), p. 390.

[4] See Andrew Higson and Richard Maltby (eds), *'Film Europe' and 'Film America': Cinema, Commerce and Cultural Exchange, 1920–1939* (Exeter, 1999).

5   *Daily Express*, 18 March 1927, quoted in Dickenson and Street, *Cinema and State*, p. 30, and also in Ross McKibbin, *Classes and Cultures: England, 1918–1951* (Oxford, 1998), p. 427.

6   Terry Ramsaye, *A Million and One Nights: A History of the Motion Picture* (London, 1926), p. xxxviii.

7   Andre Bazin, *What is Cinema?* (Berkeley and Los Angeles, 1967), p. 21.

8   Michael Chanan, *The Dream That Kicks: The Prehistory and Early Years of Cinema in Britain* (London and New York, 1996 edn), p. 10.

9   Peter Stead, *Film and the Working Class: The Feature Film in British and American Society* (London and New York, 1989), pp. 6, 13.

10 E. P. Thompson, *The Making of the English Working Class* (London, 1963), pp. 63–4.

11 Rachael Low and Roger Manvell, *The History of the British Film: Vol. 1, 1896–1906* (London, 1948), p. 37.

12 Michael Chanan, *Labour Power in the British Film Industry* (London, 1976), p. 13.

13 G. Robinson to A. Andrews, 22 June 1920, Glamorgan Record Office [GRO hereafter], D/D A/B 18/5/48.

14 A. Gambold to A. Andrews, 23 April 1920, GRO, D/D A/B 18/14/17.

15 *Kinematograph Weekly*, 22 January 1920, 151.

16 This Act related to music halls and variety theatres. See Jeffrey Richards, 'The cinema and cinema-going in Birmingham in the 1930s', in John K. Walton and James Walvin (eds), *Leisure in Britain, 1780–1939* (Manchester, 1983), pp. 32–52.

17 Rachael Low, *The History of the British Film: Vol. 2, 1906–1914* (London, 1948), p. 11.

18 Richards, 'The cinema and cinema-going in Birmingham', p. 38.

19 Stead, *Film and the Working Class*, pp. 5, 6, 13.

20 Low, *History*, Vol. 2, pp. 16–17.

21 Stead, *Film and the Working Class*, p. 11.

22 See Andy Medhurst, 'Music hall and British cinema', in Charles Barr (ed.), *All Our Yesterdays: 90 Years of British Cinema* (London, 1986), pp. 168–88; Jeffrey Richards, 'Tod Slaughter and the cinema of excess', in Jeffrey Richards (ed.), *The Unknown 1930s: An Alternative History of the British Cinema, 1929–1939* (London, 1998), pp. 139–59.

23 A. Gambold to A. Andrews, 15 April 1926, GRO, D/D A/B 18/15/98.

24 Peter Stead, 'By the light of the silvery moon', *Planet*, 116 (April/May 1996), p. 37.

25 G. Robinson to A. Andrews, 6 June 1920, GRO, D/D A/B 18/5/44.

26 A. Gambold to A. Andrews, 3 January 1923, GRO, D/D A/B 18/15/14.

27 Hugh Louden, *My Hollywood: A Nostalgic Look at Films of the Thirties and Forties* (Upton-upon-Severn, 1991), p. 49.

28 Stead, 'By the light', p. 41.

29 Louden, *My Hollywood*, p. 48.

30 Louden, *My Hollywood*, p. 49.

31 Andrews to Temple Morris MP, *c*.1937, GRO, D/D A/B 43/1/58.

32 Robinson to Andrews, 29 July 1920, GRO, D/D A/B 18/5/57ii.

33 Robinson to Andrews, 26 November 1920, GRO, D/D A/B 18/5/87.

34 Pearl White appears in the recollections of the following: Herbert James, in Jeffrey Grenfell-Hill (ed.), *Growing up in Wales: Collected Memories of Childhood in Wales, 1895–1939* (Llandysul, 1996), p. 94; Florence David, quoted in the *South Wales Echo*, 14 February 1985, 13; letters to the author by Mr T. H. Jones, 24 February 1997, and Robert Parry, 18 February 1997.

35 Dick Lewis, quoted in the *South Wales Echo*, 17 May 1971, 5.

36 Louden, *My Hollywood*, pp. 18–19.

[37] William Norman Thomas, whose reminiscences are held at Caernarfon Archives, XM/T/353.

[38] Townsend to Andrews, 5 August 1937, GRO, D/D A/B 42/3/2.

[39] *Kinematograph Weekly*, 30 April 1931, 65.

[40] *Kinematograph Weekly*, 16 April 1925, 57.

[41] *Kinematograph Weekly*, 20 August 1925, 109.

[42] Paul Rotha and Richard Griffith, *The Film Till Now: A Survey of World Cinema* (London, 1949 edn), pp. 516, 119.

[43] Peter Baechlin and Maurice Muller-Strauss, quoted in Anthony Aldgate, *Cinema and History: British Newsreels and the Spanish Civil War* (London, 1979), p. 17.

[44] Cheetham's work, which consisted entirely of actuality films, is discussed in David Berry, *Wales and Cinema: The First Hundred Years* (Cardiff, 1994), pp. 35–42.

[45] Nicholas Pronay, 'British newsreels in the 1930s: 1. audiences and producers', *History*, 56, 188 (1971), 415–16.

[46] Sir Arthur Elton, quoted in Aldgate, *Cinema and History*, p. 8.

[47] Terry Ramsaye, quoted in Aldgate, *Cinema and History*, p. 64.

[48] The tenuous claims of British documentarists to be developing a more realist approach to film-making in the 1930s is critically examined in Brian Winston, *Claiming the Real: The Documentary Film Revisited* (London, 1995).

[49] *Kinematograph Weekly*, 12 November 1931, 48; and 10 December 1931, 40.

[50] Aldgate, *Cinema and History*, p. 62.

[51] Jeffrey Richards, *The Age of the Dream Palace: Cinema and Society in Britain, 1930–1939* (London, 1984), p. 106.

[52] Nicholas Pronay, 'British newsreels in the 1930s: 2. their policies and impact', *History*, 57, 189, (1972), 67.

[53] Richards, *Age of the Dream Palace*.

[54] Albert Shaw, in the *South Wales Echo*, 3 September 1936, 6.

[55] Gambold to Andrews, 8 March 1923, GRO, D/D A/B 18/15/21.

[56] Gambold to Andrews, 2 May 1923, GRO, D/D A/B 18/15/27.

[57] Robinson to Andrews, 26 April 1921, D/D A/B 18/6/25.

[58] Gambold to Andrews, 26 January 1927, GRO, D/D A/B 18/15/124.

[59] Low Warren (ed.), *The Cinematograph Exhibitors' Diary: 1928* (London, 1928), p. 69.

[60] Fletcher Clayton, in a supplement to *Kinematograph Weekly*, 5 February 1920, xiii.

[61] Ibid., p. xv.

[62] Robinson to Andrews, 29 July 1920, GRO, D/D A/B 18/5/57 ii–iii.

[63] *Kinematograph Weekly*, 26 March 1925, 72.

[64] GRO, D/D A/B 19/6/10.

[65] Reg Pickard to A. Andrews, 25 January 1937, GRO, D/D A/B 20/3/16i.

[66] This information comes from the cinema's surviving records, held at Ceredigion Museum, Aberystwyth.

[67] Ruthin Public Record Office, DD/DM/204/1.

[68] GRO, D/D A/B 19/6/93.

[69] Gwyn Thomas, *A Few Selected Exits* (London, 1968), p. 66.

[70] H. E. Browning and A. A. Sorrell, 'Cinemas and cinema-going in Great Britain', *Journal of the Royal Statistical Society*, 117, II (1954), 138–40.

[71] *Kinematograph Weekly*, 1 January 1931, 41.

[72] *Kinematograph Weekly* (supplement), 8 January 1931, 53, and 1 January 1931, 41.

[73] *Kinematograph Weekly*, 26 November 1931, 52.

[74] *South Wales Echo*, 23 February 1976, 9.

[75] *South Wales Echo*, 4 April 1938.

[76] Stephen Ridgwell, 'South Wales and the cinema in the 1930s: the functioning and reception of a mass cultural form' (M.Phil. thesis, Swansea, 1993), p. 74; Brian Hornsey, *Ninety Years of Cinema in Swansea* (Stamford, 1994), p. 16.

[77] *Kinematograph Weekly*, 30 July 1931, 50; Brian Hornsey, *Ninety Years of Cinema in Cardiff* (Stamford, 1997), p. 16.

[78] Michael Freeman, *The Coliseum: The History of a Cinema and Theatre in Pictures* (Aberystwyth, 1994).

[79] *Kinematograph Weekly*, 15 January 1925, 74.

[80] D. Griffiths to A. Andrews, GRO, D/D A/B 20/2/39ii; the only other written complaint contained in this file is that of J. Edwards to A. Andrews, GRO, D/D A/B 20/2/42.

[81] A. Andrews to D. Griffiths, GRO, D/D A/B 20/2/39i.

[82] Jeffrey Richards and Dorothy Sheridan (eds), *Mass-Observation at the Movies* (London and New York, 1987), pp. 34, 32.

[83] Anthony Aldgate and Jeffrey Richards, *Britain Can Take It: The British Cinema in the Second World War* (Oxford, 1986); Robert Murphy, *Realism and Tinsel: Cinema and Society in Britain, 1939–1948* (London and New York, 1989).

[84] Ross McKibbin, *Classes and Cultures: England, 1918–1951* (Oxford, 1998), p. 456.

[85] See Dilys Powell, *Films Since 1939* (London, 1947).

[86] John Russell Taylor (ed.), *The Pleasure Dome: The Collected Film Criticism of Graham Greene, 1935–1940* (London, 1972), p. 229.

[87] The actual amounts taken in the respective weeks were £130 and £259. GRO, D/D A/B Box 41.

[88] Aldgate and Richards, *Britain Can Take It*, pp. 152, 155.

[89] Townsend to Twentieth Century Fox, 3 April 1943, GRO, D/D A/B 42/3/4.

[90] Aldgate and Richards, *Britain Can Take It*, p. 149.

[91] David Smith, *Aneurin Bevan and the World of South Wales* (Cardiff, 1993), p. 195.

[92] The two films were *Bridal Suite* and *I Take This Woman*. GRO, D/D A/B, box 41 / 5.

[93] GRO, D/D A/B box 41.

[94] The other two were *Gone With the Wind* (which took over two-and-a-half times as much at the box-office as any other film) and *Snow White and the Seven Dwarves*.

[95] The film is not mentioned in Charles Barr (ed.), *All Our Yesterdays: 90 Years of British Cinema* (London, 1986), nor does its director receive an entry in Brian McFarlane, *An Autobiography of British Cinema* (London, 1997).

[96] See David Berry, *Wales and Cinema: The First Hundred Years* (Cardiff, 1994), pp. 234–6; Peter Miskell, 'Imagining the nation: the changing face of Wales in the cinema, 1935–1955' (unpublished MA thesis, Aberystwyth, 1996).

[97] The information comes from the cashbooks of the Coliseum Cinema, which are part of an uncatalogued collection of records held at the Ceredigion Museum, Aberystwyth.

6. Critics

[1] A. J. P. Taylor, *English History, 1914–1945* (Oxford, 1965), p. 313.

[2] C. A. Lejeune, '"Eyes and no eyes": what to look for in films', in R. S. Lambert (ed.) *For Filmgoers Only: The Intelligent Filmgoers Guide to the Films* (London, 1934), pp. 82–3.

[3] George Orwell, 'The lion and the unicorn: socialism and the English genius. Part I: England your England', in *The Penguin Essays of George Orwell* (Harmondsworth, 1994 edn), pp. 154–6.

[4] Jen Samson, 'The film society, 1925–1939', in Charles Barr (ed.), *All Our Yesterdays: 90 Years of British Cinema* (London, 1986), p. 306.

[5] Charles Barr, 'Introduction: amnesia and schizophrenia', in Barr (ed.), *All Our Yesterdays*, p. 5.

[6] The letter was written by one Thomas Wood, *The Times*, 5 March 1932, 13.

[7] Ibid., 13.

[8] Commission on Educational and Cultural Films, *The Film in National Life* (London, 1932), pp. 126, 139.

[9] See Rachael Low, *The History of the British Film, 1918–1929* (London, 1971), pp. 89–90.

[10] Julian Petley, 'Cinema and state', in Barr (ed.), *All Our Yesterdays*, pp. 31–46.

[11] Paul Rotha and Richard Griffith, *The Film Till Now: A Survey of World Cinema* (London, 1949 edn), p. 313. Also quoted in Andrew Higson, *Waving the Flag: Constructing a National Cinema in Britain* (Oxford, 1995), p. 36.

[12] In 1929 Leon Moussinac wrote that '*L' Angleterre n'a jamais produit un vrai film anglais*' (The English have never produced a truly English film). In 1930 Paul Rotha described this remark as 'miserably true', and even in 1949 he argued 'that the dictum of the famous French critic is still even partly true'. Rotha and Griffith, *The Film Till Now*, pp. 313, 544.

[13] For a much more detailed discussion of *Comin' Thro' The Rye* see Higson, *Waving the Flag*, pp. 26–97.

[14] There has been much discussion of the role of the countryside in shaping British culture and identity, see, for example, A. Potts, 'Constable country between the wars', in R. Samuel (ed.), *Patriotism, Vol. 3: National Fictions* (London and New York, 1989), pp. 160–86; Malcolm Chase, 'This is no claptrap: this is our heritage', in Christopher Shaw and Malcolm Chase (eds), *The Imagined Past: History and Nostalgia* (Manchester and New York, 1989), pp. 128–46; A. Howkins, 'The discovery of rural England', in R. Colls and P. Dodds (eds), *Englishness: Politics And Culture, 1880–1920* (Beckenham, 1986), pp. 62–88; Angus Calder, *The Myth of the Blitz* (London, 1991), pp. 180–208; Martin Weiner, *English Culture and the Decline of the Industrial Spirit, 1850–1980* (Cambridge, 1981).

[15] Christopher Cook (ed.), *The Dilys Powell Film Reader* (Manchester, 1991), pp. ix–x.

[16] Peter Miskell, 'Seduced by the silver screen: film addicts, critics and cinema regulation in Britain in the 1930s and 1940s', *Business History*, 47, 3 (July 2005).

[17] Guy Morgan, 'Critic or reporter?', in *Sight and Sound*, 7, 26 (1938), 54.

[18] Graham Greene, 'Is it criticism?', in *Sight and Sound*, 5, 19 (1936), 64–65.

[19] Lejeune, '"Eyes and no eyes" ', pp. 80, 85.

[20] Paul Rotha, 'The development of cinema', in Lambert (ed.), *For Filmgoers Only*, pp. 33–4.

[21] The cast of *Kameradschaft*, as with documentary films, was not entirely made up of professional actors, many of the miners in the film were playing themselves.

[22] Francis Birrell, 'A film as a serious subject', *The New Statesman and Nation*, 5 March 1932.

[23] Roger Manvell, in *Sight and Sound*, 19, 7 (November 1950), 299.

[24] These included *The Stars Look Down* (Carol Reed, 1938), *The Proud Valley* (Pen Tennyson, 1940) and *Blue Scar* (Jill Craigie, 1949). See Peter Stead, '"Kameradschaft" and after: the miners and film', *Llafur: Journal of Welsh Labour History*, 5, 1 (1988), 37–44.

[25] *The Times*, 7 March 1932, 10.

[26] Sue Harper, *Picturing the Past: The Rise and Fall of the British Costume Film* (London, 1994), p. 20.

27 See Harper, *Picturing the Past*, pp. 16, 22, 23; *The Times*, 25 October 1933, 10.

28 Alistair Cooke, 'Films of the quarter', *Sight and Sound*, 3, 12 (Winter, 1934–5), 165.

29 David Smith, 'Wales through the looking glass', in David Smith (ed.), *A People and a Proletariat: Essays in the History of Wales, 1780–1980* (London, 1980), pp. 215–39. The essay can also be found in David Smith, *Aneurin Bevan and the World of South Wales* (Cardiff, 1993).

30 Quoted in Smith, 'Wales through the looking glass', p. 222.

31 Ibid., p. 219.

32 These figures are taken from John May, *Reference Wales* (Cardiff, 1994), pp. 18–19.

33 The actual figure is 64 per cent and it is taken from the year 1921, ibid., p. 19.

34 Gwyn A. Williams, *When Was Wales? A History of the Welsh* (Harmondsworth, 1985), p. 239.

35 Gareth Elwyn Jones, *Modern Wales: A Concise History* (Cambridge, 1994 edn), p. 318.

36 *Western Mail*, 16 October 1926, 9.

37 Ibid., 6.

38 *Western Mail*, 18 March 1927, 7.

39 Ifor Evans, for example, expressed the view that 'when the history of the changed attitude of the Indians to the British comes to be studied I think it will be found that an important cause lies in the introduction of the cinema into India'. *Western Mail*, 4 August 1925, 6.

40 Peter Miskell, 'Imagining the nation: the changing face of Wales in the cinema, 1935–1955' (unpublished MA thesis, Aberystwyth, 1996).

41 *Western Mail*, 16 October 1926, 9.

42 *Western Mail*, 23 October 1936, 7.

43 *Western Mail*, 30 October 1936, 8.

44 The film made by the Cardiff Amateur Film Society was *The Secret of the Chinese Cabinet*. It was not their first, the previous year they had produced a picture called *Nothing Ever Happens*, see the *Western Mail*, 13 and 16 December 1937.

45 *Western Mail*, 21 December 1938, 9.

46 *Western Mail*, 30 December 1938, 9.

47 *Western Mail*, 4 January 1939, 9.

48 *Western Mail*, 6 January 1939, 9.

49 *Western Mail*, 10 January 1939, 9.

50 *Western Mail*, 14 January 1939, 11.

51 *Western Mail*, 9 January 1939, 9.

52 *Western Mail*, 16 January 1939, 9.

53 *Western Mail*, 4 April 1939, 11.

54 See programmes and second annual report of the New Film Society, Colwyn Bay, Denbighshire Record Office, DD/DM/962/18–19.

55 *Western Mail*, 5 November 1951, 2.

56 *Western Mail*, 28 March 1940, 9.

57 B. L. Coombes, *Miners Day* (Harmondsworth, 1945), p. 85.

58 *South Wales Evening Post*, 6 July 1937, 7 and 13 December 1937, 6.

59 See Stephen Ridgewell, 'Pictures and proletarians: south Wales miners' cinemas in the 1930s', *Llafur: Journal of Welsh Labour History*, 7, 2 (1997), 74.

60 Coombes, *Miners Day*, p. 85.

61 South Wales provided the setting for various documentary films in the 1930s such as *Today We Live* (Ralph Bond and Ruby Grierson, 1937); *Eastern Valley* (Donald Alexander, 1937); *Rhondda* (Donald Alexander, 1935). See Bert Hogenkamp, 'Today

we live: the making of a documentary in a Welsh mining valley', *Llafur: Journal of Welsh Labour History*, 5, 1 (1988), 45–52; David Berry, *Wales and Cinema: The First Hundred Years* (Cardiff, 1994), pp. 127–44.

62	Ridgewell, 'Pictures and proletarians', p. 79.

63	Bert Hogenkamp, 'Miners' cinemas in south Wales in the 1920s and 1930s', *Llafur: Journal of Welsh Labour History*, 4, 2 (1985), 64, 67.

64	*Western Mail*, 20 April 1934, 15.

65	D. J. Davies, *Ninety Years of Endeavour: The Tredegar Workman's Hall, 1861–1951* (Cardiff, 1951), p. 88; Hogenkamp, 'Miners' Cinemas', p. 73.

66	See, for example, the reviews of *The Citadel* and *The Stars Look Down* in the *Cambrian News*, 28 July 1939, 9 and 19 April 1940, 4.

67	Joanne M. Cayford, 'The Western Mail 1869–1914: a study in the politics and management of a provincial newspaper' (unpublished Ph.D. thesis, Aberystwyth, 1992), p. 212.

68	Aled Jones, 'The New Journalism in Wales', in Joel H. Wiener (ed.), *Papers for the Millions: The New Journalism in Britain, 1850s to 1914* (Westport, 1988), p. 166.

69	*South Wales Echo*, 19 March 1932, 5.

70	*South Wales Echo*, 16 December 1933, 5.

71	*South Wales Echo*, 5 March 1932, 5.

72	*South Wales Echo*, 19 March 1932, 5.

73	*South Wales Echo*, 30 April 1932, 5.

74	*South Wales Echo*, 1 August 1936, 3.

75	*South Wales Echo*, 27 January 1934, 5.

76	Hollywood actually proved far more effective than the British industry in presenting 'British' films to the rest of the world. Britain was much the largest of the US industry's export markets in the 1930s and 40s, and the major studios consciously produced pictures that would appeal to British tastes. See H. Mark Glancy, *When Hollywood Loved Britain: The Hollywood 'British' Film, 1939–1945* (Manchester, 1999).

77	Smith, 'Wales through the looking glass', p. 225.

7. Censorship and control

1	Some of the best accounts of British film censorship are to be found in Annette Kuhn, *Cinema, Censorship and Sexuality, 1909–1925* (London and New York, 1988); James C. Robertson, *The Hidden Cinema: British Film Censorship in Action, 1913–1975* (London and New York, 1989); James C. Robertson, *The British Board of Film Censors: Film Censorship in Britain, 1896–1950* (London, 1985); Guy Phelps, *Film Censorship* (London, 1975); Jeffrey Richards, *The Age of the Dream Palace: Cinema and Society in Britain, 1930–1939* (London, 1934), pp. 89–152; Rachael Low, *The History of the British Film, 1918–1929* (London, 1971), pp. 55–70; Rachael Low, *The History of the British Film, 1929–1939: Film Making in 1930s Britain* (London, 1985), pp. 54–72.

2	The BBFC did not grant 'A' certificates to those films it considered unsuitable for children. The purpose of the classification was to alert parents to their responsibility of judging whether their children should see the film. The CEA, however, were consistently prevented from making this point to the local magistrates, who refused to receive their deputation, and failed to read out their letter of protest in a meeting. It was not until the north-west branch of the CEA wrote personally to each city councillor that their voice was finally heard, and the ban was dropped. See Low, *Film Making in 1930s Britain*, pp. 59–60.

3   In order to watch films banned by the local authority but passed by the BBFC inhabitants of Beckenham were prepared to travel to neighbouring districts. In one case weekly attendance at a Beckenham cinema dropped by 36 per cent and local exhibitors, many of whom were threatened with closure, refused to pay their rates in protest. See Dorothy Knowles, *The Censor, The Drama and the Film, 1900–1934* (London, 1934), p. 181; also Low, *Film Making in 1930s Britain*, p. 59.

4   Michel Foucault, 'Truth and power', in *Power/Knowledge: Selected Interviews and Other Writings, 1972–1977* (Hemel Hempstead, 1980), p. 119.

5   For a fuller discussion of how Foucault's notion of power can be applied to censorship, see Kuhn, *Cinema, Censorship and Sexuality*, pp. 4–8.

6   Kuhn, *Cinema, Censorship and Sexuality*, p. 16. There may have been no major cinema fires in Britain by this time, but public opinion could have been influenced by events overseas, most notably the disastrous fire at the Paris *Bazaar de Charitée* in 1897.

7   *Kinematograph Weekly*, 11 March 1920, 123.

8   *Kinematograph Weekly*, 5 February 1920, 155.

9   *Kinematograph Weekly*, 4 March 1920, 127.

10   P. Morton Shand, *Modern Theatres and Cinemas* (London, 1930), p. 9.

11   Leslie Halliwell, *Seats in All Parts: Half a Lifetime at the Movies* (London, 1985), p. 115.

12   The quotation comes from a feature advertising 'Ultrazone', in Low Warren (ed.), *The Cinematograph Exhibitors' Diary: 1928* (London, 1928), p. 70.

13   *Cambrian News*, 3 January 1936.

14   *Kinematograph Weekly* (supplement), 5 February 1920, xii.

15   Lleufer Thomas has been described as 'one of the most useful Welshmen of his generation'. See David Smith, 'Wales through the looking glass', in David Smith (ed.), *A People and a Proletariat: Essays in the History of Wales, 1780–1980* (London, 1980), p. 229.

16   *Western Mail*, 10 May 1920, 7.

17   Thomas's audacious suggestion could easily be dismissed as hopelessly optimistic, though it might also serve as a poignant reminder of the spirit of self-confidence that existed in south Wales prior to the inter-war depression.

18   Concerns about the effect of the flickering screen were frequently voiced in this period, though little evidence was ever produced to prove that this was a real threat.

19   *Kinematograph Weekly*, 18 March 1920, 136.

20   Robinson to Andrews, 12 March 1920, GRO, D/D A/B 18/5/23.

21   *Kinematograph Weekly*, 8 April 1920, 123; *Western Mail*, 31 March 1920, 5.

22   *Western Mail*, 23 April 1921, 6.

23   The issue of Sunday opening is discussed more fully below, pp. 173–181.

24   *Western Mail*, 13 June 1931, 11.

25   Cinema Commission of Inquiry, *The Cinema: Its Present Position and Future Possibilities* (London, 1917), p. xxv.

26   One of the correspondents who wrote to the author to describe their cinema-going experiences in this period had vivid memories of being harassed during a cinema performance. Like many others, no doubt, she said nothing about it to anyone at the time.

27   The chief constables of Edinburgh, Dundee, Guildford, Hull and Margate had

expressed such sentiments. See Cinema Commission of Inquiry, *The Cinema*, pp. xxiv–xxix.

28 Robinson to Andrews, 5 February 1920, GRO D/D A/B 18/5/14.

29 *Kinematograph Weekly*, 8 April 1920, 123.

30 Gwyn Thomas, quoted in the *South Wales Echo*, 18 May 1971, 5.

31 See N. M. Hunnings, *Film Censors and the Law* (London, 1967), pp. 79–80.

32 Kuhn, *Cinema, Censorship and Sexuality*.

33 O'Connor took over as president following the death of G. A. Redford in November 1916. He continued in this position until his own death in November 1929 and was succeeded by Lord Tyrrell.

34 Richards, *The Age of the Dream Palace*, pp. 89–107.

35 Quoted in the *Western Mail*, 18 March, 1930, 8.

36 Richard Maltby, ' "D" for disgusting: American culture and English criticism', in Geoffrey Nowell-Smith and Steven Ricci (eds), *Hollywood and Europe: Economics, Culture and National Identity 1945–95* (London, 1998), p. 106.

37 Quoted in Richards, *Age of the Dream Palace*, p. 92.

38 Mrs George Bowen, quoted in *Kinematograph Weekly*, 25 March 1920, 139.

39 Mr G. Percy Thomas, quoted in the *Western Mail*, 3 May 1932, 14.

40 Canon D. W. Thomas, quoted in the *Western Mail*, 8 May 1934, 11.

41 See Richard Ford, *Children in the Cinema* (London, 1939).

42 R. G. Burnett and E. D. Martell, *The Devil's Camera: Menace of a Film-Ridden World* (London, 1932), pp. 10, 123.

43 For reports of such meetings in Llanelli and Swansea see the *Western Mail*, 23 November 1937, 11, and 4 May 1938, 6.

44 *Western Mail*, 13 November 1920, 5.

45 Miss Spender, quoted in the *Western Mail*, 11 June 1924, 9.

46 Quoted in *Kinematograph Weekly*, 8 April 1920, 122. See also the *Western Mail*, 29 March 1920, 8.

47 Quoted in the *Western Mail*, 17 February 1931, 7.

48 Councillor Jenkins, quoted in *Kinematograph Weekly*, 3 September 1931, 47.

49 See *Western Mail*, 21 January 1931, p. 7; 22 January 1931, 11.

50 The Chief Constable was quoted in *Kinematograph Weekly*, 3 September 1931, 47.

51 Burnett and Martell, *The Devil's Camera*, pp. 78, 81.

52 Robinson to Andrews, 5 February 1920, GRO D/D A/B 18/5/14.

53 Mrs H. D. Williams, quoted in the *Western Mail*, 3 August 1929, 11.

54 *Western Mail*, 14 November 1933, 13.

55 *Western Mail*, 13 May 1947, 2.

56 *Western Mail*, 23 November 1937, 11.

57 *Western Mail*, 11 June 1924, 9.

58 The failed attempts of Liverpool and Beckenham Councils to ban minors from 'A' certified films is discussed above.

59 *Western Mail*, 3 May 1932, 14.

60 Rachael Low, *The History of the British Film 1929–1939: Film Making in 1930s Britain* (London, 1985), p. 59.

61 Burnett and Martell, *The Devil's Camera*, p. 51.

62 *Western Mail*, 10 May 1920, 7.

63 *Western Mail*, 3 August 1929, 11.

64 *Western Mail*, 22 January 1930, 6.

65 *Kinematograph Weekly*, 12 February 1931, 40.

66 *South Wales Daily Post*, 10 November 1926, 9. See also GRO D/D A/B 18/15/114ii.

[67] Far from being apologetic about screening the film in the first place, the only regret Mr Gambold expressed to his superiors was that he had to withdraw the picture on a Thursday (traditionally a popular night): 'I wish that Armistice Day had been earlier in the week, say Tuesday, I believe we should have done big business for the remainder of the week, as it is we have only Friday and Saturday.' Gambold to Andrews, 12 November 1926, GRO D/D A/B 18/15/114i.

[68] Browning and Sorrell, 'Cinema and cinema-going in Great Britain', p. 147.

[69] This attitude to cinema performances on Sundays is similar to that of the Reithian Sunday on the BBC.

[70] *Western Mail*, 29 January 1921, 8.

[71] Ibid., 8.

[72] *Kinematograph Weekly*, 8 January 1931, 80.

[73] *Western Mail*, 29 January 1921, 8, and 8 February 1921, 9.

[74] This brief summary of the Sunday cinema legislation is based on the ongoing, and extensive, coverage the Sunday opening question in the *Western Mail* throughout the passage of the 1931 and 1932 bills.

[75] Two years after the Swansea referendum, the people of Cardiff voted overwhelmingly in support of Sunday cinemas.

[76] *Wrexham Advertiser and Star*, 11 December 1942, 1.

[77] *South Wales Echo*, 7 March 1928, 9.

[78] *Western Mail*, 5 July 1932, 10.

[79] *Western Mail*, 13 June 1931, 11.

[80] *Western Mail*, 14 April 1932, 7.

[81] W. R. Lambert, 'The Welsh Sunday Closing Act, 1881', *Welsh History Review*, 6, 1 (1972), 184.

[82] *Western Mail*, 29 January 1921, 8.

[83] *Western Mail*, 13 June 1931, 11.

[84] Stephen J. Ridgwell, 'South Wales and the cinema in the 1930s: the functioning and reception of a mass cultural form' (M.Phil. thesis, Swansea, 1993), pp. 50–1.

[85] Ridgwell, 'South Wales and the cinema', 59.

[86] Ibid. pp. 60–1.

[87] Peter Stead, 'Working-class leadership in south Wales, 1900–1920', *Welsh History Review*, 6, 2 (1973), 350–1.

[88] The six were: W. G. Cove (Lab., Aberavon); Reginald Clarry (Con., Newport); Capt. D'Arcy Hall (Con., Brecon and Radnor); David Grenfell (Lab., Gower); Morgan Jones (Lab., Caerphilly); and Capt. Arthur Evans (Con., Cardiff South).

[89] Kenneth O. Morgan, *Rebirth of a Nation: Wales 1880–1980* (Oxford, 1981), p. 191.

[90] H. Victor Davies, quoted in *Kinematograph Weekly*, 30 April 1931, 25.

[91] Saunders Lewis, 'The Deluge 1939', in Alan R. Jones and Gwyn Thomas (eds), *Presenting Saunders Lewis* (Cardiff, 1983), p. 177.

[92] *Western Mail*, 14 April 1932, 7.

[93] Morgan, *Rebirth of a Nation*, 36.

[94] *Western Mail*, 17 June 1932, 13.

[95] *Western Mail*, 8 January 1940, 6.

[96] *Western Mail*, 6 February 1940, 7.

[97] *Western Mail*, 27 March 1940, 9.

[98] T. Brennan, E. W. Cooney and H. Pollins, *Social Change in South-West Wales* (London, 1954), pp. 156–7.

SELECT BIBLIOGRAPHY

Primary sources

Archive materials

Caernarfon Record Office
Letters of contemporary cinema-goers, XM / T / 242, 353, 428.
Miscellaneous cinema documents, XD55 / B31, D55; XM / 345 / 83; XM / 4016 / 791; XM / 1395 / 262; XM / 5257; D28 / 254, 2565.

Ceredigion Museum
Cash books and lists of attractions for the Coliseum Cinema, Aberystwyth.

Denbighshire Record Office
Records of the Picture House, Ruthin, DD / DM / 149 / 4–5.
Records of the New Film Society, Colwyn Bay, DD / DM / 962 / 18–19.
Booklet from the Rialto Picture House, Colwyn Bay, DD / DM / 204 / 1.

Glamorgan Record Office
Andrews Collection, D/D A/B Boxes 18–20 and 41–3.

Museum of Welsh Life
Letters of contemporary cinema-goers, MWL / 3682 / 1–12.
Transcripts of interviews with cinema-goers, MWL Tapes 7583 and 7633–4.

The National Archives
BT 55/3; 60/21
CUST 49/1946; 153/3
Lab 17/7
T 172/1406–1408; 233/94

Swansea City Archives
Miscellaneous information on Swansea cinemas, D/D RMD 1 / 16–17.

Wisconsin Historical Society Archives, Madison, Wisconsin
United Artists Collection: Series 6B, Arthur Kelly papers
                             Series 8B, Gradwell Sears papers
                             Series 1F, Black Books
                             Series 4F, Walter Gould papers

Reports, Surveys and Statistical Studies

The Bernstein Film Questionnaire 1946–7, in Guy Morgan, *Red Roses Every Night* (London, 1948), pp. 94–101.

Board of Trade, *Tendencies to Monopoly in the Cinematograph Film Industry* (the Palache Report) (London, 1944).

Box, Kathleen, *The Cinema and the Public: An Enquiry into Cinema Going Habits and Expenditure Made in 1946* (London, 1946).

Browning, H. E. and Sorrell, A. A., 'Cinemas and cinema-going in Great Britain', *Journal of the Royal Statistical Society*, Vol. 117, 1954, 133–65.

Carnegie United Kingdom Trust, *Disinherited Youth: A Survey, 1936–39* (Edinburgh, 1943).

Cinema Commission of Inquiry, *The Cinema: Its Present Position and Future Possibilities* (London, 1917).

Cinematograph Films Council, *Distribution and Exhibition of Cinematograph Films* (London, 1950).

Cole, G. D. H. and Cole, M. I., *The Condition of Britain* (London, 1937).

Commission on Educational and Cultural Films, *The Film in National Life* (London, 1932).

Durant, Henry, *The Problem of Leisure* (London, 1938).

Hannington, W., *The Problem of the Distressed Areas* (London, 1937).

Jack Jones, 'Social effects of the coming of broadcasting', NLW manuscript, No. 146, 1938.

Jennings, Hilda, *Brynmawr: A Study of a Distressed Area* (London, 1934).

Klingender, F. D. and Legg, Stuart, *Money Behind the Screen: A Report Prepared on Behalf of the Film Council* (London, 1937).

Lush, A. J., *The Young Adult in South Wales* (Cardiff, 1941).

Ministry of Labour and National Service, 'Weekly expenditure of working-class households in the United Kingdom in 1937–1938', unpublished report, July 1949.

Ministry of Labour and National Service, *Report of an Enquiry into Household Expenditure in 1953–54* (London, 1957).

Moss, Louis and Box, Kathleen, 'The cinema audience: an inquiry made by the Wartime Social Survey for the Ministry of Information', an appendix to J. P. Mayer, *British Cinemas and their Audiences: Sociological Studies* (London, 1948), pp. 250–75.

The Pilgrim Trust, *Men Without Work* (Cambridge, 1938).

Political and Economic Planning, *The British Film Industry: A Report on its*

History and Present Organisation, with Special Reference to the Economic Problems of British Feature Film Production (London, 1952).

Psychological Research Committee of the National Council of Public Morals, *The Cinema in Education* (London, 1925).

Rowntree, B. Seebohm, *Poverty and Progress* (London, 1941).

Rowson, Simon, 'Statistical survey of the cinema industry in Great Britain in 1934', *Journal of the Royal Statistical Society* vol. XCIX, 1936, 67–119.

Smith, H. L. (ed.), *The New Survey of London Life and Labour: Vol. IX, Life and Leisure* (London, 1935).

Stewart, Mary, *The Leisure Activities of Schoolchildren* (London, 1947).

Wall, W. D. and Simson, W. A., 'The effects of cinema attendance on the behaviour of adolescents as seen by their contemporaries', *British Journal of Educational Psychology*, 19 (1949), 53–61.

Contemporary journals

Bioscope
The Cinematograph Exhibitors' Diary
Cinema Quarterly
Close Up
Kinematograph Weekly
Kinematograph Year Book
Monthly Film Bulletin
New Statesman and Nation
Penguin Film Review
Picture Post
Picturegoer
Punch
Sight and Sound
Spectator

Newspapers

Local and regional papers
Aberdare Leader
Caernarfon and Denbigh Herald
Cambrian News
Cardiff and South Wales Times
Cardiff and Suburban News
Cardigan and Tivyside Advertiser
Carmarthen Journal
Flintshire Evening Leader
Liverpool Post and Mercury

Merthyr Express
South Wales Argus
South Wales Daily Post
South Wales Echo
South Wales Evening Post
Western Mail
Wrexham Advertiser and Star
Wrexham Leader

National papers
Daily Express
Daily Herald
Daily Mail
Daily Mirror
News of the World
Sunday Express
The Times

Correspondence with contemporary cinema-goers

The author has received letters from the following cinema-goers:
Brian Beard
Judy Godfrey Brown
Beryl Davies
Cora Edwards
Tom Hillier
J. A. Hollowood
P. F. Hughes
J. C. James
E. Annwen Jones
Laura Eilwyn Jones
T. H. Jones
Graham Owens
Robert Parry
Valerie Puckering
Brenda Roberts
Wilfred Stanley

Secondary sources

Books

Aaron, Jane, Rees, Teresa, Betts, Sandra and Vincentelli, Moira (eds), *Our Sisters' Land: The Changing Identities of Women in Wales* (Cardiff, 1994).

Aldgate, Anthony, *Censorship and the Permissive Society: British Cinema and Theatre 1955–1965* (Oxford, 1995).

Aldgate, Anthony, *Cinema and History: British Newsreels and the Spanish Civil War* (London, 1979).

Aldgate, Anthony and Richards, Jeffrey, *Best of British: Cinema and Society 1930–1970* (Oxford, 1983).

Aldgate, Anthony and Richards, Jeffrey, *Britain Can Take It: The British Cinema in the Second World War* (Oxford, 1986).

Amin, Ash (ed.), *Post-Fordism* (Oxford, 1994).

Anderson, Benedict, *Imagined Communities: Reflections on the Origin and Spread of Nationalism* (London, 1991 edn).

Ashby, Justine and Higson, Andrew (eds), *British Cinema: Past and Present* (London, 2000).

Armes, Roy, *A Critical History of British Cinema* (London, 1978).

Atwell, David, *Cathedrals of the Movies: A History of British Cinemas and their Audiences* (London, 1980).

Balio, Tino, *Grand Design: Hollywood as a Modern Business Enterprise, 1930–1939* (Berkeley and Los Angeles, 1993).

Balio, Tino, *United Artists: The Company Built by the Stars* (Madison, 1976).

Balio, Tino (ed.), *The American Film Industry* (Madison, 1976).

Barr, Charles, *Ealing Studios* (London, 1993 edn).

Barr, Charles (ed.), *All Our Yesterdays: 90 Years of British Cinema* (London, 1986).

Barry, Iris, *Lets Go to the Pictures* (London, 1926).

Bazin, Andre, *What is Cinema?* (Berkeley and Los Angeles, 1967).

Beddoe, Deirdre, *Back To Home and Duty: Women Between the Wars 1918–1939* (London, 1989).

Benson, John, The *Rise of Consumer Society in Britain, 1880–1980* (London, 1994).

Berry, David, *Wales and Cinema: The First Hundred Years* (Cardiff, 1994).

Betts, Ernest, *The Film Business: A History of the British Cinema, 1896–1972* (London, 1973).

Bordwell, David, Staiger, Janet and Thompson, Kristen, *The Classical Hollywood Cinema: Film Style and Mode of Production to 1960* (London, 1985).

Boughey, Davidson, *The Film Industry* (London, 1921).

Brennan, T., Cooney, E. W., Pollins, H., *Social Change in South-West Wales* (London, 1954).

Brewer, John and Porter, Roy (eds), *Consumption and the World of Goods* (London, 1993).

Burnett, J., Vincent, D. and Mayall, D. (eds), *The Autobiography of the Working Class: An Annotated, Critical Bibliography, Vols. II and III* (Hemel Hempstead, 1987 and 1989).

Burnett, R. G. and Martell, E. D., *The Devil's Camera: Menace of a Film-Ridden World* (London, 1932).

Calder, Angus, *The Myth of the Blitz* (London, 1991).

Calder, Angus, *The People's War: Britain, 1939–1945* (London, 1969).

Chanan, Michael, *Labour Power in the British Film Industry* (London, 1976).

Chanan, Michael, *The Dream That Kicks: The Prehistory and Early Years of Cinema in Britain* (London and New York, 1980 and 1996).

Charney, Leo and Schwartz, Vanessa R. (eds), *Cinema and the Invention of Modern Life* (Berkeley, Los Angeles and London, 1996).

Christie, Ian, *Arrows of Desire* (London, 1985).

Christie, Ian, *Powell, Pressburger and Others* (London, 1973).

Christie, Ian, *The Last Machine: Early Cinema and the Birth of the Modern World* (London, 1994).

Clair, Rene, *Reflections on the Cinema* (London, 1953).

Clark, John and Critcher, Chas, *The Devil Makes Work: Leisure in Capitalist Britain* (Basingstoke, 1985).

Clegg, Rosemary, *Odeon* (Birmingham, 1985).

Cohen, Robin, *Frontiers of Identity: The British and the Others* (London and New York, 1994).

Colley, Linda, *Britons: Forging the Nation 1707–1837* (New Haven and London, 1992).

Colls, R. and Dodds, P. (eds), *Englishness: Politics and Culture, 1880–1920* (Beckenham, 1986).

Cook, Christopher (ed.), *The Dilys Powell Film Reader* (Manchester, 1991).

Cook, Pam, *Fashioning the Nation: Costume and Identity in British Cinema* (London, 1996).

Coombes, B. L., *Miners Day* (Harmondsworth, 1945).

Croll, Andy, *Civilizing the Urban: Popular Culture and Public Space in Merthyr, c.1870–1914* (Cardiff, 2000).

Cronin, James E., *Labour and Society in Britain 1918–1979* (London, 1984).

Curtis, Tony (ed.), *Wales: The Imagined Nation, Essays in Cultural and National Identity* (Bridgend, 1986).

Daunton, M. J., *Coal Metropolis: Cardiff, 1870–1914* (Leicester, 1977).

Daunton, Martin and Hilton, Matthew, *The Politics of Consumption: Material Culture and Citizenship in Europe and America* (Oxford, 2001).

Davies, Charlotte Aull, *Welsh Nationalism in the Twentieth Century: The Ethnic Option and the Modern State* (New York, 1989).

Davies, D. Hywel, *The Welsh Nationalist Party 1925–1945: A Call to Nationhood* (Cardiff, 1983).

Davies, D. J., *Ninety Years of Endeavour: The Tredegar Workman's Hall, 1861–1951* (Cardiff, 1951).

Davies, James A., *The Heart of Wales: An Anthology* (Bridgend, 1994).

Davies, John, *A History of Wales* (London, 1993).

Davies, Walter Haydn, *Ups and Downs* (Swansea, 1975).

Davy, Charles (ed.), *Footnotes to the Film* (London, 1937).

Dibbets, Karel and Hogenkamp, Bert (eds), *Film and the First World War* (Amsterdam, 1995).

Dickenson, Margaret and Street, Sarah, *Cinema and State: The Film Industry and the British Government, 1927–1984* (London, 1985).

Docherty, David, Morrison, David and Tracey, Michael, *The Last Picture Show? Britain's Changing Film Audiences* (London, 1987).

Duberman, Martin B., *Paul Robeson* (London, 1991).

Dunne, Philip, *How Green Was My Valley: The Screenplay for the John Ford Directed Film* (Santa Barbara, 1990).

Durgnat, Raymond, *A Mirror for England: British Movies from Austerity to Affluence* (London, 1970).

Dyer, Richard, *Brief Encounter* (London, 1993).

Dyer, Richard, *Heavenly Bodies: Film Stars and Society* (Basingstoke, 1986).

Dyer, Richard, *Stars* (London, 1998 edn).

Edwards, H. W. J., *The Good Patch* (London, 1938).

Elley, Derek (ed.), *Variety Movie Guide* (London, 1991).

Elwyn-Jones, Lord, *In My Time* (London, 1983).

Evans, Neil (ed.), *National Identity in the British Isles: Occasional Papers in Welsh Studies* (Harlech, 1989).

Eyles, Allen, *ABC: The First Name in Entertainment* (Burgess Hill, 1993).

Eyles, Allen, *Gaumont British Cinemas* (Burgess Hill, 1996).

Field, Audrey, *Picture Palace: A Social History of the Cinema* (London, 1974).

Fine, Ben and Leopold, Ellen, *The World of Consumption* (London, 1993).

Foot, Michael, *Aneurin Bevan: Volume Two, 1945–1960* (London, 1973).

Ford, Richard, *Children in the Cinema* (London, 1939).

Foucault, Michel, *Power/Knowledge: Selected Interviews and Other Writings, 1972–1977* (Hemel Hempstead, 1980).

Francis, Hywel, *Miners Against Facism: Wales and the Spanish Civil War* (London, 1984).

Francis, Hywel and Smith, David, *The Fed: A History of the South Wales Miners in the Twentieth Century* (London, 1980).

Frayling, Christopher, *Things to Come* (London, 1995).

Freeman, Michael, *The Coliseum: The History of a Cinema and Theatre in Pictures* (Aberystwyth, 1994).

Gifford, Dennis, *The British Film Catalogue, 1895–1985* (Newton Abbott and London, 1986).

Glancy, H. Mark, *When Hollywood Loved Britain: The Hollywood 'British' Film, 1939–1945* (Manchester, 1999).

Gledhill, Christine and Swanson, Gillian, *Nationalising Femininity: Culture, Sexuality and British Cinema in the Second World War* (Manchester and New York, 1996).

Glynn, S. and Booth A., *Modern Britain: An Economic and Social History* (London, 1995).

Godson, E. A., *Digest of the Cinematograph Films Act 1927 and other Legislation* (London, 1927).

Grenfell-Hill, Jeffrey (ed.), *Growing up in Wales: Collected Memories of Childhood in Wales, 1895–1939* (Llandysul, 1996).

Halliwell, Leslie, *Seats in all Parts: Half a Lifetime at the Movies* (London, 1985).

Hanke, Ken, *Charlie Chan at the Movies: History, Filmography and Criticism* (North Carolina and London, 1989).

Harding, James, *Ivor Novello: A Biography* (London, 1987).

Harper, Sue, *Picturing the Past: The Rise and Fall of the British Costume Film* (London, 1994).

Herbert, Trevor and Jones, Gareth Elwyn (eds), *Wales Between the Wars* (Cardiff, 1988).

Herbert, Trevor and Jones, Gareth Elwyn (eds), *Post-War Wales* (Cardiff, 1995).

Higson, Andrew, *Waving the Flag: Constructing a National Cinema in Britain* (Oxford, 1995).

Higson, Andrew (ed.), *Dissolving Views: Key Writings on British Cinema* (London, 1996).

Higson, Andrew and Maltby, Richard (eds), *'Film Europe' and 'Film America': Cinema, Commerce and Cultural Exchange, 1920–1939* (Exeter, 1999).

Hill, John, *Sex, Class and Realism: British Cinema 1956–1963* (London, 1986).

Hill, John, McLoone, Martin and Hainsworth, Paul (eds), *Border Crossing: Film in Ireland, Britain and Europe* (Belfast, 1994).

Hilton, Matthew, *Consumerism in 20th-Century Britain* (Cambridge, 2003).

Hobsbawm, Eric, *Age of Extremes: A Short History of the Twentieth Century, 1914–1991* (Harmondsworth, 1994).

Hobsbawm, Eric and Ranger, Terence, *The Invention of Tradition* (Cambridge, 1983).

Hogenkamp, Bert, *Deadly Parallels: Film and the Left in Britain, 1929–1939* (London, 1986).

Hornsey, Brian, *Cinemas of North Wales* (Stamford, 1996).

Hornsey, Brian, *Ninety Years of Cinema in Cardiff* (Stamford, 1997).

Hornsey, Brian, *Ninety Years of Cinema in Newport* (Stamford, 1997).

Hornsey, Brian, *Ninety Years of Cinema in Swansea* (Stamford, 1994).

Hornsey, Brian, *Ninety Years of Cinema in Wrexham* (Stamford, 1990).

Houston, Penelope, *Went the Day Well?* (London, 1992).

Howkins, A. and Lowerson, J., *Trends in Leisure* (London, 1979).

Hunnings, Neville March, *Film Censors and the Law* (London, 1967).

Hurd, Geoff, *National Fictions: Second World War in British Films and Television* (London, 1984).

Hutt, Allen, *The Post-War History of the British Working Class, 1918–1937* (London, 1937).

Jenkins, Philip, *A History of Modern Wales, 1536–1990* (London and New York, 1992).

Jeremy, David (ed.), *Dictionary of Business Biography* (London, 1984).

John, Angela V. (ed.), *Our Mothers' Land: Chapters in Welsh Women's Hisory, 1830–1939* (Cardiff, 1991).

Jones, Aled G., *Press, Politics and Society: A History of Journalism in Wales* (Cardiff, 1993).

Jones, A. R. and Thomas, G. (eds), *Presenting Saunders Lewis* (Cardiff, 1983).

Jones, Gareth Elwyn, *Modern Wales: A Concise History* (Cambridge, 1994 edn).

Jones, Jack, *Me and Mine: Further Chapters in the Autobiography of Jack Jones* (London, 1946).

Jones, Stephen G., *The British Labour Movement and Film, 1918–1939* (London and New York, 1987).

Jones, Stephen G., *Workers at Play: A Social and Economic History of Leisure, 1918–1939* (London, 1986).

Kael, Pauline, *I Lost it at the Movies* (London, 1966).

Kaplan, E. Ann, *Women and Film: Both Sides of the Camera* (New York, 1983).

Kirby, M. W. and Rose, M. B. (eds), *Business Enterprise in Modern Britain* (London, 1994).

Knowles, Dorothy, *The Censor, The Drama and the Film, 1900–1934* (London, 1934).

Kuhn, Annette, *An Everyday Magic: Cinema and Cultural Memory* (London, 2002).

Kuhn, Annette, *Cinema, Censorship and Sexuality, 1909–1925* (London and New York, 1988).

Kuhn, Annette, *Women's Pictures: Feminism and Cinema* (London, 1994 edn).

Kuhn, Annette and Stacey, Jackie (eds), *Screen Histories: A Screen Reader* (Oxford, 1998).

Kulik, Karol, *Alexander Korda: The Man Who Could Work Miracles* (London, 1975).

Lambert, R. S., *For Filmgoers Only: The Intelligent Filmgoers Guide to the Films* (London, 1934).

Landy, Marcia, *British Genres: Cinema and Society, 1930–1960* (New Jersey and Oxford, 1991).

Lant, Antonia, *Blackout: Reinventing Women for Wartime British Cinema* (New Jersey, 1991).

Lee, R. L., *The Town That Died* (London, 1975).

Lejeune, C. A., *Chestnuts in Her Lap* (London, 1948 edn).

Lejeune, C. A., *Cinema: A Review of Thirty Years' Achievement* (London, 1931).

Lewis, Howard T., *The Motion Picture Industry* (New York, 1933).

Lewis, Jane, *Women in Britain Since 1945: Women, Family, Work and the State in the Post-War Years* (Oxford, 1992).

Libby, Harry, *The Mixture: Mumbles and Harry Libby* (Swansea, 1962).

Lindgren, Ernest, *The Cinema* (London, c.1944).

Llobera, Josep R., *The God of Maternity: The Development of Nationalism in Western Europe* (Oxford and Providence, 1994).

Louden, Hugh, *My Hollywood: A Nostalgic Look at Films of the Thirties and Forties* (Upton-Upon-Severn, 1991).

Low, Rachael, *The History of the British Film*, Vols I–VII (London, 1948–1985).

McArthur, Colin (ed.), *Scotch Reels: Scotland in Cinema and Television* (London, 1982).

McBain, Janet, *Pictures Past: Recollections of Scottish Cinemas and Cinema-Going* (Edinburgh, 1985).

McFarlane, Brian, *An Autobiography of British Cinema* (London, 1997).

McKendrick, N. Brewer, J. and Plumb, J. H., *The Birth of a Consumer Society: The Commercialisation of Eighteenth Century England* (London, 1982).

McKibbin, Ross, *Classes and Cultures: England 1918–1951* (Oxford, 1998).

Macnab, Geoffrey, *J. Arthur Rank and the British Film Industry* (London and New York, 1993).

Maltby, Richard, *Hollywood Cinema* (Oxford, 2003 edn).

Manvell, Roger, *A Seat at the Cinema* (London, 1951).

Manvell, Roger, *A Survey of the Cinema and its Public* (London, c.1947).

Manvell, Roger, *Film* (Harmondsworth, 1946 edn).

Marwick, Arthur, *British Society Since 1945* (Harmondsworth, 1990 edn).

May, John, *Reference Wales* (Cardiff, 1994).

May, Lary, *Screening Out the Past: The Birth of Mass Culture and the Motion Picture Industry* (Oxford, 1980).

Mayer, J. P., *British Cinemas and their Audiences: Sociological Studies* (London, 1948).

Mayer, J. P., *Sociology of Film: Studies and Documents* (London, c.1946).

Miles, Peter and Smith, Malcolm, *Cinema, Literature and Society: Elite and Mass Culture in Interwar Britain* (London, 1987).

Montagu, Ivor, *Film World: A Guide to the Cinema* (Harmondsworth, 1964).

Montagu, Ivor, *The Political Censorship of Films* (London, 1929).

Morgan, Guy, *Red Roses Every Night: An Account of London Cinemas Under Fire* (London, 1948).

Morgan, Kenneth O., *Rebirth of a Nation: Wales, 1880–1980* (Oxford, 1981).

Morgan, Robert, *My Lamp Still Burns* (Llandysul, 1981).

Morton, H. V., *In Search of Wales* (London, 1932).

Murphy, Robert, *Realism and Tinsel: Cinema and Society in Britain, 1939–1948* (London and New York, 1989).

Murphy, Robert (ed.), *The British Cinema Book* (London, 1997).

Nairn, Tom, *The Break-Up of Britain: Crisis and Neo-Nationalism* (London, 1981 edn).

Nowell-Smith, Geoffrey and Ricci, Stephen (eds), *Hollywood and Europe: Economics, Culture and National Identity, 1945–1995* (London, 1998).

Oakes, Philip, *The Film Addicts Archive: Poetry and Prose of the Cinema* (London, 1977).

O'Brian, Margaret and Eyles, Allen (eds), *Enter the Dream House: Memories of Cinemas in South London from the Twenties to the Sixties* (London, 1993).

Orwell, George, *Keep the Aspidistra Flying* (London, 1936).

Orwell, George, *The Penguin Essays of George Orwell* (Harmondsworth, 1994 edn).

Osmond, John (ed.), *The National Question Again: Welsh Political Identity in the 1980s* (Llandysul, 1985).

Parkinson, David, *History of Film* (London and New York, 1995).

Paynter, Will, *My Generation* (London, 1972).

Perry, George, *Forever Ealing* (London, 1981).

Phelps, Guy, *Film Censorship* (London, 1975).

Philip, Alan Butt, *The Welsh Question: Nationalism in Welsh Politics 1945–1970* (Cardiff, 1975).

Porter, Vincent and Curran, James (eds), *British Cinema History* (London, 1983).

Powdermaker, Hortense, *Hollywood the Dream Factory* (London, 1951).

Powell, Dilys, *Films Since 1939* (London, 1947).

Priestly, J. B., *English Journey* (London, 1934).

Pugh, Martin, *Women and the Women's Movement in Britain, 1918–1959* (London, 1992).

Ramdin, Ron, *Paul Robeson: The Man and His Mission* (London, 1987).

Ramsaye, Terry, *A Million and One Nights: A History of the Motion Picture* (London, 1926).

Reynolds, Frank, *Off to the Pictures* (London, 1937).

Richards, Jeffrey, *Films and British National Identity: From Dickens to Dad's Army* (Manchester, 1997).

Richards, Jeffrey, *The Age of the Dream Palace: Cinema and Society in Britain, 1930–1939* (London, 1984).

Richards, Jeffrey, *Visions of Yesterday* (London, 1974).

Richards, Jeffrey (ed.), *The Unknown 1930s: An Alternative History of the British Cinema, 1929–1939* (London, 1998).

Richards, Jeffrey and Sheridan, Dorothy (eds), *Mass-Observation at the Movies* (London and New York, 1987).

Robertson, James C., *The British Board of Film Censors: Film Censorship in Britain, 1896–1950* (London, 1985).

Robertson, James C., *The Hidden Cinema: British Film Censorship in Action, 1913–1972* (London and New York, 1989).

Robeson, Paul, *Here I Stand* (London, 1958).

Rotha, Paul and Griffith, Richard, *The Film Till Now: A Survey of World Cinema* (London, 1949 edn).

Ryall, Tom, *Alfred Hitchcock and the British Cinema* (London, 1986).

Samuel, R. (ed.), *Patriotism, Vol. 3: National Fictions* (London and New York, 1989).

Schatz, Thomas, *The Genius of the System: Hollywood Film-making in the Studio Era* (New York, 1988).

Schonfield, Hugh J. (ed.), *The Book of British Industries* (London, 1933).

Scott, Joan Wallach, *Gender and the Politics of History* (New York, 1988).

Sedgwick, John, *Popular Filmgoing in 1930s Britain: A Choice of Pleasures* (Exeter, 2000).

Seldes, Gilbert, *Movies for the Millions: An Account of Motion Pictures, Principally in America* (London, 1937).

Shand, Philip Morton, *Modern Theatres and Cinemas: The Architecture of Pleasure* (London, 1930).

Sharp, Dennis, *The Picture Palace and Other Buildings for the Movies* (London, 1969).

Shaw, Christopher and Chase, Malcolm (eds), *The Imagined Past: History and Nostalgia* (Manchester and New York, 1989).

Short, K. R. M. (ed.), *Feature Films as History* (London, 1981).

Sissons, Michael and French, Philip (eds), *The Age of Austerity, 1945–51* (London, 1964).

Smith, Anthony D., *National Identity* (London, 1991).

Smith, David, *Aneurin Bevan and the World of South Wales* (Cardiff, 1993).

Smith, David, *Wales! Wales?* (Hemel Hempstead, 1984).

Smith, David and Williams, Gareth, *Fields of Praise: The Official History of the Welsh Rugby Union, 1881–1981* (Cardiff, 1980).

Smith, David (ed.), *A People and a Proletariat: Essays in the History of Wales, 1780–1980* (London, 1980).

Smith, Harold, *War and Social Change: British Society in the Second World War* (Manchester, 1986).

Smith, Harold (ed.), *British Feminism in the Twentieth Century* (Amherst, 1990).

Spencer, D. A. and Waley, H. D., *The Cinema Today* (London, 1956).

Stacey, Jackie, *Star Gazing: Hollywood Cinema and Female Spectatorship* (London, 1994).

Staiger, Janet, *Interpreting Films: Studies in the Historical Reception of American Cinema* (Princeton, NJ, 1992).

Stead, Peter, *Film and the Working Class: The Feature Film in British and American Society* (London and New York, 1989).

Stokes, Melvyn and Maltby, Richard (eds), *Identifying Hollywood's Audiences: Cultural Identity and the Movies* (London, 1999).

Stone, R. and Rowe, D. A., *The Measurement of Consumers' Expenditure and Behaviour in the United Kingdom, 1920–1938*, 2 vols (Cambridge, 1954).

Strasser, Susan, McGovern, Charles and Judt, Matthias (eds), *Getting and Spending: European and American Consumer Societies in the Twentieth Century* (Cambridge and New York, 1998).

Street, Sarah, *British National Cinema* (London and New York, 1997).

Summerfield, Penny, *Women Workers in the Second World War: Production and Patriarchy in Conflict* (London, 1984).

Swann, Paul, *The Hollywood Feature Film in Postwar Britain* (London, 1987).

Tanner, Duncan, Williams, Chris and Hopkin, Deian (eds), *The Labour Party in Wales, 1900–2000* (Cardiff, 2000).

Taylor, A. J. P., *English History, 1914–1945* (Oxford, 1965).

Taylor, John Russell (ed.), *The Pleasure Dome: The Collected Film Criticism of Graham Greene, 1935–1940* (London, 1972).

Taylor, Philip M., *Munitions of the Mind: A History of Propaganda from the Ancient World to the Modern Era* (Manchester, 1995).

Taylor, Philip M. (ed.), *Britain and the Cinema in the Second World War* (Basingstoke, 1988).

Thomas, Brinley (ed.), *The Welsh Economy: Studies in Expansion* (Cardiff, 1962).

Thomas, Dylan, *Quite Early One Morning* (New York, 1954).

Thomas, Gwyn, *A Few Selected Exits* (London, 1968).

Thomas, Gwyn, *Selected Short Stories* (Bridgend, 1988).

Thomas, Leslie, *In My Wildest Dreams* (London, 1984).

Thomas, Sari (ed.) *Film/Culture: Explorations of Cinema in its Social Context* (Metuchen and London, 1982).

Thompson, E. P., *The Making of the English Working Class* (London, 1963).

Thompson, Kristen, *Exporting Entertainment* (London, 1985).

Trevelyan, John, *What the Censor Saw* (London, 1973).

Trosset, Carol, *Welshness Performed: Welsh Concepts of Person and Society* (Tucson and London, 1993).

Trumpbour, John, *Selling Hollywood to the World: US and European Struggles for Mastery of the Global Film Industry, 1920–1950* (Cambridge, 2002).

Turner, Graham, *Film as Social Practice* (London and New York, 1993 edn).

Veblen, Thorstein, *The Theory of the Leisure Class* ([1899], New York, 1965).

Wakelin, Michael, *J. Arthur Rank: The Man Behind the Gong* (Oxford, 1996).

Walton, John K. and Walvin, James (eds), *Leisure in Britain, 1780–1939* (Manchester, 1983).

Weiner, Martin, *English Culture and the Decline of the Industrial Spirit, 1850–1980* (Cambridge, 1981).

Wiener, Joel H. (ed.), *Papers for the Millions: The New Journalism in Britain, 1850s to 1914* (Westport, 1988).

Williams, Chris, *Capitalism, Community and Conflict: The South Wales Coalfield, 1898–1947* (Cardiff, 1998).

Williams, Chris, *Democratic Rhondda: Politics and Society 1885–1951* (Cardiff, 1996).

Williams, Emlyn, *George* (London, 1961).

Williams, Gareth, *1905 and all that: Essays on Rugby Football, Sport and Welsh Society* (Llandysul, 1991).

Williams, Gareth, *Valleys of Song: Music and Society in Wales, 1840–1914* (Cardiff, 1998).

Williams, Gwyn A., *The Welsh in their History* (London, 1982).

Williams, Gwyn A., *When Was Wales? A History of the Welsh* (Harmondsworth, 1985).

Williams, John, *Digest of Welsh Historical Statistics*, 2 vols (Welsh Office, 1985).

Williams, John, *Was Wales Industrialised? Essays in Modern Welsh History* (Llandysul, 1995).

Williams, Stewart, *The Cardiff Book* (Barry, 1973).

Winnington, Richard, *Film Criticism and Caricatures 1943–1953* (London, 1975).

Winston, Brian, *Claiming the Real: The Documentary Film Revisited* (London, 1995).

Zimmern, Alfred E., *My Impressions of Wales* (London, 1921).

Zweig, F., *Men in the Pits* (London, 1948).

Articles

Atkinson, Robert, 'The design of the picture theatre', *Journal of the Royal Institute of British Architects*, third series, XXVIII (June, 1921), 441–55.

Bakker, Gerben, 'Building knowledge about the consumer: the emergence of market research in the motion picture industry', *Business History*, 45, 1 (2003), 101–27.

Bakker, Gerben, 'Entertainment industrialized: the emergence of the international film industry, 1890–1940', *Enterprise and Society*, 4, 4 (2003), 579–85.

Bakker, Gerben, 'Selling French films on foreign markets: the international strategy of a medium-sized film company', *Enterprise and Society*, 5, 1 (2004), 45–76.

Bakker, Gerben, 'Stars and stories: how films became branded products', *Enterprise and Society*, 2, 3 (September 2001), 461–502.

Bakker, Gerben, 'The decline and fall of the European film industry: sunk costs, market size and market structure, 1890–1927', LSE working paper no. 70/03 (February 2003).

Colli, A., Perez, P. F. and Rose, M. B., 'National determinants of family firm development? Family firms in Britain, Spain and Italy in the nineteenth and twentieth centuries', *Enterprise and Society*, 4, 1 (2003), 28–64.

Cromie, Robert, 'What I really think of present day cinemas', *Architectural Design and Construction*, VIII, 3 (March, 1938), 88–9.

Edwards, Sir Ifan ab Owen, 'The Welsh language: its modern history and its present day problems', *Hesperia*, No. 6/7 (1951), 39–57.

Gruffudd, Pyrs, 'Remaking Wales: nation-building and the geographical imagination, 1925–1950', *Political Geography*, 14, 3 (1995), 219–39.

Harper, Sue and Porter, Vincent, 'Cinema audience tastes in 1950s Britain', *Journal of British Popular Cinema*, 2 (1999), 66–82.

Harper, Sue and Porter, Vincent, 'Moved to tears: weeping in the cinema in postwar Britain', *Screen*, 37, 2 (1996), 152–73.

Hiley, Nicholas, '"Let's go to the pictures": the British cinema audience in the 1920s and 1930s', *Journal of Popular British Cinema*, 2 (1999), 39–53.

Hogenkamp, Bert, 'Miners' cinemas in south Wales in the 1920s and 1930s', *Llafur: Journal of Welsh Labour History*, 4, 2 (1985), 64–76.

Hogenkamp, Bert, 'Today We Live: the making of a documentary in a Welsh mining valley', *Llafur: Journal of Welsh Labour History*, 5, 1 (1988), 45–52.

John, Angela V., 'A miner struggle? Women's Protests in Welsh Mining History', *Llafur: Journal of Welsh Labour History*, 4, 1 (1984), 72–90.

Johnson, Paul, 'Conspicuous consumption and working class culture in late Victorian and Edwardian Britain', *Transactions of the Royal Historical Society*, series 5, 38 (1988), 27–42.

Jones, R. Merfyn, 'Beyond identity? The reconstruction of the Welsh', *Journal of British Studies*, 31, 4 (1992), 330–57.

Jones, Stephen G., 'Trade union policy between the wars: the case of holidays with pay in Britain', *International Review of Social History*, 31 (1986), 40–67.

Lambert, W. R., 'The Welsh Sunday Closing Act, 1881', Welsh History Review, 6, 1 (1972), 161–89.

Miskell, Peter, 'Film exhibition in Wales: a study of circuits and cinemas', Llafur: Journal of Welsh Labour History, 7, 2 (1997), 53–68.

Miskell, Peter, 'Seduced by the silver screen: film addicts, critics and cinema regulation in Britain in the 1930s and 1940s', Business History, 47, 3 (2005), 433–48.

Pronay, Nicholas, 'British newsreels in the 1930s: 1. audiences and producers', History, 56, 188 (1971), 411–18.

Pronay, Nicholas, 'British newsreels in the 1930s: 2. their policies and impact', History, 57, 189 (1972), 63–72.

Ridgwell, Stephen, 'Pictures and proletarians: south Wales miners' cinemas in the 1930s', Llafur: Journal of Welsh Labour History, 7, 2 (1997), 69–80.

Ridgwell, Stephen, 'South Wales and the cinema in the 1930s', Welsh History Review, 17 (1995), 590–615.

Ridgwell, Stephen, 'The people's amusement: cinema and cinema-going in 1930s Britain', The Historian, 52 (1996), 18–21.

Scott, Peter, 'The state, internal migration, and the growth of new industrial communities in inter-war Britain', English Historical Review, CXV, 461 (April, 2000), 329–53.

Sedgwick, John, 'Product differentiation at the movies: Hollywood, 1946–1965', Journal of Economic History, 62, 3 (2002), 676–705.

Sedgwick, John and Pokorny, Michael, 'The risk environment of film making: Warner Bros in the inter-war years', Explorations in Economic History, 35 (1998), 196–220.

Stead, Peter, 'By the light of the silvery moon', Planet, 116 (1996), 35–43.

Stead, Peter, 'Hollywood's message for the world: the British response in the nineteen thirties', Historical Journal of Film, Radio and Television, 1, 1 (1981), 19–32.

Stead, Peter, '"Kameradschaft" and after: the miners and film', Llafur: Journal of Welsh Labour History, 5, 1 (1988), 37–44.

Stead, Peter, 'Working-class leadership in south Wales, 1900–1920', Welsh History Review, 6, 2 (1973), 329–53.

Williams, Gwyn A., 'Women workers in Wales, 1968–1982', Welsh History Review, 11, 4 (1983), 530–48.

Zweiniger-Bargielowska, Ina, 'Miners' militancy: a study of four south Wales collieries during the middle of the twentieth century', Welsh History Review, 16, 3 (1992), 356–83.

Unpublished theses

Cayford, Joanne, 'The Western Mail 1869–1914: a study in the politics and management of a provincial newspaper' (Ph.D. thesis, Aberystwyth, 1992).

Chandler, Andrew James, 'The re-making of a working class: migration from the south Wales coalfield to the new industry areas of the midlands, *c*.1920–1940' (Ph.D. thesis, Cardiff, 1988).

Miskell, Peter, 'Imagining the nation: the changing face of Wales in the cinema, 1935–1955' (MA thesis, Aberystwyth, 1996).

Ridgwell, Stephen, 'South Wales and the cinema in the 1930s: the functioning and reception of a mass cultural form' (M.Phil. thesis, Swansea, 1993).

Roberts, Dafydd, 'The slate quarrying communities of Caernarfonshire and Merioneth, 1911–1939' (Ph.D. thesis, Aberystwyth, 1982).

INDEX